Contemporary Masculinities in Fiction, Film and Television

Contemporary Masculinities in Fiction, Film and Television

Brian Baker

Bloomsbury Academic
An imprint of Bloomsbury Publishing Inc

B L O O M S B U R Y
NEW YORK · LONDON · OXFORD · NEW DELHI · SYDNEY

Bloomsbury Academic

An imprint of Bloomsbury Publishing Inc

1385 Broadway	50 Bedford Square
New York	London
NY 10018	WC1B 3DP
USA	UK

www.bloomsbury.com

BLOOMSBURY and the Diana logo are trademarks of Bloomsbury Publishing Plc

First published 2015
Paperback edition first published 2016

Library of Congress Cataloging-in-Publication Data
Baker, Brian, 1969–
Contemporary masculinities in fiction, film and television/
Brian Baker.
pages cm
Includes bibliographical references and index.
ISBN 978-1-62356-747-7 (hardback: alk. paper) 1. Masculinity in motion pictures.
2. Men in motion pictures. 3. Masculinity on television. 4. English fiction–20th century–
History and criticism. 5. American fiction–20th century–History and criticism.
6. Masculinity in literature. 7. Men in literature. I. Title.
PN1995.9.M34B33 2015
820.9'35211–dc23
2014033054

ISBN: HB: 978-1-6235-6747-7
PB: 978-1-5013-2009-5
ePDF: 978-1-6235-6922-8
ePUB: 978-1-6235-6738-5

Typeset by Deanta Global Publishing Services, Chennai, India

Contents

Acknowledgements

Although the writing of a book can be a frustratingly isolated and isolating experience, and not only for oneself, the process cannot take place without the help and support of others. Personally, I would like to thank Katie Gallof of Bloomsbury Academic for her ongoing enthusiasm and support for this project, and Mary Al-Sayed for her diligence and professionalism; friends and colleagues with whom I have discussed the ideas and texts, and who have provided me with inspiration and a helping hand at key moments, in particular, Andrew Tate, Arthur Bradley, John Schad, Catherine Spooner, Chris Witter, Fred Botting, Bruce Bennett, Amit Thakkar, Nick Hodgin and Lindsey King; and colleagues at Lancaster University, Keele University, the University of Mainz at Germersheim, the University of Chester and the Gladstone Library at Hawarden, where parts of this book were first tried out as seminar papers and at conferences.

Parts of this book have previously been published, and I would like to acknowledge the following for their permission to reprint this material in a different form. Chapter 1, from *Revisioning 007: James Bond and Casino Royale*, by Christoph Lindner (ed.), Copyright © 2010 Columbia University Press, Reprinted with permission of the publisher. Part of Chapter 8, from *Textual Revisions: Literature and Film*, Brian Baker (ed.), Copyright © 2009 The University of Chester Press, Reprinted with permission of the publisher. Chapter 10 was published, in altered form, as 'Tape Spectra' in *The Irish Journal of Gothic and Horror Studies*, issue 11. Elements of Chapter 12, from *The Routledge Companion to Gothic*, by Catherine Spooner and Emma McEvoy (eds.), Copyright © 2007 Routledge, and *The Lure of the Dark Side: Satan and Demonology in Popular Culture* by Christopher Partridge and Eric S. Christianson (eds.), Copyright © 2009 Equinox/Routledge, Reprinted with permission of the publisher.

Finally, I must offer my deepest gratitude and appreciation to my wife Deniz and my daughters Isobel and Sophie, who have put up with the negative effects of the writing of this book with patience and kindness, and without which it would not exist.

Introduction

This book developed from my growing critical interest in the intersection of representations of gender, in particular, masculinities, and the burgeoning field in sociology known as mobility studies, of which there is a leading research centre at my own institution, Lancaster University, which is led by John Urry. Although my project has since gone beyond the conceptual frame of mobilities, strong traces of it can be found everywhere in this book, especially in the work of Tim Cresswell and John Urry, in the attempt to think through constructions of hegemonic masculinity (the dominant within Anglo-American cultural representation) in an increasingly mobile, networked and globalized society. In this, my approach is not instrumental or neutral with regard to the impact of enhanced mobility upon masculinity; as will become apparent in the course of this book, my reading of contemporary masculinities (since 2000, but largely in the era of the 'War on Terror' that followed 11 September 2001) is one that is informed by discourses of trauma, pathology and dislocation (in time and space). In short, across the range of different genre texts I look at in this book, masculinity is troubled, anxious, fissured, unable to cope with the alienating dynamics of contemporary globalized capitalism. In my previous book, *Masculinities in Fiction and Film 1945–2000*, I discussed the 'crisis of masculinity' that became culturally prominent at the very end of the 1990s, and particularly visible in films such as *Fight Club* (1999) and *American Beauty* (1999), as well as in a variety of publications, from newspaper articles to academic discourse. In a sense, the 'crisis' has become the new hegemon, in that the dominance of neoliberal economics in the global North, crises of legitimacy in 'democratic' political processes, the experience of war and the effects of terrorism, as well as emergent social and cultural formations produced by digital networks and globalized travel, have all shifted the ground for representations of masculinity, particularly white (hegemonic) masculinity, produced by the capitalist democracies of Europe and North America.

This story is, of course, as old as modernity itself. Sigmund Freud, in *Beyond the Pleasure Principle* (1920), to which I will return (most appropriately) at key points in this book, proposes that the human psychic apparatus develops a kind of shield to ward off the 'shocks' (in a physical sense, as well as the psychological and cultural one theorized by Walter Benjamin) of modern life. Although my approach is not strictly Freudian, I will make recurrent use of the discourses of trauma and its relation to cultural works (literature, film, television), some of which are Freudian in origin. The traumatized male subject has become a recognizable figure across a range of cultural representations in the United States and United Kingdom, concretized in the figure of the 'veteran' or a soldier suffering from Post-Traumatic Stress Disorder. The representation of the traumatized soldier has long historical roots, of course, back to the aftermath of World War I, which – through texts such as Pat Barker's *Regeneration* (1992) – have remained current through wars in Vietnam, and more recently in Iraq and Afghanistan. The first four chapters of this book negotiate with the figure of the damaged soldier, and the modulation of 'secret agent' narrative and figures such as James Bond and Jason Bourne through trauma and loss. The hyper-mobility I diagnose in relation to both these agents is, I propose, directly connected to an extension of military intelligence-gathering power of the United States and United Kingdom across global spaces and boundaries, recurrent motifs in contemporary cinema. These chapters will also investigate the connection between masculinity and a new Imperium, as well as draw on counter-currents with regard to hegemonic and 'damaged' masculinities, from the naval novels of Patrick O'Brian (and their film adaptation) to the film *Four Lions*, a black comedy about British Muslims who have been radicalized and attempt suicide bombings.

In the second section, the focus shifts to science fiction and uses Darko Suvin's classic statement of science fiction's capacity for 'estrangement' effects to read dystopian, post-catastrophic and alien contact/invasion narratives, as well as those concerned with genetics and the post-human. These films become a means by which the effects of war, exclusion and displacement can be imagined, in part through the return of these effects to the previously unaffected centres of power: London, in particular. Accompanying the anxieties of loss are those to do with fatherhood and the role of the father, which is recurrent in the science fiction films I will consider; but in the final chapter of this section, returning again to Freud's 'death drive', the book will consider the attractions of a sublime annihilation of the masculine subject as a means by which to escape the pain of loss, of love, of life itself.

In the third section, I turn to horror and the Gothic, in texts which investigate the pathologization of the masculine subject, from serial killers such as Hannibal

Lecter, to those who begin to present symptoms of what Freud would call traumatic neurosis as a response to loss. These texts have a recurrent fascination with the afterlife, the boundary between life and death and, in particular, spaces of Hell in which the male protagonists journey to either recover themselves or their love, or perish in a form of self-damnation.

My method throughout the book remains plural, and pluralist. A diverse range of conceptual and theoretical material is introduced, but full weight is given to close readings of the texts to bring forth their complexity. The texts themselves may be complex, or internally striated; their relation to dominant representations of masculinity do not unproblematically reproduce ideologically sanctioned subject positions, because no texts do so, even though I assume that there is a strong connection between the social and cultural formations of the text's time of production, and the ways in which they represent gender. I do not intend to offer a symptomology of contemporary masculinities, nor offer the texts as evidence of certain critical models; I hope to let the texts speak, if not exactly for themselves.

The first chapter sets out much of the conceptual ground, which is then developed over the remainder of the chapters. Although there is a logical sequence to the book's construction, there are internal 'rhymes', where chapters anticipate or echo others, both between and across sections. There is no easily stated thesis of this book, but I hope that, through close investigation of such a diverse range of popular fictions across a range of media, patterns will emerge that illuminate the ways in which dominant fictions of masculinity have been negotiated in the years since 2000.

Part One

Narratives of Power

1

Gallivanting Around the World

A helicopter shot circles a crowd in a small arena. From a low angle, we see the crowd, predominantly African faces. A title indicates that we are in Madagascar. This is a snake pit, the crowd betting on snake or on mongoose. A man, a black African, is picked out in the crowd: betting, drinking from a bottle of beer, viewing a text on a cell phone. A cut to a medium shot of this man is disrupted by a white male face entering in the foreground from the right side, saying, 'Looks like our man'. A whip pan reveals Bond standing high above the snake pit, arms folded, half-turned away from the action, leaning against a half-built wall. The film cuts again to snake and mongoose, to the African man on the phone. The white man in the foreground, who we learn is called 'Carter' and is an associate of Bond, touches his ear, and the man on the phone recognizes the gesture: he's fiddling with an earpiece. He runs. Bond is still, watching the scene, as Carter falls into the snake pit, his handgun accidentally going off. The crowd flees, in a sequence of rapid edits, hand-held camera dominant, transmitting the energy of the dispersing crowd. The man with the phone (we now see he also has a small rucksack on his back) runs up some steps, and the camera pans up to find Bond still standing in the same pose. Bond runs.

This short scene begins one of the most exhilarating chase sequences in contemporary cinema, and certainly the most kinetic in the Bond film canon: the foot race between Bond (Daniel Craig) and the 'bomb-maker' (Sebastien Foucan) in *Casino Royale*. This chapter will analyse the sequence in some detail later, but we begin this chapter here to emphasize the contrast between stasis and mobility that is central to the film's visual economy and to its politics of representation. Bond *stands* aloof, watching the snake pit; Bond *runs*. This chapter will take its critical cue from recent work done in the field of 'mobilities', particularly that of Tim Cresswell and John Urry, to investigate what I propose is *Casino Royale*'s aesthetic of total mobilization in terms of spectatorial gaze and free-running bodies in motion. This, I will argue, signals a rupture in the visual regime of the Bond series, embracing contemporary globalized capital's emphasis upon free movement: of information, of resources and of the gaze, and, at the same time, the necessity to police this movement and maintain borders or erect barriers to restrict this fluidity. I will compare *Casino Royale* to the last of the Roger Moore Bond films, *A View To A Kill* (1985), which engages a modern spectatorial sensibility through the visual insistence upon panoramas seen from great height (the top of the Eiffel Tower, the top of the Golden Gate Bridge) and tourist spectacles. At this stage in the Bond production cycle, the tourist-location *mise-en-scène* which increasingly comes to characterize the films turns self-conscious: in *A View To A Kill*, at the bottom of the Eiffel Tower, in another chase sequence (markedly less kinetic than the one in *Casino Royale*) in which Bond engages his antagonist on foot, Bond knocks over stalls displaying the bric-a-brac of tourist consumption before stealing a Parisian taxi and launching it onto the roof of the 'Paris–Istanbul' coach, itself a relic from circa 1920. Abandoning the car, he dives off a bridge over the Seine and plunges through the glass roof of a large river cruiser containing a wedding party. Tourism and consumption become part of the very fabric of the world of *A View To A Kill*; its very title indicates its emphasis on seeing and spectatorship. I will return to this sequence later in this chapter.

First, I would like to outline the conceptual framework that I will utilize in the first half of this chapter with regard to movement and vision. Tim Cresswell, in *On the Move* (2006), revisits the way in which movement has been thought in Western culture, suggesting that 'mobility' enters the English language in the seventeenth century 'when it was applied to persons, their bodies, limbs and organs' (Cresswell 2006: 20). In the eighteenth century, the Latin term *mobile vulgus* is used to characterize the 'moveable and excitable crowd' (Cresswell 2006: 20), the Latin later shortened and anglicized to the 'mob'. 'Mobility', as distinct from 'movement', is 'thoroughly socialized and often threatening' (Cresswell 2006: 20). However, it is modernity that is Cresswell's true focus, a modernity that is fissured by mobility:

> Modernity has been marked by time-space compression and staggering developments in communications and transportation. At the same time, it has seen the rise of moral panics ranging from the refugee to the global terrorist. The celebrated technologies of mobility simultaneously open up the possibility of an increasingly transgressive world marked by people out of place at all scales. (Cresswell 2006: 20–1)

We will return to the threatening figure of the global terrorist as a spectre that haunts mobile modernity in relation to *Casino Royale* later in this chapter. Cresswell's critical intervention in the field of mobilities is organized in *On The Move* around two opposing principles that he sees as underpinning much social theory of movement and human geography: a *sedentarist metaphysics* is opposed to a *nomadic metaphysics*. The term sedentarist metaphysics Cresswell appropriates from the anthropologist Liisa Malkki, and by this Cresswell means, 'ways of thinking about mobility in the Western world [that] see it as a threat, a disorder in the system, a thing to control' (Cresswell 2006: 26). A sedentarist metaphysics privileges rootedness or locatedness, 'the moral and logical primacy of fixity in space and place' (Cresswell 2006: 26). This metaphysics 'reaffirm[s] and enable[s] the commonsense segmentation of the world into things like nations, states, countries, and places' (Cresswell 2006: 28). There is a tension between mobility and place in modernity, argues Cresswell, but it is not that between an inauthentic spatial flux and an authentic sense of locatedness; rather, modernity produces an irreducible tension between free flows of capital, labour, information and populations, and the need to restrict or control this mobility, as it may destabilize the geopolitical and economic structures than enable these flows. I will turn to the economic and political implications of this tension towards the end of this chapter, but here I would like to turn to what Cresswell places in opposition to the sedentarist metaphysics: the 'nomadic metaphysics'.

The metaphysics of mobility

As Cresswell points out, in contemporary social theory, 'words associated with mobility are unremittingly positive' (Cresswell 2006: 25). Flux, fluidity, dynamic, mobile: all words that seem to offer the possibility of disrupting the ideological landscape, to resist or destabilize hegemonic forms of subjectivity, cultural representation or everyday life. 'Mobility has become the ironic foundation for anti-essentialism, antifoundationalism and antirepresentationalism' (Cresswell 2006: 46), he writes. The figure of mobility as resistance can be found in the work of Michel de Certeau, Guy Debord and contemporary psychogeographers, or the 'nomadology' of Felix Guattari and Gilles Deleuze and others. Cresswell is suspicious of 'nomad thought'. In appropriating the figure of the 'nomad', such thought falls prey to 'androcentric tendencies' and ethnocentrism, if not a repeating of 'centuries of Western romanticization of the non Western other. . . .

Insofar as nomadology looks to the representations of colonial anthropology for its conception of the nomad, it is a thoroughly Orientalist discourse' (Cresswell 2006: 54). It is no coincidence that the free-running footrace in *Casino Royale* takes place in Madagascar, just as it is no coincidence that the dangerous 'terrorist' figure is represented as a black African (although he is played by Sebastien Foucan, the French exponent of *parkour*). The connection between the nomad, the mobile subject and the colonial subject is all too evident in *Casino Royale*. I will pick up on the implicit racialization of difference in the free-running sequence shortly.

Although the binary that Cresswell deploys between a sedentarist and nomadic metaphysics may, like all binaries, appear problematic, it does provide a framework for thinking through mobility and representation that does not fall into the trap of a crude moral or ideological coding: mobility good, fixity bad. In fact, in my understanding of Cresswell's argument, modernity is characterized by an irreducible tension between mobility and fixity that insists upon their mutual implication rather than placing a final value upon one or the other. Where Cresswell attempts to deconstruct the informing premises of Western thinking about mobility, there is a long history of thought that connects mobility to vision and spectacle, and it is to this that I wish to now turn. Cresswell's proposal of opposing metaphysics provides the overarching conceptual framework for this chapter, but it is crucial to historicize and (irony notwithstanding) *locate* my discussion of mobility, the gaze and modernity in specific historical and cultural contexts and the history of theorization of these concepts.

My argument in this chapter rests upon evidence that the nineteenth century experienced the development of a particular kind of visual culture which placed the consumption of spectacle at the centre of the experience of everyday (urban) life. Gillen D'Arcy Wood, in his book *The Shock of the Real: Romanticism and Visual Culture 1760–1860* (2001), locates the rise of the 'society of the spectacle' not in the Second Empire Paris of the 1860s, but in London at the turn of the nineteenth century. Wood suggests that a growing economy of spectacular consumption, an identifiably modern visual culture, is a major motivating force behind the rise of Romanticism and its critique of industrial modernity. Wood notes that Wordsworth, in *The Prelude*, includes a section in which he visits a 'panorama' in London (a kind of large, artificial, painted vista, usually of a cityscape such as London or Paris) and then contrasts this to the *real* or unmediated experience of nature available to he or she who seeks it out – in the Lakes, for instance. In the Preface to the second edition of the *Lyrical Ballads*,

Wordsworth contrasts a modern 'degrading thirst after outrageous stimulation' (Wordsworth 1970: 161), which would include panoramas, the theatre and other elements of visual spectacle, with 'organic sensibility' and poetry as the 'spontaneous overflow of powerful feelings' (Wordsworth 1970: 160). Panoramas and spectacle paintings were in enormous vogue in the early nineteenth century, particularly in Europe, and also in the paintings of Frederick Edwin Church in the United States. Church's *Niagara* of 1857 was a huge success when exhibited, almost as huge as the canvas itself. Church frames the water thundering over the Niagara Falls as an awe-inspiring spectacle, devoid of human life and framing a moment of direct communion between spectator and Nature in its most powerful guise. The spectacle of Nature, the falls themselves, become in Church's hands, a spectacle painting, complete unto itself as a kind of marvel or 'event'. There is no Wordsworthian anxiety here.

I am not the first to note a connection between the rise of a nineteenth-century culture of spectacle and the forms of spectacular cinema at work in contemporary culture. Scott Bukatman, in 'The Artificial Infinite', writes:

> The paintings of Frederick Church are particularly appropriately considered alongside [Douglas] Trumbull's [special] effects [in the sequence that ends *2001: A Space Odyssey*]. The astonishing, bold colour experiments (special effects) that Church unleashed in depicting his twilight skies and volcanic eruptions were the result of new technologies in cadmium-based pigment production. These effects were placed at the service of atmospheric and cosmological phenomena: not just the sky, but the sun and the moon, a meteor, and the aurora borealis. . . . Through slitscan technologies, Trumbull created a set of images that were little more than organized patterns of light – the very stuff of cinema. Light, with its implications of revelation and blinding power, is also the very stuff of the sublime. (Bukatman 1999: 263–4)

In slightly different terms, Gillen D'Arcy Wood also offers a connection between early nineteenth-century forms of spectacle and the cinema when he suggests that 'the panorama anticipated the early twentieth-century newsreel. In commercial terms it operated more like the contemporary movie industry than the traditional art market' (Wood 2001: 101). Although these continuities are important, I would like to suggest a complication here in the spectacular forms of modernity that I have outlined above. The panorama, the exhibition, the arcade, are mobile forms of the gaze that rest upon static displays; the forms of contemporary cinematic spectacle conform more to what Anne Friedberg suggests is a 'virtual mobile gaze'. In *Window Shopping*, Friedberg proposes not a rupture between a modern and a postmodern visuality, but instead an 'epistemological tear along the fabric of modernity, a change produced by the increasing cultural centrality of an integral feature of both cinematic and televisual apparatuses: a *mobilized "virtual" gaze*' (Friedberg 1993: 2). The distinction Friedberg makes between the *mobilized gaze* and the *mobilized 'visual' gaze* is organized around the central term of cinema. The mobilized gaze is produced by 'cultural activities that involve walking and travel' (Friedberg 1993: 2), such as *flânerie*; tourism; mobility created by trains, bicycles, steamships, elevators, automobiles, airplanes; and cultural sites such as exhibition halls, winter gardens, arcades, department stores and museums. The gaze is mobilized because the spectating subject circulates around a fixed display of objects that are actually present (museum exhibits, tourist attractions); the gaze becomes 'virtual' when this experience is 'but a *received* perception mediated through representation' (Friedberg 1993: 2). Like Wood, Friedberg connects the panorama with cinema, suggesting that the panorama was a kind of 'building machine . . . designed to *transport* . . . the spectator-subject' (Friedberg 1993: 20) through the presentation of a vast cityscape that imitated (or perhaps 'virtualized') the experience of taking the whole of London or Paris from a great height. The cinema audience do not move themselves; their gaze is mobilized 'virtually' through what is shot and then presented on the cinema screen. The gaze is then dislocated from the actual movement of bodies in space. As a cinematic spectator, we occupy a de-realized subject-position that presents us with the illusion of corporeality through a point of view and the kind of immersive experience (and suppression of spectatorial self-consciousness) presented to us by the Hollywood continuity system.

The Tourist Gaze

The movement of bodies in space is crucial to what John Urry, in *The Tourist Gaze* (2002), argues to be a particular form of visuality produced by tourism and travel, the tourist gaze of his title. In fact, Urry's tourist gaze is analogous to what Friedberg calls the mobilized gaze, in that it is a *corporeal* mobility. Urry makes a distinction between the '"static" forms of the tourist gaze, such as that from a balcony vantage point' (Urry 2002: 153), which he associates with still photography, and a '"mobility of vision" [where] there are swiftly passing panorama, a sense of multidimensional rush and the fluid interconnections of places, peoples and possibilities' (Urry 2002: 153), which is connected to the development of the railway and then the automobile. A kind of whirling, kaleidoscopic visuality implied by Urry's second category has clear affinities with *flânerie*, the urban sensorium of shocks and energies analysed by Walter Benjamin. The 'tourist gaze' is still a mobilized gaze; however, virtuality has yet to enter the field.

The centrality of tourism and travel to Bond texts (Fleming's and the films) needs little further emphasis from me, though it is important to note how Michael Denning's analysis of Bond's 'heroic consumption' of the tourist spectacle is echoed so strongly by Urry. Denning writes, after quoting from a scene in Fleming's *From Russia, With Love*:

> Here we find the epitome of the tourist experience: the moment of relaxed visual contemplation from above, leaning on the balustrade; the aesthetic reduction of a social entity, the city, to a natural object, coterminous with the waves of the sea; the calculations of the tourist's economy, exchanging physical discomfort for a more 'authentic' view; and the satisfaction of having made the 'right' exchange, having 'got' the experience, possessed the 'view'. (Denning 1987: 104)

It is no coincidence, argues Denning, that the Bond narratives find their location in the Mediterranean, the Caribbean or certain parts of East Asia: these constitute the 'pleasure periphery', 'the tourist belt surrounding the industrialized world' (Denning 1987: 105). I should here like to emphasize the centrality of the tourist destination to the visual economy of the Bond films as well as the Fleming novels. In the novels and in the majority of the Bond film series, mobility is *horizontal*, ordered through the tourist-destination locations made available through jet-era travel infrastructures, the age of mass mobility. These locations, like the huge Ken Adam sets that dominate the *mise-en-scène* in the final sequences of all the earlier Bond films, signify the centrality of the mobilized gaze rather than the mobilized 'virtual' gaze (even though, as films, there is obviously a degree of virtuality at work here). I would like to suggest that the *mise-en-scène* of the Bond films up to the 2006 *Casino Royale* is carefully orchestrated to avoid the vertiginousness and dislocation inherent in mobility, the 'shock' of visual modernity. I will take for my example *A View To A Kill* (1985), Roger Moore's final film as Bond, whose very title indicates the centrality of looking, spectatorship or the gaze to its thematic and visual structure. The narrative of this film is a pale echo of *Goldfinger* (1964): Max Zorin (Christopher Walken), an ex-KGB agent now turned businessman and race-horse owner, plans to open up the San Andreas Fault in California and flood Silicon Valley, thereby ensuring his own monopoly of the global trade in silicon chips. The main locations of the film are Paris and the West Coast of the United States, with the final confrontation between Zorin and Bond taking place atop the Golden Gate Bridge which spans the San Francisco Bay. After the pre credit and title sequences of *A View To A Kill*, Bond is informed of the problems surrounding the Zorin Corporation and then told by the Minister and the Admiral in charge of this operation that he has 'half an hour to dress'. The scene switches to Ascot, where the morning-suited Bond and the Admiral watch not Zorin's horse win a prize race, but Zorin and his lover/accomplice Mayday (Grace Jones) celebrating in the stands. (The *mise-en-scène* is echoed later in the film in a confrontation between Zorin and the KGB general Gogol, which takes place otherwise inexplicably in a spectator stand.)

The shot that begins the next sequence is the Eiffel Tower, as seen from the Trocadero, and then the film cuts inside an Art Nouveau restaurant where Bond is lunching with one 'Aubergine', a detective who has been investigating Zorin's horse-racing activities. The name of this character is itself enough to indicate the level of banality and levity generally at work in *A View To A Kill*, but when Bond displays his customary knowledge of wine vintages, Aubergine says, 'I see you are a connoisseur.' Connoisseurship is an index of Bond's difference as a tourist/ traveller: he is possessed of knowledge that allows him to assume a cultural locatedness to make him seem somehow 'at home' in a diversity of cultures and places. (In a typical scene, when taken by Kerim to the gypsy caravanserai in *From Russia, With Love*, he is recognized by the gypsy leader as a kindred spirit and allowed to stay to see, and even make judgement upon, the otherwise taboo female fight.) It is also a marker of the sophistication of Bond's consumption, its superiority over that of the mass. In the scene in the Eiffel Tower restaurant, whose 'magic butterfly' act is at once high kitsch and an index of an 'authentic' Parisian locale, Aubergine is attacked by a disguised Mayday, who then escapes, chased by Bond. A moment to consider Mayday's costume is worth taking: she first knocks out the operator of the long boom (like a fishing rod) that is integral to the illusion of the 'magic butterfly' act, then takes over, 'hooking' Aubergine through the cheek with what we must assume is a poisoned fly. The original operator is dressed entirely in black to make him or her fade into the dimness of the restaurant's periphery; Mayday's costume repeats this, but with the addition of a seemingly superfluous cape. As Mayday runs from Bond, up the Eiffel Tower's iron steps, the cape flows out behind her, and Paris is laid out as a panorama beyond. The visual reference here is, I think, to the early twentieth-century French film serial *Fantomas*, whose costume Mayday's head-to-toe black recalls. As Mayday runs up the steps, the film intercuts shots of her running with Bond, static, firing up at the fleeing figure (and towards the raised camera). There is a significant visual coding between mobility and immobility at this point, accentuated by the then sexagenarian Roger Moore as the less-than-athletic Bond. Mayday takes off the cape, leaps upon the handrail of the stairwell and dives off: the cape has concealed a parachute, and the suicide dive is transformed into a base jump.

Bond, of course, does not follow suit: he waits for the down elevator, jumps onto its roof and travels downwards *statically*, Bond posed/poised in tuxedo against the Paris cityscape as the elevator moves downwards through the shot. At the bottom of the Tower, Bond knocks over some tourist stalls, then steals a Parisian taxi in which he pursues Mayday to a bridge crossing the Seine, as she has landed on a large tourist cruiser. Bond jumps, to fall through the glass roof and spoil a wedding party, whereupon he is bundled away by some irate cleaver-wielding chefs. This crucial sequence in *A View To A Kill* has multiple significance with regard to the film's organization of spectatorship. As I have already suggested, the tourist experience of Paris (the Eiffel Tower, the Trocadero, a river launch) is already encoded into the film's *mise-en-scène* to locate the film's own audience, the 'virtual' nature of this experience insistently lensed through the more static spectacles of the 'tourist gaze' or the mobilized gaze. As Friedberg herself notes, the Eiffel Tower and 1889 Paris Exposition were fundamentally implicated in the nineteenth century's cultures of spectacle and visual modernity:

> [I]t offered its visitors a spectacular new vista of urban space. The elevator ascension of the tower was one of the exposition's main attractions; the gaze was mobilized to a new vantage. The aerial view of Paris from the Tour d'Eiffel was previously available only to balloonists. From this lofty *passerelle*, all of Paris unfolded like a grand magasin. (Friedberg 1993: 84)

The last sentence also helps make sense of the puzzling centrality of a modern airship to Zorin's mobility (and the final sequence on the Golden Gate bridge) in *A View To A Kill*: the film self-consciously deploys an insistent perspective of height in its narrative and *mise-en-scène*, looking down from the Eiffel Tower, airship or bridge, to produce the panorama. It also seeks to limit the possible de-corporealization and vertiginousness of the *mobilized 'virtual' gaze* by offering overt, and culturally sanctioned, vantage points from which to see. To this end, *falling* is a crucial visual motif in the film, from Mayday's base jump, to the disposal of a businessman from the airship after he refuses to join in Zorin's plan for domination, to Zorin's own death, plunging from the top of the bridge into the Bay; but the film consistently displaces away from Bond himself the possibility of falling, such as in his elevator ride down the Eiffel Tower, or his absurdly long clinging to the guy rope of Zorin's airship. To sum up, I would suggest that the film offers an insistent corporealization of the gaze, connected to Moore's fairly obvious age-related immobility as an actor (an immobility only pointed up, not masked as intended, by the casting of the even more superannuated and immobile Patrick Macnee as his 'sidekick'); in *A View To A Kill*, mobility is certainly a problem for Bond. In *Casino Royale*, as I shall now go on to investigate, it is *immobility* that is problematic.

Here, then, we move from the category of Friedberg's mobilized gaze – which I have argued is coterminous with Urry's 'tourist gaze' – to the mobilized 'virtual' gaze, where movement is virtualized and mediated. Friedberg's contention is that the latter term is produced by photography, and cinema in particular; she is careful to bracket off periodization (this is not modernity opposed to postmodernity), using the metaphor of an 'epistemological tear' rather than the more conclusive 'rupture'. In terms of a shift between *A View To A Kill* in 1985 to *Casino Royale* in 2006, I am also willing to avoid over-emphasizing some kind of determining historical or cultural shift/rupture to locate the different visual strategies of the two films. It is not that *A View To A Kill* is a 'modern' film; it is that the film uses the mobilized gaze, and the spectatorial strategies of tourism, travel and the panorama to limit the disruptive effects of the cinematic spectacle. Certainly, between 1985 and 2006, the geopolitical environment has altered considerably, from the anxieties (yet securities) of the Cold War to the current post-9/11 world of 'the war on terrorism', the spectre of neo-Imperialism, and the growth of alternative poles of geopolitical power in China and India; and also a change with regard to financial, informational and population flows. There has also been a change within the dominant forms of popular cinema, and this is where I would like to begin.

Geoff King, in his chapter on 'Spectacle and Narrative in the Contemporary Blockbuster' in *Contemporary American Cinema* (2006), proposes a transformation in the kinds of spectacle that characterize Hollywood cinema in the 1900s and early 2000s. He writes,

> Spectacle in contemporary Hollywood is not just a matter of lofty vistas. . . . This is spectacle that can be understood as offering a vicarious assault on the position of the viewer through strategies such as rapid editing, unstable camerawork and, in some cases, the propulsion of objects out towards the screen. The large-scale

vista is often viewed from on high, either statically, or, more characteristically in contemporary Hollywood, via expansive wheeling, arcing or panning motions of the camera. (King 2006: 340)

King calls this 'impact aesthetic' 'Impressive spectacular realism' (King 2006: 338), which offers a tension between the immersive pleasures of a world created through 'the apparently "seamless" manner with which digital artefacts are employed, either alone or in combination with "real" live-action characters and settings' (King 2006: 338), and the 'wow-factor' of spectacle sequences which draw attention to themselves *as* spectacles. In the quotation above, King moves from an idea of spectacle as 'vista' (the localization/corporealization of the mobile gaze through the construction of a 'static' place from which to view) to one of spectacle as total mobility (the decorporealization of the gaze through camera movement and editing to radically destabilize 'the position of the viewer'). The aesthetic of the contemporary blockbuster, of which *Casino Royale* is surely a part, then corresponds to an extreme version of Friedberg's mobilized 'virtual' gaze, where the virtual element causes a radical de-location of the spectator-subject. This 'wheeling, arcing or panning' can be seen to greatest effect in *Casino Royale* in the free-running sequence with which I began this chapter, and will now return.

Vertigo and free running

In stark contrast to Roger Moore's immobility in *A View To A Kill*, Daniel Craig's Bond is characterized by aggressive movement. Throughout the film, Bond struts, Craig's shoulders twitching back and forward with the intensity of his walk; or, he runs, in a manner not seen even in the Sean Connery or Tim Dalton incarnations. In the sequence in which he pursues the 'bomb-maker' in Madagascar, Bond's mobility is in fact placed in contradistinction to that of his quarry. The 'bomb-maker' is played by Sebastien Foucan, one of the originators and leading exponent of *parkour*, the anglicized name of which is 'free-running'. *Parkour* is a kind of pedestrian urban mobility which originated in the alienating concrete landscaping of the Parisian *banlieues*, the ring of suburbs constructed to house the dispersed inhabitants of Paris's inner-city deprived areas, many of them of North African or West African descent. The *banlieues* themselves became centres of alienated youth, racial tension and violence, unemployment and deprivation, and they found their highest popular profile in Matthieu

Kassowitz's fiction film *La Haine* (1995). *Parkour* could be seen as an embodied resistance to the planned and controlled urban environments of the *banlieues*, a physical version of Michel de Certeau's formulation of the 'practices' of walking, the 'tactics' which, in a micro-political way, disrupt the determining fabric of the space of power and the 'strategies' of the state and ideological forces. Where the conforming urban walker will keep to the walkways, paths and streets, the exponent of *parkour* will jump, hurdle, run or vault, turning the urban environment into a kind of giant gymnasium in which the resisting body of the *parkour*-ist is located in space in a manner different from, and alternate to, that coded by the planners of the *banlieue*.

It was only a matter of time, however, before Hollywood filmmakers understood the visual and spectacular possibilities of *parkour* within the 'impact aesthetic' of contemporary cinema to turn resisting behaviours into a cinematic spectacle. The body in motion of the *parkour* exponent offers a kind of corporeal mobility that fully displays the imperatives of 'Impressive spectacular realism': without CGI, the body seems to perform 'impossible' acrobatic and gymnastic movements in space, creating the spectatorial 'wow' while emphasizing at the same time the *reality* of what is being filmed. It is a special effect not created by special effect technologies; however, unlike former Hollywood genres that focused upon the body in motion (the musical, in particular, which favoured the long take in order to give full expression to the dancers' performances), Foucan's free running is at the service of exactly the kind of 'wheeling, arcing and panning' camera and rapid editing that Geoff King identifies as central to the formal properties of the contemporary blockbuster. This does not restrain or undermine the spectacular nature of Foucan's stunts, however. The camera, which, as the sequence in *Casino Royale* progresses, becomes increasingly de-corporealized in the terms I discussed above (dis-located from a static point of view from which to see), performs or inhabits the same kind of mobility in space as the free runner. Camerawork and filmed body are of a piece; in fact, the camera itself could be seen to engage in a kind of visual *parkour*, a radical destabilization of the codes of representation offered by the mobilized gaze.

The bomb-maker (Foucan) runs from Bond and the snake pit to a construction site. Vaulting over the wire-mesh fence, he zigzags across the site, up a building and then on to the gridded space of the steel-frame skeleton of an under-construction curtain-wall skyscraper, of course, the signature building of a certain form of urban modernity. Bond pursues: on foot, at the wheel of an earthmover (smashing one of the buildings), and then follows the bomb-maker by ascending vertically on a crane pulley. (Bond smashes off the load to do so, which then plunges onto the workers below.) After ascending the building, the bomb-maker jumps onto a crane, followed by Bond on the pulley, where he is finally able to force a physical confrontation with his antagonist. Up to this point, the film heightens the kineticism of the action by rapid editing, shots lasting a second or less, intercutting between the fleeing Foucan and the pursuing Craig. On the crane, however, helicopter shots predominate, the camera swirling and wheeling around the figures on the huge industrial structure (which, in its visual structure, is a gigantic sign of the vertical and horizontal axes). This sequence emphasizes a fantastical, almost dream-like bodily mobility, where 'real' human beings launch themselves (seemingly impossibly) across vertiginous spaces, from building to crane, from crane to building. In keeping with this fantastical mobility, the camera of director Martin Campbell and DoP Paul Meheux is always on the move, 'tracking' almost impossibly several hundred feet in the air, circling around the protagonists, who are themselves always in energetic motion. The film does not allow the spectator a fixed point from which to view, but fully emphasizes the vertiginous, de-corporealized effect of the mobile 'virtual' gaze.

That the free-running sequence takes place largely on a building site, in Madagascar, is an index of the change in the geopolitical landscape that informs *Casino Royale* in contradistinction to some of its forerunners. Rather than being in the 'pleasure periphery', this sequence takes place in a developing-world locale in which the imperatives of contemporary capital are beginning to be inscribed, in terms of a 'Western' (or developed world) architecture, upon the topography of the country. The brilliant blue sea that forms the backdrop to Bond and the bomb-maker on the crane also signifies that this development is connected (still) to the postcard-panorama aesthetics of tourism. *Casino Royale* can be seen not only as a post-9/11 Bond film, but also as the first truly post–Bretton Woods Bond film. The Bretton Woods system is described by Robert Wade as an 'international financial system [in which] the world economy operated with fixed exchange rates; an international medium of exchange and store of value – the US dollar – backed by gold; and restrictions on capital movements' (Wade 2006: 116). Its collapse in 1973 introduced a financial world of flexible exchange rates and free capital movements, the basis for rapid credit expansion which led to a 'surge' in 'world liquidity' (Wade 2006: 116). Wade argues that this financial mobility, coupled with national policies of deregulation, was the motor of global economic expansion, but, at the same time, 'the surge of liquidity since the end of Bretton Woods and the resulting financialization of the economy have created

an inherent source of instability in the world economy' (Wade 2006: 118). That
the casino is the crucial space of (political) conflict in this narrative is indicative
of *Casino Royale*'s place in what John Urry, quoting Bauman, calls 'liquid
modernity' and its globalized system of 'free' capital flows. There is no 'super-
villain' plotting world domination as there is in *A View To A Kill*; here, Bond's
ultimate antagonist is a financier, a card player and a facilitator of the globalized
'free flow' of capital that finds its physical analogue in the free-running bomb-
maker, or terrorist. When M tells Bond, after he has killed the bomb-maker, that
he needs to think of the bigger picture rather than being satisfied with having
one less bomb-maker alive, it masks the truth that it is the very financial system
that Bond represents and protects that is the ultimate enabler of global terrorism,
rather than the bomb-maker, or even Le Chiffre.

There is evidence, in *Casino Royale*, of the irreducible tension in contemporary
capital between the imperative towards the reduction or removal of barriers to the
'free flow' of capital, and the imperative of developed nations to restrict this flow
(certainly in terms of population flows, particularly immigration) or transform this
population liquidity into a legitimated form: migrant workers who perform the
labour roles that indigenous populations do not want to do, or into tourists. Ginette
Verstraete proposes a 'contradictory logic' at the heart of the European Union's (EU)
'geopolitics of mobility' that can stand as a diagnostic case for the kind of economic
world represented in *Casino Royale* (Verstraete 2001: 27). Verstraete argues that
since the Schengen Agreement of 1986 (curiously, the same year as *A View To A
Kill* was released) the European Community, subsequently the European Union

> has implemented the gradual abolition of national border controls (which
> became common frontiers), and replaced them with limited passport and other
> document checks. . . . The Schengen agreement was meant to: minimise delays
> caused by traffic congestion and identity checks; stimulate the free and competitive
> flow of goods, money and people; create a common European market at a scale
> that would improve productivity, distribution, and consumption; attract large
> foreign investments; and enable Europe to compete with the USA and East Asia.
> (Verstraete 2001: 28–9)

The contradictory logic that Verstraete diagnoses can be seen in this abolition
of *internal* barriers that found its correlative in 'the introduction of firm
external frontiers to keep illegal immigrants, terrorists and drug-dealers out,
and guarantee internal security and stability' (Verstraete 2001: 29). Most
importantly in the context of this chapter, 'the freedom of mobility for some
(citizens, tourists, business people) could only be made possible through the

organised exclusion of others forced to move around as illegal "aliens", migrants, or refugees' (Verstraete 2001: 29). Very largely, Verstraete argues, this distinction is racialized: white Europeans are placed in the former category, non-white Europeans and others in the latter. This casts the free-running sequence in *Casino Royale* in a particular, if not peculiar, light, for the difference between the free-running bomb-maker and the chasing secret service agent is also played out as a racial or ethnic difference. Craig's aggressive, almost angular physicality is at odds with Foucan's physical agility and fluidity; where Foucan slides feet-first through a narrow head-height window, Craig bursts straight through the plasterboard wall. *Casino Royale*'s geopolitical space is an extension of Schengen space: for Bond, mobility is unrestricted (despite the fact that M is in high dudgeon and sends him to the periphery), whereas for the non-white 'bomb-maker', his free-running emphasizes danger, and the need to impose restrictions upon his movement. (For Bond, even the violation of diplomatic protocol by invading the embassy of another country in pursuit of the 'bomb-maker' has no real consequences for him, even if the 'political' realities of such an act are stressed by the film.) As I noted above in relation to Bond's 'heroic tourism', Bond is 'at home' anywhere, a condition often validated by his connoisseurship; but as Vivian Halloran notes in 'Tropical Bond', the issue of 'passing' for a local recurs in Bond texts, which consistently, she argues, 'complicate Bond's whiteness' (Halloran 2005:165). Following Edward Said's argument about Kipling's *Kim* in *Culture and Imperialism*, I would like to stress here that Bond can 'pass', even as a non-white other (see the film of *You Only Live Twice* for a concrete, if risible, example); but the non-white other (the free-running bomb-maker) most assuredly cannot. In *Casino Royale*, the bomb-maker's proficiency in *parkour* is, ideologically, another sign of his dangerous, and uncontrolled, mobility.

Casino Royale is deeply embedded in a system of representation in which can be traced the foundational tension between mobility and immobility in contemporary culture. Mobile phones and laptop computers are ubiquitous in *Casino Royale*, as are laptop computers connected to the internet; the narratively central card-game standoff between Bond and Le Chiffre emphasizes financial mobility and liquidity; Le Chiffre is a kind of financier, offering banking facilities to 'freedom fighters' (who require 'access around the world' to their deposited monies). Bond himself is a figure of almost fantasy mobility, as I have indicated above, both in terms of bodily movement and in geopolitical space. His journey around the Mediterranean on the yacht with Vesper Lynd towards the end of the film also signifies a fantasy of tourist mobility, an endlessly financed Grand

Tour ending in that most liquid of cities, Venice. In fact, it is *immobility* that is most dangerous to Bond: when captured by Le Chiffre, Bond is strapped naked to a cane chair and his genitals beaten: recovering in a wheelchair, he reveals both the password to his bank account and his love for Vesper Lynd, the loss of his secret agent 'armour'. The tension between mobility and territorialization that characterizes the unstable geopolitics of the 'financialized', post–Bretton Woods economic world can also be found in Hollywood cinema itself, and, according to Geoff King, is integral to Hollywood's productive imperatives in the age of contemporary spectacle. 'In the contemporary global-scale moving-picture economy,' he writes, 'Hollywood creates a territory on which it, alone, can compete. . . . Spectacle *as* spectacle is, thus, a matter of strongly market-driven aesthetics' (King 2006: 339). The decorporealization of the mobilized 'virtual' gaze is thereby put into the service of further territorialization. I need not elaborate on the politics of copyright, the region coding of DVDs or the campaigns by the film industry against pirated, downloaded copies of a movie to emphasize the tension between a global market (facilitated by the internet) and the desire for restrictions on the 'free flow' of capital or trade, nor the attendant ironies of this tension. As I hope to have outlined here, the Bond films are deeply implicated in systems of cultural representation which negotiate the place of the mobile subject and the mobile gaze in an increasingly, if not disturbingly, mobilized world. While some forms of mobility – economic, visual, informational, physical – are legitimated, others are shown to be radically destabilizing and dangerous to the anxious nation-states of the 'developed world'. The mobile gaze of the tourist is now haunted by the spectre of the gaze of the other, the one who sees and visits 'us': the terrorist.

After *Casino Royale*: The traumatized Bond

In the two Bond films subsequent to *Casino Royale*, *Quantum of Solace* (2008) and *Skyfall* (2012), Daniel Craig plays the secret agent less as a strutting, hyper-masculine and hyper-mobile articulation of the global power of transnational capital than as 'damaged goods', a subject struggling to deal with the death of Vesper Lynd (in *Quantum of Solace*) and with his own role as an expendable instrument in the geopolitical matrix (in *Skyfall*). *Quantum of Solace* begins with a car chase, which takes place a few hours after the end of *Casino Royale*. The editing in this and other chase sequences which provide the mobile dynamic of the film is kinetic to the point of incoherence. Time and space become chaotic, point of view fragmented and length of shot extremely short. As Bond drives his car through a traffic-crowded tunnel, pursued by assailants in other automobiles, bullets fly, car doors are ripped off, collision follows collision; but the vertiginous camerawork that was held in tension with narrative coherence in *Casino Royale* here overcomes continuous time and space, to the point that the viewer loses sense of just where they are in relation to what is being shown. In a later foot chase across the rooftops of Siena, this collapse of a continuity-based space works effectively when Bond and his antagonist plunge through a glass roof and, caught in ropes attached to scaffolding, conduct a fist-fight while swinging violently in the air. The tangle of the ropes is an analogue of the tangled nature of space itself in *Quantum of Solace*: there is no mastery over space in its articulation in the film (as in *A View to a Kill* and its panoramic views), nor negotiations of routes through it (as in *Casino Royale*). The viewer, like Bond himself, is left hanging.

Mobility in *Quantum of Solace* is plural to the point of parody. In addition to the opening car chase and rooftop footrace, there is a motor-boat chase in the harbour of Port au Prince in Haiti; an aerial dogfight in Bolivia, with Bond at the controls of an aged DC-3; and a long walk out of the desert by Bond and Camille Montes (Olga Kurylenko) after they both skydive out of the crashing plane into a large sinkhole. The motif of falling here lacks the resonance of *A View to a Kill* and its titular importance in the following film; here it is another articulation of a fantastical and fluid space. The global reach of the intelligence agencies and the 'Quantum' organization headed by Dominic Greene (Mathieu Amalric) is represented graphically in a small scene at the beginning of the film; after Bond has killed the double-agent Mitchell in the rope fight, he is briefed by M and others about some tagged money found in Mitchell's London apartment. On a table-top touchscreen, a network of financial connections is presented, a tentacular display of financial mobility which exists in parallel to the governmental/nation-state operations of Bond (and his enemies in many of the previous films). The Quantum organization is a kind of updated 'assassination bureau' for the twenty-first century; available for hire by a shadowy network of corporate organizations (symbolized by the cellular telephone network that Bond hacks at a performance of *Tosca* in Austria), it disrupts national economies and political processes at the behest of transnational actors, but in this film it is in the process of the old-fashioned capitalist practice of 'cornering the market' in a particular commodity. In *Quantum of Solace*, this commodity is water.

The film looks forward to a post–peak oil geopolitics in which water has become a key commodity rather than a natural resource, and indicates the extent to which national governments and their security operations (like the CIA) have tacitly operated in terms of mutual interest with 'extra-legal' organizations like Quantum. In a sense, this returns the Bond franchise to the world of SPECTRE, but the framing is explicitly economic rather than straightforwardly ideological. When Greene threatens the Bolivian Generalissimo whom Quantum plans to return to power, it is an index of the power of multinational finance over national sovereignty. The imagined limitation to national agency is, of course, directly countermanded by Bond himself, who operates (largely, even if he has gone 'rogue') in the British national interest.

In *Skyfall*, Bond becomes even more 'damaged'. Sent on a mission to retrieve stolen data which will compromise British agents if released (anticipating WikiLeaks and Edward Snowden), Bond is sacrificed by M when she orders another British agent to 'take the shot' to try to kill the enemy when the two fight aboard a moving train. Bond's 'fall' into the river below recapitulates the thematic emphases of *A View To A Kill*, but here (as in another earlier film, *You Only Live Twice* (1967)) Bond's 'death' is prematurely broadcasted. When he returns to London and active duty after the MI6 building on the Thames has been bombed, Craig is presented as an older, rather battered man: red of eye, gaunt, dishevelled, this Bond is a long way from the strutting masculinity of *Casino Royale*. In fact, when he is put through his paces to gauge his fitness for duty, the film indicates a physical *in*capacity that was never an issue even in the later Moore films. This sense of superannuation – that Bond might be past his physical prime – plays against Craig's own physicality: he is clearly extremely fit, but this is the body of a man in his forties, and one that bears the traces of past violence. Where, in *Quantum of Solace*, Bond is scarred emotionally by the death of Vesper Lynd, in *Skyfall* it is Craig's body that bears the marks of his traumatic history.

Pursuing the assassin 'Patrice' to Shanghai, Bond follows his quarry to the top of a large skyscraper, where he witnesses Patrice assassinate someone. The *mise-en-scène* of this sequence is extraordinary. The two men move inside an unoccupied floor of the office building, its interior divided by panes of glass. In a manner clearly echoing the 1982 science fiction film *Blade Runner*, an advertisement is projected upon the sheer glass wall of the building, and the light refracts from the interior glass walls and doors in blue and neon. The palette is grey, green and blue, an entirely unnatural environment denoting technological modernity and, in its shifting and broken sense of space, the global dislocations of contemporary capital. At one point, Bond 'hides' in plain sight by opening a door slightly, so its reflective surface shows the lights of the apartment building opposite rather than affording a transparent revelation of Bond's presence. The subsequent fist-fight, much unlike the fragmented editing of the violent scenes in *Quantum of Solace*, is done largely on one take, with Bond and Patrice silhouetted against the electric light of night-time Shanghai. The fight ends, once again, with a point-of-view shot of a vertiginous drop, here down the outside of the building as Patrice fails to hold on. This 'fall' not only recapitulates Bond's own, but also plays spatially against later scenes where Bond travels to the base of Raoul Silva (Javier Bardem), an abandoned island off the coast of Macau that echoes the ruined aesthetic of Hashima Island, close to Nagasaki in Japan, upon which a coal-mining operation and its accommodation now lie empty and abandoned. Hashima, known more popularly as 'Battleship Island', is a paradigmatic space of industrial ruin, as identified by Tim Edensor and others, a locus of discourses about the spaces of late capital. (Hashima has now been partially reopened for tourists and has been mapped by Google Street View.) This ruined space operates as a kind of emblem for the critique of Bond's own activities that Silva offers. He, like *Quantum of Solace*'s Dominic Greene, operates as an agent for hire, manipulating political and economic networks, but as the film reveals, was once a British agent himself. 'England', he says to Bond, 'The Empire. MI6. You're living in a ruin as well. You just don't know it.' This message of superannuation curiously echoes the discourses that can be found in Hollywood Westerns in the 1950s and 1960s, which I have analysed elsewhere. Where the Western proposes the death of the gunfighter as the necessary means by which 'civilization' can take root in the West, leaving the superannuated 'heroes' (and outlaws) of the West out of time and excluded from the spaces of the new *polis*, *Skyfall*'s critique is of the 'spy game' as a vestige of British Imperialism, and Bond, therefore, as outmoded in a world of transnational actors and globalized finance.

Curiously, then, *Skyfall* also returns to clearly identifiable Cold War espionage tropes in articulating the relationship between Silva, Bond and M. While Silva explicitly engages a Freudian register, telling M 'Look at your work, Mother', it is in fact the events of 1997, when Britain 'handed over' Hong Kong to the People's Republic of China, that is the political epicentre of *Skyfall*. This emblematic moment for the post-war British history of decolonization is re-inscribed as a moment of sacrifice or betrayal (echoing the sacrifice of Bond that M chooses at the beginning of the film), as Silva, a troublesome if brilliant British agent (and thereby forerunner of Bond), was himself betrayed by the British secret service in an espionage exchange: 'I gave him up,' says M. 'I got six agents and a peaceful transition.' The moment of decolonization is re-enacted, in a return not only to Cold War espionage tropes but also to those of Empire, as a 'betrayal' in the heart of Empire, London.

Skyfall clearly articulates anxieties about security and the return of violence from the Imperial periphery that overlay *Heart of Darkness* (1899) with the '7/7' bombing in London in July 2005. Much of the London sequence in *Skyfall* takes place underground (including the spectacular derailing of an Underground train), an analogue of the hidden and secret networks of power, influence and violence that underpin the Bond series and, in *Skyfall*'s critique, contemporary life. This also repeats Bond's fall from the train at the beginning of the film, and the images of Bond under water that recur when he fights beneath the ice of a frozen pond towards the end of the film. When *Skyfall* shifts from London to the eponymous mansion that was Bond's childhood home, the narrative enters much more personal territory, but is, in fact, a restatement of the 'heart of darkness' motif. A return 'home' is one to a primal scene of exile, of alienation: Bond's home has been auctioned upon his presumed death, and at the end of the film Bond reveals that he never liked the place anyway. This is not, nor has it ever been, *home*. *Skyfall* clearly articulates a critique of sentimentalized images of 'home' and 'homeland', particularly when used in the service of a 'patriotic' rationalization of the work of supranational networks of security.

The death of Judy Dench as M, as well of Silva, is an ending, but of course, considering the economic imperatives of the Bond franchise, a beginning. The last scene of the film presents a 'resurrected' Bond, ready for a new mission, with a new M (Mallory, played by Ralph Fiennes). Standing upon the roofs of Whitehall, a very ironic Union flag fluttering nearby, Bond takes in the city and nation-state whose interests he works to 'protect', but this is Bond as instrument, sacrificed and resurrected, betrayed and reborn. The ethical ambiguity of Cold War espionage texts, where the moral coding of 'us' and 'them', 'good' and 'bad', 'democratic' and 'communist' become irresolvably confused, here becomes almost an ethical evacuation. Bond operates without illusions, but goes on operating nonetheless. The strutting masculinity of *Casino Royale*, passing through traumatic loss and a symbolic 'death', is re-negotiated as something purely instrumental. Motherless, homeless, Bond finally becomes an instrument of global power as much as a British subject.

2

Masters and Commanders

This chapter considers the figure of the male soldier, particularly in British fiction and film, and especially texts that re-imagine historical constructions of the soldier in previous wars. Alan Moore and Melinda Gebbie's *Lost Girls* (2006), Tom McCarthy's *C* (2010) and Pat Barker's *Regeneration* (1991) rethink the male soldier of World War I; Patrick O'Brian's Aubrey/Maturin novels (and Peter Weir's screen adaptation, *Master and Commander: The Far Side of the World* (2003)) narrate naval warfare during the Napoleonic period. The means by which these texts renegotiate representations of masculinity, and culturally produced constructions of the soldier, have clear political urgency for the contemporary period, where British and American troops have been engaged in wars in Afghanistan and Iraq. We will look at representations of those conflicts, and the resonance they have for the period of the 'War on Terror', in the next chapter in more detail. But I would like to begin this chapter with a striking, if deliberately obscene, image that recurs in three very different texts: *Lost Girls*, Klaus Theweleit's *Male Fantasies* (1989) and Kurt Vonnegut's *Timequake* (1998). All of these images feature the exploded and dismembered male body, and, in particular, the severed penis.

The exploded male body

In Vonnegut's *Timequake*, the universe suffers a 'cosmic charley-horse', a temporal contraction, in which all the people on Earth re-enact, without volition, the last ten years of their lives. The dead are resurrected to die again, and the writer Kilgore Trout, a recurrent character in Vonnegut's fictions, is left to write again all the science fiction short stories which he composes and then disposes of (in public litter bins). One of these is called 'Albert Hardy', and he is composing this story when the 'timequake' ends and everyone is returned to free will, once again, to initially catastrophic effect (as they have forgotten that they do indeed have agency, and neglect to operate machinery or even keep walking). Writing this story bridges the transition between 'being on auto pilot' (as Trout calls it) and a return to 'normal' subjectivity and agency; writing itself a form of automatism that protects Trout from the greater consequences of a 'return' to free will. 'Albert Hardy' is about 'a guy with his head between his legs and his ding-dong atop his neck':

> Albert Hardy would be blown to pieces while a soldier in the Second Battle of the Somme in World War One.
>
> Albert Hardy's dogtags wouldn't be found. His body parts would be reassembled as though he had been like everybody else, with his head atop his neck. He couldn't be given back his ding-dong. To be perfectly frank, his ding-dong wouldn't have been what you might call the subject of an exhaustive search.
>
> Albert Hardy would be buried under and Eternal Flame in France, in the Tomb of the Unknown Soldier, 'normal at last'. (Vonnegut 1998: 79)

Vonnegut's grotesque image of bodily disruption is ironically put in the service of a somatic and ideological normativeness, where the only time in his life that Albert Hardy 'fits in' to images of masculine subjectivity is when his body is exploded and reassembled in death, with a crucial component missing. Vonnegut figures this 'normal at last' body as one that is constituted by a foundational lack, that of the penis.

This image is repeated in the second volume of Klaus Theweleit's *Male Fantasies*. In these two books, he investigates the Fascist imaginary of German militiamen in the early 1920s, ex-soldiers who were recruited into the Nazi Party's SA organization (the Brownshirts). Theweleit found that, in their diary writings and letters, these militiamen consistently imagined themselves as an armoured body, in mechanical phalanx with other 'hard-bodied' men, resisting the 'red flood' of female desire and communism (as pollution). This armour is theorized by Theweleit as being produced by social and cultural conditions that can be traced back much further than that of wartime Germany; the deep roots of the production of the armoured male subject are coterminous with the rise of an industrial and bureaucratic modernity. Theweleit, drawing upon Deleuze and Guattari, proposes an anti-Oedipal reading of masculinity, though he does accept the basic Freudian structure of the 'drives'. Indeed, Theweleit argues thus:

A psychic type whose basic structure was more or less 'psychotic' may have been the norm in Germany (at the very time that Freud was writing), and that this type was far more 'normal' and more common than Oedipus, for example. Oedipus seems likely to have been a highly unusual specimen: a fictional non-fascist citizen modelled on Freud himself. (Theweleit 1989b: 213)

Theweleit proposes that there are numerous parallels between the 'soldier males' he draws upon and the 'average man': the soldier is merely an extension of the tendencies of the more general condition of masculinity. He further suggests:

Since the 'ego' of these men cannot form from the inside out . . . they must acquire an enveloping 'ego' from the outside. [This is] a result of coercion; it is forced upon them by the pain they experience in the onslaught of external agencies. The punishments of parents, teachers, masters, the punishment hierarchies of young boys and the military, remind them constantly of the existence of their periphery (showing them their boundaries), until they 'grow' a functioning and controlling body armour, and a body capable of seamless fusion into larger formations with armorlike properties. [T]he armour of these men may be seen as constituting their ego. (Theweleit 1989b: 164)

This armour is particularly used in defence against the threat of dissolution, typed (in Fascist writings) as the 'red flood'. The 'most urgent task' of the armoured masculine subject 'is to pursue, to dam in, and to subdue any force that threatens to transform him back into the horribly disorganised jumble of flesh, hair, skin, bones, intestines, and feelings that calls itself human – the human being of old' (1989b: 160). The flood is, of course, gendered; flow, flux, the 'morass', is feminine, that which must be defended against: feminization, dissolution. At the same time, Theweleit suggests, the armour produces a desire to 'explode' out of its confines in a violent moment of ecstasy.

Part of the visual method of the books is to place imagery from a range of cultural production – from Nazi-era posters and photographs to Vietnam War–era underground comics – alongside the text, forming a largely separate 'image-track' which is placed in ironic dialogue with the main body of work. By implication, Theweleit is able to suggest that continuation of the Fascist armoured masculine subject in contemporary culture. One of these materials is a German comic from 1970, by an artist called 'Irons', published in *Radical America* (1970). Panels from this strip are given over several pages of *Male Fantasies* (187–196), many of which explicitly portray the male body exploded by weapons fire; indeed, the very first image is of a GI's head, the right side of which explodes outwards towards the edge of the panel, eyeball and ear and tongue starting away as the head disintegrates. This is not portrayed 'realistically'; the rendering is grotesque, overtly 'cartoonish'. The other panels show another GI torn apart by a fusillade of small-arms fire; another whose legs are blown off by a mine; a USAF pilot whose plane is destroyed in an explosion; and the final image is of an atomic weapon detonating, the final 'rupture' in the body politic. The penultimate death is of a North Vietnamese soldier attempting to crawl under some barbed wire on a 'sabotage' mission. An explosion takes his body apart; the panel constellates two boots, a hand, an eyeball and a helmet flying away from the blast. In the lower centre foreground is the man's penis, while the caption reads: 'What on Earth is wrong with this comic strip? The whole thing has gotten out of control!' (Theweleit 1989b: 194). The comic strip itself enacts what Theweleit elsewhere diagnoses about the control of bodily boundaries, and the desire to rupture them or explode out of them:

> The same transformation, the same eruption outward, is sought by all soldier males in the moment of attack. Ultimately, they themselves become the shots spreading outward, bullets hurtling from the military machine toward their body-targets. At these moments, they anticipate the most intense possible sensation: but it is their own velocity they continuously evoke to legitimize their movement of eruption and penetration into the body of the enemy. (Theweleit 1989b: 181)

We will return to the importance of 'velocity' shortly, in relation to Tom McCarthy's novel *C*. Here it is crucial to note the implication of 'eruption', of 'explosion', in the construction of the armoured phallic body of the male soldier. One is not antithetical to the other; in fact, explosion is intensely desired and is a culmination of the soldier-subject's trajectory.

The third of the images of the dismembered penis occurs in the Moore/Gebbie book *Lost Girls* (2006). *Lost Girls* is a graphic tale by Alan Moore and Melinda which rewrites the characters and histories of Wendy Darling (*Peter Pan and Wendy* (1911)), Alice Liddell (*Alice's Adventures in Wonderland* (1865)/*Through the Looking Glass* (1871)) and Dorothy Gale (*The Wonderful Wizard of Oz* (1900)). The book is sexually explicit, offering a fantasia of couplings, flows and desires; and it is utopian, in that its recoding of the latent sexual content of Victorian and Edwardian children's literature is released from the structures of repression into a polymorphously perverse world of unrestricted desire and sexual pleasure. *Lost Girls* takes place in the last few months before the outbreak of the Great War in 1914, and in fact the assassination of the Archduke Ferdinand in Sarajevo is depicted at the very end of Book 2. *Lost Girls* is then a retrospective *belle epoque* fiction, where the 'long Edwardian afternoon' is about to be plunged into dreadful night. As in Truffaut's *Jules et Jim* (1961), also set in the 'innocent' years prior to 1914, a transnational male friendship is a crucial index of the text's critique of the Great War as the violent expression of a corrosive nationalism. While the French Jim (Henri Serre) and Austrian Jules (Oskar Werner), close friends and two points of an erotic triangle with the beloved Catherine (Jeanne Moreau) in *belle epoque* Paris, are able to maintain their friendship despite fighting on opposite sides (friendship transcending nationalism), in *Lost Girls*, this male homosociality is deficient. As Tof Eklund writes in his contribution to an *ImageText* roundtable, 'Lost Girls posits a uniquely male tendency to sublimate sex into violence as the cause of WWI. [Wendy Darling's husband] Harold and [Dorothy's "boyfriend"] Rolf are judged harshly because each puts his national loyalty ahead of their mutual desire for each other' (Eklund 2007: par 18). Both Rolf and Harold are emblematically products of sexual repression (and thereby 'perversion'): Rolf is a shoe fetishist, who is excited by power fantasies as well as literal jackboots, and Harold's deeply closeted homosexuality is connected with his job in armament manufacture and sales, and his investment in the 'manly' icon of the battleship. Where, for Wendy, Alice and Dorothy, the polymorphous perverse is utopian, for Rolf and particularly Harold, the enjoyment of unrepressed sexual desire is temporary and abandoned in the face of the geopolitical narrative of national conflict. Their sexual 'liberation' is really an extension of their predisposition towards Fascism. Rolf and Harold, when fucking, do so with an eye to power, to domination; their ineradicable phallicism is shunned by Alice, the 'leader' of the lost girls, whose desire is, until the very end, strictly lesbian – although she does wear a dildo, and it is when she is simultaneously penetrated by Wendy and Dorothy with similar strap-on penises that she reaches her own epiphany, when she is able to let slip the reins of control. For Rolf and Harold, power holds sway over desire.

The text ultimately recapitulates the correlation of female desire with fluidity, fecundity and the polymorphous, and masculinity with Fascism, that we find critiqued in Theweleit's *Male Fantasies*. In *Lost Girls*, this imagery is found when Dorothy has sex with the Tin Man, one of the workers on her father's farm. In a fantastical tableau, consisting of a single-page panel outside of the narrative diegesis (a device repeated in many narrative episodes told by Dorothy and

Wendy), Dorothy is manacled and spreadeagled in a kind of abstract congress with a heavily robotic 'Tin Man', whose segmented metal phallus penetrates her vagina. It is a horrifying image, a violation unlike even the coercive or abusive sex found at points elsewhere in *Lost Girls*. The metal phallus, unlike the dildo, is a literal 'weapon'.

The connection between masculine phallicism and war is sealed in the final pages of part 3, which is where we find the image of the severed penis. Wendy, Alice and Dorothy, having told their stories and 'healed' their lostness, leave the empty hotel. Their room is subsequently occupied by the advancing German soldiers, some of whom build a bonfire in their room and smash Alice's abandoned mirror. The panels follow the smoke to the battlefield, where we find a soldier, legs propped apart, leaning back against the rim of a bomb crater. This, it seems, is Rolf. His boots have been blown off and lay in the foreground, on the lip of the crater – as does something else. For Rolf has been emasculated, his genitalia blown to the other side of the crater, and a gaping wound tears him from crotch to sternum. Visually, what we have here is an invagination, a monstrous perversion of the imagery of the opened vulva that stands for the utopian possibilities of polymorphous sexual desire (aligned with the female body) throughout the text. This is the terminal image of lost innocence in *Lost Girls*. The 'lost innocence' of Wendy, Dorothy and even Alice is recuperable on the Freudian stage of storytelling and unrepressed sexual desire, but it is not so for Rolf. His Fascist body armour is undone by a bursting shell, his body exploded by the very military phallicism that seemed to armour it. While Alice can leave her mirror behind, having found a kind of wholeness, Rolf's dead eyes stare sightlessly into the dark future, his body fatally disintegrated.

The soldier and trauma

These images of the male body attest to a discourse of bodily and psychological trauma that has become central to the ways in which soldier masculinity has been presented, certainly since World War I, where work on the 'war neuroses' by Army psychiatrists, and also by Freud and psychoanalytical practitioners, has been formative to the way in which the experience of World War I, and of all subsequent wars, has been presented. In his 'Introduction to *Psycho-Analysis and the War Neuroses*' (a literal Introduction to a book), Freud initially differentiates war neuroses from 'the ordinary neuroses of peace-time' by his emphasis on trauma: they 'are to be regarded as traumatic neuroses whose occurrence has been made possible or has been promoted by a conflict in the ego' (Freud 1955a: 209). Freud proposes a kind of psychological splitting or doubling caused by the experience of war (in a mass or conscript army: 'there would be no possibility of it arising in an army of professional soldiers' (Freud 1955a: 209)), one in which the 'peace-ego realizes what danger it runs of losing its life owing to the rashness of its newly formed, parasitic double' (Freud 1955a: 209). Neurosis is manifested by the peace-ego defending itself not only from intense physical danger, but also from the effects of the war-ego upon it. This pressure externally *and* internally leads Freud to argue:

> In traumatic and war neuroses the human ego is defending itself from a danger which threatens it from without or which is embodied in a shape assumed by the ego itself. In the transference neuroses of peace the enemy from which the ego is defended is actually the libido, which demands seem to it to be menacing. In both cases the ego is afraid of being damaged. (Freud 1955a: 210)

By the end of the Introduction, then, Freud makes a clear analogy between peace-time neuroses, caused by the libido (desire) and its repression, and war-time neuroses, caused by the fear of external violence. Freud completes the logical circuit at the very end of the Introduction when he states, 'we have a perfect right to describe repression, which lies at the basis of every neurosis, as a reaction to a trauma – as an elementary traumatic neurosis' (Freud 1955a: 210). The implication of this statement is that the war neurosis is in no sense *originary*: it replicates the conditions of repression which forms the pattern of subjectivity that Freud outlines in his theory of Oedipal conflict (and, ultimately, as the motive force which provides the energies for cultural and social production, for 'civilization'). In *Moses and Monotheism* (1939), Freud argues that 'it is correct to say that there are cases which we single out as "traumatic" ones because the effects unmistakably go back to one or more strong impressions of this early period [of infancy]' (Freud 1951: 118). If war neurosis is analogous to peace-time neurosis in the ego defending itself from trauma, then trauma becomes foundational to the operation of repression in the peace-time ego itself. In a paper called 'Memorandum on the Electrical Treatment of War Neurotics', unpublished until the 1955 *Collected Works*, Freud notes:

> There were plenty of patients even in peace-time who, after traumas (that is, after frightening and dangerous experiences such as railway accidents, etc.)

exhibited severe disturbances in their mental life and in their nervous activity, without physicians having reached an agreed judgement on these states. (Freud 1955b: 211)

Freud insists that the symptoms exhibited by soldier-patients were entirely unconscious; these men were not 'malingerers', consciously avoiding battle, but the sufferers of 'an unconscious inclination in the soldier to withdraw from the demands, dangerous or outrageous to his feelings, made upon him by active service' (Freud 1955b: 212). Illness becomes an unconscious means by which to withdraw the subject from the source of trauma. The most important source of the conflict makes revealing reading: 'Fear of losing his own life, opposition to the command to kill other people, rebellion against the ruthless suppression of his own personality by his superiors' (Freud 1955b: 212). Only one of the causes is a reaction to physical danger; another is almost an ethical revulsion from obedience, the third a result of the internal doubling or splitting produced by the apparatus of ideological instruction and psychological and physical training. This is the disciplinary apparatus outlined by Theweleit; but he has a very different conception to Freud of masculine subjectivity at work.

The connection between trauma and modernity, however, and not just between trauma and the experience of war, that is emphasized by Freud in his analogy between peace-time and war time neurosis, is revealed in his reference to 'railway accidents etc'. As Lynne Kirby explores in *Parallel Tracks: The Railroad and Silent Cinema* (1997), the extended mobility of modernity itself produces 'shock' or trauma, and is symbolized in 'a condition known as "railway spine", later called "traumatic neurosis"' (Kirby 1997: 57–8). This is particularly pertinent to the production of masculinities within a technological environment in which speed and mobility become increasingly important. 'Hysteria', the term used in Freud (and Joseph Breuer's) first book on psychological disturbance, *Studies on Hysteria* (1895/1956), is, of course, a gendered term, used to denote psychological disturbance in women (and connected, in classical medicine, to the *mobility* of the womb around the female body). Kirby notes that in the work of Jean-Martin Charcot, 'the similarity of the symptoms [of "male hysteria"] to those of female hysterics' was apparent, as was the surprising number of 'stereotypically virile working-class men' who presented these symptoms (Kirby 1997: 66). Charcot connected the symptoms of male hysteria to displacement and mobility in men, 'vagabonds, tramps, society's peripatetic disenfranchised ... who experience in their own bodies and lives the metaphor of a characteristic trait of hysteria – mobility' (Kirby 1997: 67). Kirby suggests that hysteria can be understood as being produced by the conditions of modernity itself:

> One can see that cultural displacement as massive as nineteenth-century mechanization and urbanization – railway-assisted – traumatized its victims into a condition akin to female hysteria. In other words, it 'emasculated' men, and not only those men of a certain class. Women, proletarian men, tramps, and other social marginals were made to bear the brunt of the shocks of modernity. (Kirby 1997: 67)

Just as Theweleit connects the soldier-male to wider constructions of masculinity – even suggesting that Freud's Oedipal male was rather uncommon – Kirby argues that 'the working-class male hysterics pointed to what all men were potentially capable of becoming' (Kirby 1997: 68). The hysteria and trauma suffered by the soldier, by the displaced and by proletarian masculinity haunts all forms of male subjectivity.

If, as E. Ann Kaplan suggests in *Trauma Culture*, 'Trauma is often seen as inherently linked to modernity' (Kaplan 2005: 24), it is also indissolubly connected to memory, and to memorialization. Indeed, Kaplan's own book was partly produced from her own experiences of the destruction of the World Trade Center in 2001, and investigates practices of memorialization within discussion of the theorization of trauma. That trauma has become central to the representation of the World War I, particularly in retrospective narratives (though as we can see from Freud's writing, the discourses of trauma are indelibly traced upon the writings of that historical period), has a particular bearing upon the works I will discuss in the remainder of this chapter, for it suggests that the texts themselves work as a means by which to manifest (and deal with) traumatic experiences, as forms of cultural memory; and also that war traumatizes not only individuals, but also systems of thought and representation, which (after Freud) insistently return to the scene of trauma to try to make sense of it. Analysing texts that represent masculine subjects in World War I is, then, a means by which to approach the legacy of that war and others upon the cultural representation of masculinity in the contemporary period.

One of the key British novels that deals with the traumatic effects of warfare upon masculinity is Pat Barker's *Regeneration* (1992), filmed by Gilles MacKinnon in 1997. *Regeneration* concerns the relationships between Dr W. H. R. Rivers, an eminent psychiatrist working for the British Army at Craiglockhart hospital in 1917, and two of his patients: Siegfried Sassoon, the poet, whose

'Declaration' against the 'political errors and insincerities for which the fighting men are being sacrificed' opens the novel (Barker 1992: 3), and Billy Prior, a working-class junior officer whose rebellious and conflicted masculinity casts Sassoon's (and Rivers') assumptions about the ethics of the war, and of psychiatric treatment, into stark relief. Sassoon's Declaration begins: 'I am making this statement as an act of willful defiance of military authority, because I believe the war is being deliberately prolonged by those who have the power to end it' (Barker 1992: 3); as we shall see later in this chapter, the problematics of military authority are central to formations of masculinity, and it is important to note that Sassoon self-identifies as a protestor through a 'defiance of military authority'. It is clear from the text that although Sassoon suffers from war trauma – he sees the bodies of dead comrades moving in waking dreams – he is not, in any sense, 'mad'; he has been sent to Craiglockhart for Rivers to 'cure' him of his political refusal to carry on fighting. Although Sassoon inhabits a prototypical warrior masculinity – he cares deeply for the men he commands, and is brave in combat to the point of physical heedlessness – this is striated by his homosexuality which, although largely implied rather than stated, is crucial to a late dialogue between himself and Rivers:

> Sassoon looked downcast: 'I thought things were getting better.'
>
> 'I think they were. Before the war. *Slightly*. But it's not very likely, is it, that any movement towards greater tolerance would persist in wartime? After all, in war, you've got this *enormous* emphasis on love between men – comradeship – and everybody approves. But at the same time there's always this little niggle of anxiety. Is it the right *kind* of love? Well, one of the ways you make sure it's the right kind is to make it crystal clear what the penalties for the other kind are.' (Barker 1992: 204)

The ideological functions of constructions of masculinity are spelt out here, but ones which the remainder of the novel is careful to complicate or blur; Sassoon is capable of feeling different kinds of love for men (homosociality/homosexuality) without apparent conflict. He returns to active service at the end of the novel, not because he has changed his mind or been 'cured' of dissident opinions, but because he feels that the lives of his men will be better protected if he is in France to lead them.

Rivers, who (the text suggests) is himself homosexual, eventually begins to exhibit the same symptoms of neurosis as his patients, through transference, and is ordered on leave. Rivers' own sense of masculinity is problematized when he remembers a former patient, Layard, saying 'I don't see you as a *father*, you know.' Looking up from the rug in front of the fire. Laughing. 'More a sort of . . . *male mother*' (Barker 1992: 107). Rivers does not like this characterization because 'he distrusted the implication that nurturing, even when done by a man, remains female, as if the ability were in some way borrowed, or even stolen, from women' (Barker 1992: 107). There is also the strong sense that Rivers resists feminization here, and is himself keen to negotiate a sense of 'fatherhood' that embraces 'a relationship between officers and men that was . . . domestic. Caring' (Barker 1992: 107). The repetition of ellipses, here and in Layard's speech, is revealing: there is something that is difficult to express about masculinity, and about the relationships between men, even in the psychiatric and analytical discourse of Rivers.

The theme of mutism, of being unable to express what is of crucial import, is central to *Regeneration*, not least because that is a symptom of working-class soldiers that is presented by Prior (an officer) at the beginning of the novel. (In a horrifying late scene, Rivers witnesses the 'treatment' of a traumatized soldier with electric shocks to the back of the throat to make him speak, a forced 'cure' that is indistinguishable from torture.) There is also a self-reflexive element at work, in Barker's use of Freudian paradigms of trauma and repression placing *Regeneration* as a text that is able to speak what is latent in culture and political discourse. Prior is able to fully participate in the 'talking cure' to the extent of challenging Rivers on his own ground: Prior himself discusses mutism as 'spring[ing] from a conflict between *wanting* to say something, and knowing that if you *do* say it the consequences will be disastrous' (Barker 1992: 96). Here is Freud's traumatic conflict between the peace-ego (who wants to speak) and war-ego (who demands silent obedience) made manifest.

The most traumatized of all the soldiers, who remains outside of the paradigm of the 'talking cure', is Burns, who had been pitched head first by an explosion into a putrefying corpse. In the moment of Rivers' most extreme alienation from the project of state violence that he serves, during a visit to Burns a storm arises, and Rivers finds his patient huddled and rocking himself in the moat of a ruined castle: 'He looked up at the tower that loomed squat and menacing above them, and thought, *Nothing justifies this. Nothing nothing nothing*' (Barker 1992: 180). Rivers' discourse descends into a terminal negation, a nihilism that shadows the war and his role in it. For a psychiatrist, who must make meaning of the symptoms with which he is presented, this moment is one where that diagnostic and meaning-making facility deserts him, leaving only the ethical truth of the war that he otherwise represses in himself. Burns is seen earlier in the text in a moment of isolation that returns us to the imagery of bodily separation, and in particular, the penis, that we analysed above: 'he looked down at himself. His naked body was white as a root. He cupped his genitals in his hands, not because he was ashamed, but because they looked incongruous, they didn't seem to belong with the rest of him' (Barker 1992: 39). Like the other soldiers we have seen, Burns is physically and figuratively *unmanned*; unlike the others, he seems to have no armour with which to protect himself.

In *Manipulating Masculinity: War and Gender in Modern British and American Literature*, Kathy J. Phillips argues: 'War, which authorizes hurting and self-hurting on a grand scale, serves as a remarkably efficient sadomasochistic machine' (Phillips 2006: 61). While noting again the discourse of authority, the idea of the war machine reflects Klaus Theweleit's somewhat anti-Oedipal reading of the soldier-male. Following the work of Gilles Deleuze and Felix Guattari (in particular, *Anti-Oedipus: Capitalism and Schizophrenia* (1983)), Theweleit argues that 'the results of our investigations so far suggest that the "ego" in the Freudian sense of a mediator "between the world and the id" exists only in a very fragmented form, or, indeed, hardly at all, in soldier males. There is some question whether it has ever really been formed in them at all' (Theweleit 1989a: 204). Instead, Theweleit follows Deleuze and Guttari in proposing a 'machinic' theorization of 'the mode of production of the unconscious' (Theweleit 1989a: 211). Theweleit explains:

> It does not require *whole* persons for its productions. It achieves satisfaction when parts of itself are joined to parts of other objects, forming transitory productive connections that are afterwards dissolved so that new productive connections can be formed.
>
> Deleuze and Guattari call this mode of production *machinic*. The unconscious is a desiring-machine and the body parts, components of that machine. In suckling, the sucking mouth and nourishing breast form a sucking-pumping machine, which continues to run until hunger is satiated. For Freud, the pattern is different: *son* Sigmund suckles at the breast of *mother* Amalie, who is later recognized as the *wife* of the *father*, Jakob Freud, and a triangle is constituted in which the son becomes 'Oedipus'. (Theweleit 1989a: 211 [italics in original])

In Theweleit's conception, the armoured body of the soldier-male is not a Freudian 'subject', a unitary individual with an internal psychic apparatus, but rather a set of components capable of articulation and combination with other similar soldier-components. This makes new sense of the images of bodily dismemberment we have seen so far: in proto-Fascist writings, the soldier's limbs are described as if severed from their bodies: they are fused together to form new totalities. The leg of the individual has a closer functional connection to the leg of his neighbor than to his own torso. In the machine, then, new totalities are formed: bodies no longer identical with the bodies of individual human beings. (Theweleit 1989b: 154)

The dismembered bodies in *Timequake, Lost Girls* and *Regeneration* attest to a non-Fascist understanding of the male body, much more closely aligned with (in the latter two particularly) Freudian discourses of trauma. Here, dismemberment, the severed penis, can be considered as *lack*, a rupture of the male body that is an invagination or feminization and which is analogous to the feminization of male subjects we saw earlier in the theories of male hysteria. These men not only lack a penis, but also a phallus; their castration is a symbol of the *subjection to* power.

Modernism and the war machine

Tom McCarthy's *C* (2010) is a novel that claims a Modernist inheritance. Narrating the early life of Serge Carrefax, who is born to a father obsessed with telegraphy and who runs a school for deaf children, through Serge's experiences as an airman in World War I through to Weimar Berlin and his experiences in Imperial espionage, *C* not only explores the male subject in war, but also makes Carrefax an emblematic male subject of modernity. Born around the turn of the century, Carrefax seems to inhabit an entirely affectless mode of existence. Deeply informed by Freud but presenting an anti-traumatic model of subjectivity, as I will investigate, McCarthy's text presents a masculine subject who thinks of himself as a machine, not only during war, but also from an early age. *C* is suffused with metaphors and images derived from communications: circuits, codes, transmissions, signals. The text itself is explicitly *coded*, even in its title; it asks, what does 'C' signify? We will discuss McCarthy's apprehension of the centrality of transmissions to modernity in more detail in Chapter 11, but here we will begin with another sense of circuitry: those networks that enable the operation of machines.

Simeon Carrefax, Serge's father, gives an address, almost a sermon, to the schoolchildren at the beginning of the novel. 'The human body', he states,

is a mechanism. When its engine-room, the thorax, a bone-girt vault for heart and lungs whose very floor and walls are constantly in motion – when this chamber exerts pressure sufficient to open the trap-door set into its ceiling and send air rushing outwards through the windpipe, sound ensues. It's as simple as that. (McCarthy 2010: 15)

The body is a machine in motion; it is not static, but active. The analysis of human sound production in terms of mechanism implies, first, the possibility of its perfection (or repair, if broken) and, second, that it may be replicated in mechanical form by pressure chambers and pipes. Friedrich Kittler, in *Gramophone, Typewriter, Film* (1999), elaborates on this techno-cultural process and practice, and cites examples in actuality and in fiction where mechanical heads, fitted with pipes, are designed to reproduce the human voice. This reproduction of sound leads to the circuitry of global mass communications that McCarthy's novel thematizes; *C* also narrates the period of its birth. For Serge Carrefax, who internalizes the discourses of mechanism to the extent that he views himself as a machine, this legacy is problematic. Later, while watching cinematic images projected onto a bed sheet as a youth, he feels a 'rush of anticipation run through the cogs and sprockets of his body' as he watches 'empty linen springing into artificial life' (McCarthy 2010: 46); as Lynne Kirby notes in *Parallel Lines*, the birth of 'railway spine' and the diagnoses of the trauma and 'shock' of modernity (in the words of Walter Benjamin) are historically coterminous with the advent of cinematic technology. Carrefax is far from a traumatized subject, however. His self-perception *as a machine* precludes this possibility. Carrefax is an emblematic figure of modernity, not traumatized by the circuits of communications, mobility and war, but produced directly from them. If not a ghost in the machine, Carrefax is something akin to Poe's 'Man of the Crowd' (1840), a somewhat phantasmic emanation of the imperatives of modernity itself.

In World War I, Carrefax takes up the position of aerial observer, a position, through the use of camera technology, that allows him 'the mechanical command of landscape and its boundaries that flight affords him, the mastery of hedgerows, fields and lanes, the shapes and volumes' (McCarthy 2010: 127). We encounter here the language of 'mastery' that will be central to our investigations in the last part of the chapter, but it is a mastery produced by the camera technology he operates. In essence, Carrefax becomes a Modernist 'kino-eye', his subjectivity intimately connected to the machines of vision that direct his gaze. Filming allows the mastery enjoyed during flight: not, one should note, the typical encoding of flight as freedom, but of flight as enabling a God's eye view, a mastery associated with an aerial perspective. Serge Carrefax not only *sees*, he *commands* what he sees. At some points, Carrefax seems to become the airplane itself: 'the idea that his flesh could melt and fuse with the machine parts pleases him' (McCarthy 2010: 164). He and his comrades sing a song:

> *Take the cylinder out of my kidneys,*
> > *The connecting rod out of my brain, my brain,*
> *From the small of my back take the camshaft*
> > *And assemble the engine again.*

(McCarthy 2010: 163)

When he thinks about this song, Carrefax 'imagines the whole process playing itself out backwards: his back quivering in pleasure as pumps and pistons plunge into it, heart and liver being spliced with valve and filter to create a whole new, streamlined mechanism' (McCarthy 2010: 164). Playing the process backwards is reversing the film; but the insistence on pleasure here is crucial. This is not a traumatic acknowledgement of the likely fate of the airmen, bodies crushed and lacerated by machine parts; instead, it is inscribed into desire, into what Theweleit diagnosed as the soldier male's desire for explosion, for fusion. The combination of component parts, of machine and flesh, is ecstatic and deeply expressive of Carrefax's proximity to the psychological structures of Theweleit's proto-Fascist militiamen. It also signifies the implication of sexual desire and war that *Regeneration* acknowledges, as is typical with the expression of taboos, through the experiences of Billy Prior. Rivers is visited by Prior outside of normal consulting hours, in the evening, and Prior tells the psychiatrist that his nightmares are: 'Nothing you won't have heard a hundred times before . . . Except that *sometimes* they get muddled up with sex. So I wake up, and. . .' (Barker 1992: 100). Prior's confession suggests that beneath the discourses of trauma and wounding that Barker both inhabits and explores, there is something more troubling: an implication of sexual desire in violence and horror, and not just in what Kathy J. Phillips called the 'sadomasochistic machine' of war. McCarthy is still more explicit when Carrefax, after the war has finished, says 'I liked the war' (McCarthy 2010: 214).

The connection between machinery and sexuality is made much earlier in the novel. Carrefax's older sister Sophie, a prodigy with codes and cryptography, enters into an apprenticeship with the older spymaster Widsun, which develops into a transgressive sexual relationship. After the performance of a play on the grounds of the Carrefax house, Serge witnesses a form of primal scene as a cinematic shadow play,

> like a film made up only of silhouettes. It's some kind of moving thing made of articulated parts. One of the parts is horizontal, propped up on four stick legs

like a low table; the other is vertical, slotted into the underside of the table's rear
end but rising above it, its spine wobbling as the whole contraption rocks back
and forth. (McCarthy 2010: 60)

This scene is a direct, albeit cinematic and mechanical replication of the primal
scene that Freud analyses in his case study 'The Wolf-Man'. In that study, Freud
pursues the origin of the man's neurosis back to an image from childhood, 'a
picture of a wolf standing on its hind legs and stepping out' that the man's older
sister used to torment him when he was a small child (Freud 2010: 11). Freud
connects this to a dream the child had, of '*white wolves sitting in the big walnut
tree outside the window.* . . . *Obviously fearful that the wolves were going to gobble
me up I screamed* and woke up' (Freud 2010: 29 [italics in original]). Freud's
analysis takes him to what is proposed to be a moment of originary trauma, a
primal scene in which the Wolf Man saw his father and mother having sex *a
tergo*. The standing wolf in the tormenting picture is a repetition of this image in
a form filtered through the screen of repression, and the dream a manifestation
of this trauma. McCarthy re-imagines this scene as a mechanical spectacle that
Carrefax can only understand in abstract terms, horizontal and vertical. He also
takes the character of Sophie almost directly from the pages of the Wolf Man
study; the Wolf Man's sister is sexually precocious and undergoes 'a dazzling
intellectual development distinguished by an acute and realistic understanding',
but whose accomplishments lead her away from social contact and whose
suicide (by poisoning) Freud speculatively attributes to the probable 'onset of
dementia praecox' (Freud 2010: 18). Incest haunts the story of the Wolf Man's
sister, both in tales of sexual precociousness and in the Wolf Man's confession
that, at the age of thirteen, he had 'ventured to approach her with a view to
physical intimacy' (Freud 2010: 19). Incest and insects are crucial to Vladimir
Nabokov's *Ada* (1969), another clear influence on *C*; but in McCarthy's novel,
these are themselves suppressed in the foregrounding of a machinic modernity.

    As we will see with regard to McCarthy's writings on Orpheus in Chapter 11,
he is in some sense a critic as well as an author of novels. With his semi-parodic
organization, the International Necronautical Society (INS), McCarthy has
published a series of communiqués and memoranda that replicate the style and
emphases of Modernist groups such as the Futurists, the Surrealists and the
Situationists. It is the Futurists, and the figure of F. T. Marinetti, who appear most
regularly in the INS writings. McCarthy refers directly to the Futurist manifesto
in the INS essay 'INS Declaration on the Notion of the "Future"', he suggests that
'the future, culturally speaking, begins with a car crash. Or rather, an account

of one' (McCarthy 2012b: 267). As McCarthy notes, in the Futurist manifesto, when Marinetti and his friends pile into 3 'roaring' cars and hurtle through the night, the cause of the crash – where Marinetti's car ends up in the ditch – is the approach of two *cyclists*. McCarthy reads this moment as emblematic of late modernity's catastrophic circuits, and of the capacity for the avant-garde to instantaneously derail itself: 'the roaring surge towards the future is arrested no sooner than it begins' (McCarthy 2012b: 268). The Futurists' emphasis on speed, on technology, on the machine, is also crucial to *C* and its representation of Carrefax's masculinity: like Theweleit's soldiers, the Futurist body is clean, masculine and mechanical, and it is also aligned with Fascism.

Patrick O'Brian's Aubrey/Maturin novels

The discourse of trauma in relation to masculinity and war is so pervasive that McCarthy's text is unusual in its accession to the potentiality for ecstatic and explosive pleasure, even if this is at the cost of rupturing the masculine subject entirely. As we shall see in the next chapter, representations of American involvement in war, even in a 'just war' such as World War II, have more recently been presented in terms of shock and terror (as in the opening sequence of Spielberg's *Saving Private Ryan* (1998)), of trauma and loss. To conclude this chapter, we will turn to a long series of novels published by Patrick O'Brian, the Aubrey/Maturin series that began with *Master and Commander* (1970) and ended with *Blue at the Mizzen* (1999), the last completed text before O'Brian's death. A film version was directed by Peter Weir, *Master and Commander: The Far Side of the World* (2003), which combined elements from several of the books, but most notably *The Far Side of the World* (1984). The book series can be considered a *roman fleuve*, a continuous narrative in which the naval officer Jack Aubrey ascends, via a series of naval battles, financial catastrophes, domestic interludes and ill-advised infidelities from the 'Master and Commander' of the first novel (his first command) to the Admiral of the Blue of the last; and in which his companion, the doctor, natural philosopher and espionage agent Stephen Maturin, attends to a range of secret missions accompanying Aubrey's ships. These men inhabit markedly different forms of masculinity: Aubrey is English, robust, physical, largely conventional in politics, but humane, inquisitive and energetic; Maturin is Irish, irascible, intellectually curious and deeply sympathetic to both radical causes and fellow human beings, and prey to obsessions and addictions.

They operate, although each marries in the course of the series, as a homosocial pair, and spend far more time with each other than they do with their respective wives. There is often tension between the men, however, often to do with the issue of command and authority. Aubrey, who sometimes uncomfortably inhabits his Captain's uniform (he has strong homosocial bonds with both officers and men, albeit regulated through the Navy's hierarchical structures, and in his youth was reduced to the ranks for disciplinary reasons) is self-reflective enough to understand, and interrogate the tensions inherent in Captaincy: in *The Mauritius Command*, Aubrey declares that 'When you are in command, you get so sick of the loneliness of playing the great man and so on that you long to break out of it' (O'Brian 2010: 32). It is Maturin, however, who most often articulates a critique of command. In *Master and Commander*, Maturin says, 'Authority is the great enemy – the assumption of authority. I know few men over fifty that seem to me entirely human: virtually none who has exercised authority' (O'Brian 2002: 181). Towards the end of the series of novels, Aubrey is in just that position, and despite being 'authority incarnate', must retain his more humane, sympathetic and empathetic aspects of masculinity to maintain his effectiveness as a commander. In the O'Brian novels, the necessity of command within the hierarchical structures of naval discipline comes at the cost of one's own humanity, embodied in the many irascible and untrustworthy admirals that populate the books; Aubrey is one of the few who does so.

In *The Far Side of the World*, Aubrey promises Maturin that he can visit the Galapagos islands when they are in the vicinity, then is forced to renege: 'The promise was subject to the requirements of the service: listen, Stephen, here I have my tide, my current and my wind all combined – my enemy with a fine head start so that there is not a moment to be lost – could I conscientiously delay for the sake of an iguano or a beetle?' (O'Brian 2003: 229). Stephen replies with, what is for him, and in relation to his friend and colleague, an extremity of anger:

> Very well, sir; I must submit to superior force, I find. I must be content to form part of a merely belligerent expedition, hurrying past all inestimable pearls, bent solely on destruction, neglecting all discovery – incapable of spending five minutes on discovery. I shall say nothing about the corruption of power or its abuse; I shall only observe that for my part I look upon a promise as binding and that until the present I must confess it had never occurred to me that you might not be of the same opinion – that you might have two words. (O'Brian 2003: 230)

Maturin here opposes homosocial, personal bonds to the official bonds of the navy (to which he himself, as ship's doctor, is subject); Aubrey asserts that the personal must be subject to the official, to the 'requirements of the service'. Maturin's heated accusations of corruption and abuse of power point to the sovereignty wielded by a Captain at sea, but ignore the military practicalities of what he proposes. He knows, of course, that Aubrey is not to be swayed; the 'requirements of the service' countermand all else.

In Peter Weir's film *Master and Commander: The Far Side of the World* (2003), Maturin (Paul Bettany) says of Aubrey (Russell Crowe) that he is 'an exception to the rule that authority corrupts', but in the scene where Maturin is refused his walk upon the Galapagos, Aubrey says 'men must be governed', to which his friend replies, 'that's the excuse of every tyrant in history'. The Napoleonic context is strong in the novels, for a hatred of tyranny is Maturin's reason for serving with the British Navy, as a United Irishman; here, the political aspect of Maturin is less present, as are his espionage activities. There is still an ongoing critique of leadership and authority, but this is displaced on to the unfortunate Midshipman Hollom, deficient in terms of both masculinity and authority; Aubrey counsels him: 'it's leadership [the men] want, strength. You find that within yourself.' This authority, 'naturally' inhabited by Aubrey's strong and active personality, cannot be found 'within' Hollom; physically small, lacking assertiveness and, the film suggests, physical bravery, Hollom is persecuted by the crew until he commits suicide. After his death, group identity and the bonds of homosociality are asserted: 'Not all of us become the men who we might be,' Aubrey declares, and asks the crew to look to their own conduct if they 'failed him in respect of fellowship'. In this sense, what N. A. M. Rodger calls the 'wooden world', the spatial proximity and shared (homosocial) values in the ship (albeit striated by class and the men/officer divide), becomes the key, and even highly prized members of the crew are sacrificed in order to preserve the ship and her company. (Not Maturin, however; when he is mortally wounded, the ship finally puts into Galapagos so he can operate upon himself.)

Released in 2003 *Master and Commander: The Far Side of the World* offers a representation of the global reach of warring superpowers (French and British ships fighting in the Pacific Ocean) that is softened by the bonds between men that remain central to the film's fabric. If the 'oceans are battlefields', as a title at the beginning of the film proposes, this is a battlefield in which the attributes of traditional masculinity – physical courage, homosocial bonds, martial prowess – are to the fore. This is also, notably, a text about men at war which does not present their experiences as traumatic. The young Midshipman Calamy (Max Benitz), whose arm is lost in an engagement, recovers to take his place at the helm of the *HMS Surprise* at the end of the film, and takes part in the final action. Violence and death are not presented as horrific, if not quite heroic; they are simply a fact of existence aboard a man o' war. This matter-of-factness indicates the distance of the film, and the Aubrey/Maturin novels, from the discourses of trauma that dominate representations of modern and contemporary warfare. These men are subject to the 'requirements of the service', which may require that they give their limbs or lives, but they are not traumatized by it. This pragmatism about violent death may end up as a form of comfort for the reader; it certainly suggests that there is little investment in these texts in demonstrating the terrifying experience of warfare. In the next chapter, which considers American texts and their relation to Empire, both horror and ecstatic release are presented as deformations to masculine subjectivity caused by war.

3

American Hearts of Darkness

Between the secret agent, discussed in the figure of James Bond in Chapter 1, and the figure of the soldier, discussed in the last chapter in relation to British texts and the focus of this chapter on American films, stands the figure of Jason Bourne. Created by Robert Ludlum, Bourne was the central character in three films made during the early 2000s, all starring Matt Damon in the title role: *The Bourne Identity* (2002), directed by Doug Liman; and *The Bourne Supremacy* (2004) and *The Bourne Ultimatum* (2007), both directed by Paul Greengrass. The first two of these films have a clear influence upon the re-imagined, hyper-mobile Bond that features in *Casino Royale* (2006) and subsequent films, not only in terms of a globalized imaginary but also in the colour palette and mode of editing. Bourne has none of the markers of sophistication that attend Bond (from clothing to food to the martinis he drinks); Matt Damon is an American, but removed from class or geographical locators in terms of his speech, behaviour or dress. He is a kind of Everyman, a status that is associated with the motive force behind the overarching narrative of the three films: he does not know who he is, and he needs to find out. At the beginning of *The Bourne Identity*, Bourne is fished from the Mediterranean by a Marseilles trawler, and when he awakes, he suffers from amnesia. He follows clues back to an apartment in Paris, where it becomes apparent that he is a highly trained espionage operative; when an assassin breaks in to the apartment to kill him, the fight scene that ensues indicates that Bourne is indeed a skilled agent and capable of a high degree of violence. What marks his difference, besides his amnesia, is a degree of ethical ambiguity at work: in the first film, Bourne acts violently and kills others only when attacked, and to protect himself or Marie Kreutz (Franka Potente), who is helping him to recover a sense of his own identity. In subsequent films, Bourne is capable of killing in order to exact revenge, but it is clear that his 'mission', to pursue his own lost identity and to understand the reason why he was found, without memories, floating in the Mediterranean, leads him into actions that he finds ethically problematic. Indeed, at the end of the first film, he and Marie attempt to flee entirely, to escape the grid of globalized security and espionage; this temporary escape comes to an end at the beginning of the second film.

Bourne, then, is a rather different figure from Bond, whose role as an instrument of British (and thereby 'Western') interests is only interrogated in *Skyfall* (2012), where his expendability is made all too apparent. Bourne is outside the institutional frameworks that rationalize and validate Bond's violent hyper-mobility, and is pursued by agents of those networks (including those on his own 'side', the CIA agents that are part of the Treadstone programme that produced him). Bourne does not use the transnational circuits of global mobility that are the enablers of Bond's narratives: there *is* international mobility in the Bourne films, but *not* by air; in fact, the only time he tries to board a plane is in *The Bourne Supremacy*, when he deliberately plans to be caught, in order to find out information. (He soon escapes again.) He does travel by boat, train and automobile, however. At the beginning of *The Bourne Identity*, Bourne escapes from a US consulate in Zurich and pays Marie Kreutz to drive him to Paris in her old VW Beetle; here, as in the later films, the *mise-en-scène* shows Bourne in thought against the window while an undifferentiated landscape passes in a blur behind him. This visual index of his alienation is markedly different from the means by which travel is presented in the Bond films, in which the actual process of travel is itself elided and we are shown departure or (more often) arrival in a destination in what Michael Denning calls the 'pleasure periphery'. Bourne's physicality, the movement of his body in space in fight sequences, is an articulation of a masculine warrior subjectivity, encoding power and domination; yet this is an empty subjectivity, purely instrumental, reduced to machinic reflexes over which Bourne himself seems to have little conscious control.

Daniel Craig, as James Bond, bears the marks of both ageing and the physical punishment he endures as the films proceed (he is made up to look ragged and weary in *Skyfall*, in particular, when he returns from his 'death' to visit M's London home, where Craig is presented as a rather anti-heroic figure, like one of the 'displaced' vagrant men that Lynne Kirby noted as male hysterics in Chapter 2). Damon, as Bourne, suffers a different kind of damage or trauma. Bourne, it transpires as the trilogy unfolds, has been 'produced' or created as a soldier/ assassin by the 'Treadstone' programme that he pursues. A volunteer from the US army, the conditioning programme he undergoes erases his previous identity and replaces it with the instrumental 'cover' Jason Bourne. When he encounters Dr Albert Hirsch (Albert Finney), the head of the Treadstone programme in

The Bourne Ultimatum, it appears that Bourne has been a kind of 'Patient Zero' for the programme of 'behaviour modification' that constructs assassins and agents who have no ethical qualms about their actions. The soldier subjectivity assumed by Bourne is analogous to the machine-masculinity diagnosed by Klaus Theweleit as a Fascist masculinity, as we saw in Chapter 2:

> Since the 'ego' of these men cannot form from the inside out ... they must acquire an enveloping 'ego' from the outside. [This is] a result of coercion; it is forced upon them by the pain they experience in the onslaught of external agencies. The punishments of parents, teachers, masters, the punishment hierarchies of young boys and the military, remind them constantly of the existence of their periphery (showing them their boundaries), until they 'grow' a functioning and controlling body armour, and a body capable of seamless fusion into larger formations with armorlike properties. [T]he armour of these men may be seen as constituting their ego. (Theweleit 1989b: 164)

Bourne's psychic 'armour' is Bourne himself, a fabricated subjectivity that occludes (even erases) the prior 'original'. His encounter with Hirsch is a confrontation with the source of trauma, a primal scene, which allows him access to memory: 'I remember everything. I'm no longer Jason Bourne', he states, after re-living his training in a flashback sequence.

The construction of 'Jason Bourne' is a kind of birth in which his previous subjectivity is deliberately erased; the memory loss that he experiences prior to the beginning of *The Bourne Identity* could be seen as a psychological mechanism of trauma and repression, as outlined by Freud in *Moses and Monotheism*: 'the experiences in question are as a rule entirely forgotten and remain inaccessible to memory. They belong to the period of infantile amnesia which is often interrupted by isolated fragmentary memories, the so-called "screen memories"' (Freud 1951: 120). Bourne does indeed suffer a series of fleeting memories during the films, all of which are associated with his role as an assassin: the killing of Russian politician Neski in *The Bourne Supremacy*; his conditioning at the hands of Hirsch in *The Bourne Ultimatum*; and the failed assassination of the former Nigerian dictator Nykwana Wombosi in *The Bourne Identity*, which results in the original loss of memory. Bourne finds Wombosi with a child, and cannot bring himself to kill. He is chased from the yacht and shot during his escape; it is after this trauma that he is rescued from the sea. The Wombosi and Neski 'scenes' are merely waypoints on the path back to the originary trauma, which is his psychological breakdown and reconstruction in Hirsch's programme. The rationales Hirsch offers – 'you volunteered, even after you were warned'; 'your missions will save American lives' – are ironized not only by Bourne's trauma, but also by the words spoken by The Professor (Clive Owen), another Treadstone agent sent to assassinate Bourne: 'Look at us. Look at what they make you give', he says as he lays dying. What they have to give 'to the program' (not just Treadstone, but the ideological fabric of a post-9/11 'War on Terror') is life itself. What they are left with is not 'bare life', in Giorgio Agamben's terms (exclusion from political subjectivity and rights, as will be explored in Chapter 5), but pure instrumentality. Bourne and the other agents who are part of Treadstone – nearly all white men in their 30s, dressed in dark civilian clothes with a backpack containing their weaponry – are killing machines.

The failure of this process to completely erase Bourne's originary self is both a sign of Bourne's difference – he retains an ethical sensibility when other operatives, including his superiors, do not – and a sign of the film's belief in a residuum of humanity that ultimately countermands the programme of assassination. This is, in a sense, the trilogy's ethical alibi: that Bourne has been 'programmed', and therefore is not culpable for his actions; and that ideological and strategic circuits may ultimately be circumvented by recourse to an irrecuperable 'human' autonomy. (It is interesting to compare the dystopian films analysed in Chapter 6, and, in particular, the influence of Orwell's *Nineteen Eighty-Four* (1949) in this regard.) While not quite sentimental, Bourne's recovery of his 'true' self at the end of the trilogy is comforting in its assertion that systems of power and domination may ultimately *not* prevail, and it seems that his trauma or psychological damage is undone at the point of recovery of memory. It is here that he may truly step off the stage, which is itself a somewhat problematic formulation, considering the networks of communications and surveillance that particularly inform the narrative of *The Bourne Ultimatum*.

From Republic to Empire

Part of the speech that Hirsch gives to Bourne, as recruitment propaganda, signifies a crucial imaginative shift with regard to the means by which several genre films of the period – as we shall see, science fiction and the heroic 'epic' as well as the espionage thriller – have conceptualized changing political and ideological structures. Hirsch, rationalizing the use of the 'killing machine' soldiers, says 'the Republic lives on a knife's edge', implying that anti-democratic and unethical means are necessary to protect the democratic Republic (of the

United States) in the post-9/11 period. This, of course, is a familiar tactic in contemporary political discourse, from the 'ticking bomb' or 'it works' rationales for torture (see the analysis of *The Ghost* in Chapter 4) to the use of rendition or extra-legal imprisonment at Guantanamo Bay. What is common to *The Bourne Ultimatum*, to the *Star Wars* prequel trilogy (*The Phantom Menace*, 1999; *Attack of the Clones*, 2002; *Revenge of the Sith*, 2005) and to the films *Gladiator* (2000) and *Coriolanus* (2011) is the sense that the Republic is in the process of becoming an Empire. Gore Vidal, a long-time critic of 'Imperial America', argued that 'from the beginning of our republic, we have had imperial longings' (Vidal 2004: 44), but the visibility of this shift is such that Perry Anderson, in a *New Left Review* special issue on 'American Foreign Policy and its Thinkers', named its historical overview 'Imperium'. Jason Bourne, the agent (and defender) of the Republic, is in fact a sign of that Republic's ethical vacuity, its political blindness and its lack of care even for its own citizens. Bourne, Anakin Skywalker and Maximus are figures who presume to defend the Republic, but whose violent prowess as a warrior only succeeds in making the identification of Republic with Empire still more evident.

Will Brooker, in his BFI Classic essay on *Star Wars*, notes the ceremonies and massed ranks of warriors that form the *mise-en-scène* of both *Star Wars* and *Attack of the Clones* suggests a slightly more sophisticated (visual) expression of the impulse towards Empire than is generally admitted for the prequel films:

> The prequels show that the Empire grew from the Republic's order, and so the mission to restore that old system of structure and ritual, represented by the medal ceremony, seems like a return to the same familiar cycle; and the ceremony itself, with its obvious parallels to the military rally that concludes *Attack of the Clones*, less of a cause for celebration. The New Republic will surely be little different from the Old Republic, which spawned the Empire – and in their shared penchant for hierarchy and rank within military, monarchic or spiritual orders, their displays of identical troops, their cleans lines and symmetry, the systems offer little to choose between them. (Brooker 2009: 80–1)

While Brooker is right to identify a more subtle articulation of this correspondence between New Republic, Old Republic and the Empire in the visual fabric of the films than is presented in the actual narratives, the figure of Anakin Skywalker, who will of course become Darth Vader, is central to the films' presentation of the way in which moral rigour slides into ambiguity and thence to outright amorality and the application of force indiscriminately. This is most effectively handled in the television series *Star Wars: The Clone Wars* (2008–13), which takes place between *Attack of the Clones* and *Revenge of the Sith*. The Anakin of *The Clone Wars* is heroic, his reckless courage the resolution to many of the narratives, but he is also placed in the role of mentor to his female *padawan* (apprentice) Ahsoka Tano. This 'father' role presents Anakin in a far more sympathetic light, and also modulates Anakin's somewhat ambivalent relation to his own 'master', Obi-Wan Kenobi. *The Clone Wars*, with far more space and time at its disposal over multiple seasons, is able to reveal just what Anakin has been trained to be, and what the clone wars are turning all the Jedi into, becomes increasingly apparent.

In the season 2 episode 'Voyage of Temptation', Obi-Wan accompanies the Mandalorean Duchess Satine (an avowed pacifist) and protects her from assassination by a warmongering dissident group from a Mandalorean moon. It is revealed, as the episode goes on, that Obi-Wan and Satine were once unrequited lovers, the object of ironic commentary from Anakin, who expresses surprise that Obi-Wan has come close to violating the Jedi code not to allow personal emotional entanglements to cloud their judgement. At the end of the episode, a traitor kidnaps Satine and is pursued by Obi-Wan. Satine escapes the traitor's grasp, and she holds a blaster on him, while Obi-Wan has his light sabre in close attendance. The traitor baits them both, noting that if Obi-Wan kills him and saves the ship (the traitor has a device to cause the ship to explode), he will be a hero, except to the ultra-pacifist Satine, who will abhor him; if Satine kills the traitor, she will violate everything she holds dear. This no-win situation is ended when Obi-Wan calls up the need for a 'cold-blooded killer'; the next moment, a light sabre protrudes from the chest of the traitor, wielded by Anakin, who catches the device as it falls. 'What?' Anakin asks, to their horrified looks. 'He was going to blow up the ship.' The insouciance with which Anakin dispatches the Mandalorean (no mere droid) is purposely chilling: the act has no ethical weight for Anakin. He has become so inured to battle, to violence, to killing, that this moment of ethical decision is entirely lost on him.

But who is to blame? Is it Anakin himself, or is it the Jedi training and warrior role he has assumed? *The Clone Wars* is able to complicate the portrayal of Obi-Wan, not only by offering romantic entanglements in the past, but also to suggest that his judgement is awry at crucial stages of the narrative. This is most evident in the final confrontation in *Revenge of the Sith*, during the light-sabre battle between him and Anakin. In a pause, Anakin (Hayden Christianson) declares that to him, 'the Jedi are evil'. Obi-Wan (Ewan Macgregor) shouts back, 'then you are lost!' Though one of the most striking lines of the film, it points out Obi-Wan's failure as a mentor to Anakin: even here, he could explain things, try to show Anakin where he has done wrong; but instead he only repeats that he has 'failed' Anakin. Later in the sequence, he calls Anakin 'brother', not 'son'; it is, in a sense, the failure of patriarchal authority that is encoded in Jedi hierarchical structures. Anakin becomes what the Jedi need him to be, the warrior nonpareil; unfortunately, the warrior prince finds another father (the future Emperor) and brings about the doom of the Jedi that made him. *The Clone Wars* reveals that it is not a failure of heroic action which is at the root of the Republic's downfall: it is an ethical, strategic and political failure on the part of the Jedi – a 'peace-keeping' order who assumes the role of pursuing martial victory – that is the real cause of defeat.

Just as the 'crisis in masculinity' can be identified as a crucial discourse with regard to discussions of gender roles and constructions, particularly in popular media, in the years 1999–2000, one can also find in the same two years, immediately prior to 9/11 and the advent of the 'War on Terror', a cluster of films and texts which articulate anxieties about American (or perhaps late capitalist) neoimperialism. A great, and unexpected, popular success was Michel Hardt and Antonio Negri's *Empire* (2000), which proposed thus:

> Empire is materializing before our very eyes. Over the past several decades, as colonial regimes were overthrown and then precipitously after the Soviet barriers to the capitalist world market finally collapsed, we have witnessed an irresistible and irreversible globalization of economic and cultural exchanges. Along with the global market and global circuits of production has emerged a global order, a new logic and structure of rule – in short, a new form of sovereignty. Empire is the political subject that effectively regulates these global exchanges, the sovereign power that governs the world. (Hardt and Negri 2000: xi)

Hardt and Negri proposed a new mode of sovereignty which, in some senses, countermanded the system of economic and political regulation that had grown during the era of the nation-state. As we saw in Chapter 1, the Bond films articulate a new mobility and anxieties about policing a world of deregulated flows of capital, information and people; as we shall see in Chapter 5, science fiction films of the decade following 2000 often figure conflict about borders and securitized spaces. Hardt and Negri define 'Empire' thus:

> [t]he sovereignty of nation-states, while still effective, has progressively declined. The primary factors of production and exchange – money, technology, people, and goods – move with increasing ease across national boundaries; hence

the nation-state has less and less power to regulate these flows and impose its authority over the economy.... *The decline in sovereignty of nation-states, however, does not mean that sovereignty as such has declined.* Our basic hypothesis is that sovereignty has taken a new form, composed of a series of national and supranational organisms united under a single logic of rule. This new global form of sovereignty is what we call Empire. (Hardt and Negri 2000: xii)

By 'Empire', however, Hardt and Negri do not propose an extension or renewal of the imperatives of Imperialism, which they see as coterminous with the period of the hegemony of the nation-state and its determination to control territory. Instead, 'Empire establishes no territorial center of power and does not rely on fixed boundaries or barriers. It is a *decentered* and *deterritorializing* apparatus of rule that progressively incorporates the entire global realm within its open, expanding frontiers' (Hardt and Negri 2000: xii). As Wendy Brown analyses in *Walled States, Waning Sovereignty* (2010), one of the responses of the nation-state to the fluid dynamics of late capitalism or globalization is the erection of actual walls, from the 'peace Wall' that divides the state of Israel from Palestine, to the fences and walls that line the Rio Grande and separate the United States from Mexico. In a sense derived from Klaus Theweleit, the contemporary nation-state itself becomes 'armoured' as a defence against the disruptive and dissolving flows of financialized capital (rather than communism).

Empire masculinities

The emblematic masculinities of the 'waning' nation-state are themselves in a continuum with the 'hard-body' males of the 1980s, which, as Susan Jeffords, in *Hard Bodies: Hollywood Masculinity in the Reagan Era*, suggested, has been 'closely affiliated with the foreign policy imaginary of the Reagan era' (Jeffords 1994: 141). Jeffords argued that a recuperation of 'masculine' ideals of strength, activity and self-confidence accompanied, and were embodied in, the election of Ronald Reagan to the presidency in 1981, and that the rise of the 'New Man' was a return to family, the sign of a conservative cultural politics. Yvonne Tasker, in *Spectacular Bodies: Gender, genre, and the action cinema* (1993), took a different approach, and argued thus:

> During the 1980s, action films such as *Indiana Jones and the Temple of Doom*, *Commando*, *Die Hard* and *Predator* paraded the bodies of their male heroes in advanced stages of both muscular development and undress. (Tasker 1993: 91)

Tasker insisted on the visibility of 'built' bodies as an index of a cultural shift in modes of representation: 'The visibility of the built male body, in both film and advertising images, represents part of the wider shift in the male image, and in the range of masculine identities, that are on offer in western popular culture' (Tasker 1993: 73). Scott Bukatman, in *Terminal Identity: the Virtual Subject in Postmodern Science Fiction* (1993), explicitly used Klaus Theweleit's *Male Fantasies* (1978) to read similar imagery at work in the 1980s science fiction film, where the re-emergence of the imagery of the armoured male body in the form of Schwarzenegger's *Terminator* and in *RoboCop* (1987) reveals a disturbing cultural anxiety about masculinity in the mid- to late 1980s. The male 'hard body' or armoured body is an anxious body, whose boundaries are constantly reaffirmed in musculature and violent action sequences. The visibility of such armoured bodies suggests not a progressive politics of representation, however, so much as a manifestation of the need to defend both the masculine subject and the nation-state against the burgeoning flows of global capital.

Such a return to the representational strategies of the 'built' body can be seen in the Ridley Scott film *Gladiator* (2000), in which the Roman General Maximus (Russell Crowe) becomes a gladiator in the Colosseum in Rome, and prevails largely due to his martial prowess (and re-inscription of his vengeful return into regimes of spectacular violence). *Gladiator* also articulates similar anxieties about the trajectory from Republic to Empire found in the Bourne films and the *Star Wars* prequels. It begins in 'Germania', where Maximus leads the Roman legions against the last of Rome's strategic enemies, in the service of Emperor Marcus Aurelius (Richard Harris). After winning a great victory, Maximus is called to the Emperor, who reveals that he has decided against the hereditary succession of his son Commodus (Joaquin Phoenix): 'Commodus is not a moral man,' the Emperor explains, 'he must not rule'. Instead, he asks Maximus to succeed as Protector, as a temporary measure, to enable Rome to make a transition back from Empire to Republic. Marcus Aurelius, the 'philosopher-Emperor', intriguingly turns to a 'clean' and uncorrupted masculine subject, the man who has never seen Rome itself (Maximus is from the Iberian provinces) and who is unsullied by political or personal corruption. Maximus then embodies a *moral* reading of the body of the soldier, one who can realize (through violent action) the 'dream of Rome' that is twice articulated in the film, and in particular in the encomium delivered by Marcus Aurelius's daughter, Lucilla (Connie Nielsen) upon Maximus's death in the arena: 'There was a dream of Rome. It shall be realized. . . . He [Maximus] was a soldier of Rome. Honour him. Now we are free.' Maximus's sacrifice on the floor of the Colosseum, where he gives his own life in order to kill Commodus in direct combat, is read heroically, but it runs somewhat against the grain of the film itself. When Senator Gracchus (Derek Jacobi) says of Commodus's plans for prolonged gladiatorial games 'He will bring them death – and they will love him for it', it exposes the violence that is at the heart of the hegemony of Rome, the very violence that subdued the Germanic tribes at the start of the film. The gladiatorial games lay bare the ideological structures of the Roman 'civilising mission', one that is the cultural and ideological work of Imperial expansion: that civilization, the 'light' in the darkness that is Roman values and virtues (as Maximus himself calls it before his fall), is merely the alibi of the political and martial logics of spectacular violence. This violence is one that *Gladiator* itself incorporates into its own fabric, of course; its diagnosis of spectacular 'bread and circuses' is deeply ironic. It is also somewhat proleptic, for the film was made and released prior to 9/11 and the 'War on Terror', but its analysis of the deep implication of the state in what may be called 'shock and awe' military tactics, and its suspicion of Imperial tendencies in the body politic, align it with films made later in the decade.

Stella Bruzzi, in *Bringing Up Daddy: Fatherhood and Masculinity in Post-War Hollywood* (2005), reads the film in terms of fatherhood. Bruzzi suggests that Marcus Aurelius's act, to return Rome to Republican virtue, 'would mean breaking the dictatorial, patrilinear rule of the Caesars, but to be a good father necessitates also being able to release Rome/the child from subservience' (Bruzzi 2005: 160). Crowe's assumption of a heroic paternal masculinity – 'just the sort of dad (part boot-boy, part protector) you would want to call to your defence' (Bruzzi 2005: 162) – then re-inscribes a rather less troubled model of masculine subjectivity and fatherhood than is diagnosed elsewhere in Bruzzi's book. The concatenation of political struggle and paternity suggests, perhaps, a desire for the 'strong man', the patriarchal 'protector' who will deliver the state from corruption and downfall; that Maximus sacrifices his life to bring Commodus's corrupt reign to an end somewhat defrays the ideological cost of such a resolution.

Masculinity in Imperial cultures does not always revert to the traditional, patriarchal type, however. Jonathan Rutherford, in *Forever England: Reflections on Masculinity and Empire* (1997), articulates the kind of Imperial masculinity fostered within Victorian Britain by public schools, a culture of physical adventurism and courage, and the virtues of homosociality and discipline embodied in team sports. 'Games encouraged physical courage and self-reliance in a context which subordinated the self to the team. They were a collective practice of asceticism intent on transforming the feminine bodies of young boys into the hardened musculature of imperial warriors' (Rutherford 1997: 16). There are inescapable echoes here of Theweleit's armoured proto-Fascist men, whose psychic apparatus was also formed within institutional systems of discipline and privation. Rutherford takes as one of his emblematic Imperial males T. E. Lawrence ('of Arabia'), whose sympathy for and identification with Arabic culture and the desert led ultimately to a dislocation from both a British cultural identity and his adopted Arabic one to the point at which he tried to enlist as a common soldier under an assumed name (T. E. Shaw) to recover what Rutherford calls 'an intense, often homoerotic, nostalgia for a lost masculine community of soldiers' (Rutherford 1997: 73). The asceticism that Rutherford diagnoses as crucial to Imperial masculinity – discipline, self-denial and self-sacrifice – achieves an almost ecstatic embodiment in Lawrence, who 'already had a predilection for acts of endurance and self-denial' by the time he attended university, but which eventually 'expressed [a] growing aversion to his body' (Rutherford 1997: 83). This asceticism, and a desire for an unsullied, pure body, is to be found in Lawrence's own writings, in particular *The Seven Pillars of Wisdom* (1935/1997). Relating the experience of the rigours of the desert, this rejection or transcendence of the body is made explicit from the beginning:

> The body was too coarse to feel the utmost of our sorrows and of our joys. Therefore, we abandoned it as rubbish: we left it below to march forward, a breathing simulacrum, on its own unaided level, subject to influences from which in normal times our instincts would have shrunk. . . . In horror of such commerce [with 'public women'] our youths began indifferently to slake one another's few needs in their own clean bodies – a cold convenience that, by comparison, seemed sexless and even pure. (Lawrence 1997: 12)

The explicit connection between homosociality and homosexuality, and its representation as 'pure' and 'clean', can be read as analogous to the *Freikorps* men's own imagery, wherein the pure, clean (and machine-like) male body is defended from the 'red flood' of sexuality, femininity, fluidity and communism. The body here, abandoned 'as rubbish', not only assumes a sexual agency that is at once separate from the ascetic mental relation of mind to desert, but also expresses it in terms of purity and sanctity. Lawrence's presentation of Arabic masculinity dovetails with his own asceticism:

> [The desert dweller's] sterile experience robbed him of compassion and perverted his human kindness to the image of the waste in which he hid. Accordingly

he hurt himself, not merely to be free, but to please himself. There followed a delight in cruelty which was more to him than goods. The desert Arab found no joy like the joy of voluntarily holding back. He found luxury in abnegation, renunciation, self restraint. (Lawrence 1997: 24)

This passage brings together sadomasochism with a self-renunciation that almost ascends to annihilation. As we will see in Chapter 9, where we will analyse science fiction texts that present an ecstatic or transcendent annihilation of the masculine subject, this desire is not for death, but for *nothingness*, is a recurrent motif in representations of masculinity in genre texts. (In the opening minutes of the film *Prometheus* (2013), the android David (Michael Fassbender) physically imitates Peter O'Toole in *Lawrence of Arabia* (1961), and is seen watching the film.) This annihilation or self-abnegation finds its expression not only in the clean, pure body (placed in conjunction with other clean bodies) but also in the desert itself. When Dahoum, Lawrence's soulmate, offers him the 'sweetest scent of all', it is 'the effortless, empty, eddyless wind of the desert', which is the best because it has no taste (Lawrence 1997: 23). This absence, a total emptiness, is an external manifestation of the to-be-longed-for emptying out of the male subject, its ultimate renunciation and transcendence into the spiritual body of the desert itself. The failure of this transcendent self-denial, the insistence of the body, is transmitted in Lawrence's text through the counter-discourse of corruption, that polluting flood against which the hygienic male body defends itself. Kaja Silverman, in *Male Subjectivity at the Margins* (1992), suggests that 'the subject who is diminished through the eclipse of the ideal is Lawrence himself' (Silverman 1992: 316), and Lawrence's subsequent history becomes one of wilful degradation.

Lawrence's alienation through his experience of the Imperial project, his failure to be able to 'come home' and his death in a motorcycle accident, which Rutherford reads in terms of Modernism and 'the new sensation of speed and the impersonal power of machinery' (Rutherford 1997: 96), mark him as a prototypical masculine subject with regard to the effects of war. Robert Jay Lifton's book on his experiences with the 'rap groups' formed by Vietnam War veterans is called *Home from the War* (1973), the title exposing the sense that the veterans no longer feel 'at home' in the United States. (One of the earliest Hollywood Vietnam War films was Hal Ashby's *Coming Home* (1978).) Lifton pursues the feelings of 'survivor guilt' felt by the veterans, resulting in psychological disturbance and dislocation:

The predominant emotional tone . . . is all-encompassing absurdity and moral inversion. The absurdity has to do with a sense of being alien and profoundly lost, yet at the same time locked into a situation as meaningless as unreal as it is deadly. The moral inversion, eventuating in a sense of evil, has to do not only with the absolute reversal of ethical standards but with its occurrence in absurdity, without inner justification, so that the killing is rendered naked. (Lifton 1973: 37)

These men are not the 'killing machines' of the Bourne films' 'Treadstone' project; indeed, 'Treadstone' is predicated on the very problematic that Lifton's work approaches but cannot resolve. The veterans are men, human beings, not machines; they are capable of atrocity, of killing civilians or mutilating bodies, but they are not pathological. How one deals with effects of actively or passively participating in such horror, horror that is 'absurd' because it is without meaning in terms of the discourses of war and its ostensible aims, is implicit in American war films after the Vietnam period. In the remainder of the chapter, I will take two films as emblematic of the two largest overseas involvements of US troops and its deforming effects on masculinity: *Apocalypse Now* (1979/2000) and *The Hurt Locker* (2008).

Apocalypse Now (Redux)

I have chosen *Apocalypse Now*, rather than one of the films which more overtly present the effects of the trauma of war upon the soldiers who experience it (such as *Coming Home* or *Born on the Fourth of July* (1989)) for three reasons; first, it most clearly articulates American involvement in Vietnam as an Imperial project; second, it was re-released in 2000 as *Apocalypse Now Redux*, a re-edit with additional material including the 'French Plantation' sequence which directly ties in American military involvement to the colonial history of Indochina; and third, because it presents war not simply as a horrifying experience which traumatizes soldiers and civilians alike, but one in which spectacle and violence are inextricably connected. *Apocalypse Now*, as is well known, is derived, albeit loosely, from Joseph Conrad's novella *Heart of Darkness* (1899), and maps the American military presence in Vietnam onto Belgian colonial exploitation of the resources in the Congo. The river Congo (like the one at the Imperial centre, the Thames) flows to the sea from 'the heart of an immense darkness' (Conrad 1994: 111), and a journey upriver is one into moral confusion and ultimately a confrontation with the true 'horror' of the colonial project. In both the texts, the protagonist's journey towards an interview or confrontation with Kurtz, the embodiment of the Imperial project, is emblematic of the texts' investigation of the ethical corrosion that accompanies Western involvement in colonial possession and exploitation. Where Marlowe, in *Heart of Darkness*, is a sailor, a wanderer who, as a child, 'had a passion for maps', and when he identified one of the 'blank spaces of the earth. . . . I would put my finger on it and say, When I grow up I will go there' (Conrad 1994: 11), *Apocalypse Now*'s Willard is a captain in the US Special Forces, and is first seen 'going soft' while waiting for a mission in Saigon. The opening scene of *Apocalypse Now*, famously soundtracked by The Doors' 'The End', shows Willard (Martin Sheen) as a dislocated, troubled man. He sleeps fitfully, with a gun beneath his pillow; by the bedside of his hotel room is a letter from his wife asking for a divorce; at a cataclysmic point of the song, Willard becomes drunk, accidentally smashes a mirror while gazing at himself, and then is seen sobbing and covered with his own blood. He is a psychological and physical mess, and although the 'mission' brings with it the promise of a solution to his problems, it is so in different terms from the one he expects. His confrontation with Kurtz is, in a sense, a confrontation with his own fragmentation, the consequences of his own involvement in the war.

When Willard reaches Kurtz's compound, he is taken into a deeply shadowed room, in which Kurtz (Marlon Brando) interrogates him. Kurtz asks: 'Are you an assassin?', to which Willard replies, 'I'm a soldier.' (Kurtz ends the scene by telling Willard: 'you're neither. You're an errand boy, sent by grocery clerks to collect the bill.') Of course, Willard, like Jason Bourne, is both: an assassin-soldier, whose subjectivity has been constructed (through a programme of training 'that damn near wasted me') to enable him to effectively function as a killer. Willard's killings are political murders, however, sanctioned by the state's secret intelligence service. Unlike Bourne, who is created simply to follow orders without ethical qualm, Willard, particularly in his voice-over narration, evinces an ethical framework that problematizes his relation to his mission: 'This time it was an American, and an officer. That wasn't supposed to make any difference to me, but it did. . . . I took the mission. What the hell else was I going to do? But I didn't know what I'd do when I found him.' Willard appears to inhabit a closed, instrumental psychological framework that allows him to kill without qualm, but the voice-over reveals something else: not necessarily a psychological reaction to trauma, but a dislocation and *philosophical* enquiry into what the war might mean and his and Kurtz's roles in it. The narrative of *Apocalypse Now*, the journey upriver, is, in part, Willard's trajectory out of the soldier-assassin subjectivity into something else. By the time he kills Kurtz, he is 'not even in their fucking army any more'. Where Marlowe sits on the yawl *Nellie*, recounting his story in the middle of the Thames, Willard's own narration comes from an unstated *elsewhere* in time and space, a form of transcendence that is entirely related to film form, not the narrative diegesis.

In *Apocalypse Now Redux*, the crew of the Navy PB boat, who are ferrying Willard upriver (into the illegal war zone of Cambodia, where lies Kurtz's compound), enter a fog, from which emerges a ruined landing stage. As they tie up the boat, figures appear ghost-like from the mist. These are French colonials, 'hanging on' in an isolated part of Vietnam, whose plantation house and dinner party is meant to reproduce that of the *haute bourgeoisie* back in Paris. Director Francis Coppola, disappointed that the sequence did not represent the otherworldly sumptuousness he required, asked editor Walter Murch to excise it in its entirety from the original release in 1979, but its restitution in *Redux* reinserts the film into a deeper Indochinese history. By journeying upriver, the crew of the boat journey back in time; the plantation sequence also makes explicit the connection, even continuity, between American military involvement and the more directly colonial imperatives of French possession of Indochina. In response to Willard asking why the family do not 'go home', the patriarchal head of the family plantation Hubert de Marais (Christian Marquand) asserts that Vietnam *is* their home, and that 'You don't understand our mentality – the French officer mentality. At first, we lose in Second World War. I don't say that you Americans win, but we lose. In Dien Bien Phu, we lose. In Algeria, we lose. In Indochina, we lose! But here, we don't lose! This piece of earth, we keep it. We will never lose it, never!' Here, although de Marais diagnoses that the Americans are 'fighting for the biggest nothing in history' (its ideological commitment to 'democracy' and its will to prevent the fall of Southeast Asian 'dominoes' to communism), his own colonial discourse is ironized by history itself; the French, like the Americans, will 'lose' Vietnam to its indigenous inhabitants, the Vietnamese.

The historical pertinence of the release of *Apocalypse Now Redux* in 2000 determines its inclusion in Slavoj Žižek's *Welcome to the Desert of the Real*

(2002), his response to the 9/11 events. Žižek reads the film through a Lacanian lens, arguing that the film

> stages the co-ordinates of [the] structural excess of state power in the clearest possible way. Is it not significant that in the figure of Kurtz, the Freudian 'primordial father' . . . is presented not as the remainder of some barbaric past, but as the necessary outcome of modern Western power itself? Kurtz was a perfect soldier – as such, through his overidentification with the military power system, he turned into the excess which the system has to eradicate. Power generates its own excess, which it has to annihilate in an operation that has to imitate what it fights. (Žižek 2002: 27)

Žižek proposes that Kurtz is an emblem of the 'embodiments of radical evil' that pervade popular discourses in the 'War on Terror', from the suicide bomber to Osama Bin Laden to the Taliban, the 'radical evil' that must be fought by means of secret wars, drone strikes, renditions, or assassinations. *Apocalypse Now Redux* not only looks back to a historical point at which American foreign policy assumed an overtly Imperial guise, but its release in 2000 also demonstrates the extent to which Willard's mission foreshadows the operation of the secret state that must eliminate the antagonists that its own policies have produced. What Žižek does not foreground is the insistently *spectacular* practice of war that *Apocalypse Now* both inhabits (in Vittorio Storaro's sumptuous cinematography) and critiques (in the 'Ride of the Valkyries' sequence, or in Lance's insistence (played by Timothy Bottoms) that Vietnam is 'Disneyland'). As the Retort group suggested in their early consideration of the 'new world order' post-9/11 and the invasion of Iraq:

> What are the moment's defining features? On the one side, a resurgent imperialism, with 'modernity' and 'democracy' its watchwords, replacing the old promise of 'civilization'. And a sovereign power at the center of things that no longer hesitates to declare unending War its *raison d'être*, and to push towards a ghost form of government – a second and authoritative policy – in which secrecy is of the essence and bureaucracy is not required to answer, even formulaically, to the rule of law. The *first* polity of this sovereign power – and no-one is denying the continuing necessity to the US of control in the non-secret realm – is more and more attuned to the cluster of techniques and priorities called spectacle. (Retort 2005: 174–5)

Rather than offering a critique of war that foregrounds trauma and psychological disruption, *Apocalypse Now* gives weight to the elements of fantasy, exhilaration and spectacle that are present in contemporary configurations of warfare. In *Apocalypse Now* and in *The Hurt Locker*, the protagonists cannot go home not simply for reasons of alienation and dislocation, but because they do not want to.

The Hurt Locker

Kathryn Bigelow's *The Hurt Locker* (2008) is an Oscar-winning film that focuses on the experience of US army bomb-disposal teams in the aftermath of the invasion of Iraq in 2003. A title at the beginning of the film seems to express its own diagnosis of the relation of male soldiers to combat: 'war is a drug'. This signifies in particular the response to the conditions of war and bomb disposal of Sgt William James (Jeremy Renner), criticized as 'reckless' by his colleague (and in terms of rank, subordinate) Sanborn (Anthony Mackie). The film begins, however, with a different leader of the bomb disposal team, Sgt Thompson (Guy Pierce), whose preparation for a mission is meticulous, and his adherence to protocols expresses his professionalism and his care for the lives of himself and of his team. In the opening sequence, such care is to no avail: he is killed when a bomb is set off, probably by accident, by the signal transmitted by an Iraqi civilian making a call on his cell phone. That preparation and professionalism cannot protect the lives engaged in these operations casts a different light on Sgt James's seeming disregard for both discipline and the rules; although Ralph Donald and Karen MacDonald, in *Reel Men at War* (2011), suggest that 'James is a war lover, a thrill junkie seeking the adrenaline high of putting his life on the line' (Donald and MacDonald 2011: 176), his seeming recklessness is as rational a response as Thompson's diligence. Death seems to come no matter the preparation and the care taken; Sgt James puts his faith in his own responses rather than the rule book. His appreciation is that the risk of death is so total that he dispenses with protocol. In this, he is a maverick, the kind of Hollywood masculinity that is usually presented as heroic and attractive, although his conflict with Sanborn indicates the extent to which that he risks their lives as well as his own; Sanborn and others are 'short-timers', coming towards the end of their tours in Iraq, and they want to get home. Sgt James, however, is more 'at home' in Iraq. After completing his tour, the film shows scenes of a rather troubled domesticity: James wanders, rather lost, around a supermarket; playing with his young son, he tells the boy that as he grows, he will end up losing everything he loves, 'except one' (and this, for James, is not constituted by his wife and family); and he talks with his wife during the making of dinner and professes his desire to return. The last shots of the film show Sgt James once again walking towards a device on the streets of Iraq, his tour clock reset to 365 days.

In this scene, and in others shown throughout the film, James is costumed in a protective suit, a literal armour that helps to absorb some of the energy of the blast if a bomb detonates. (This suit, like the protocols he follows, does not protect Sgt Thompson.) This armouring of the masculine body operates not only as a form of physical protection, but also as a kind of ideological insulation: there are many shots of James, and the other American soldiers, being stared at by Iraqi civilians as they patrol the streets of the city, a spectacle that encodes ethnic and cultural difference as well as the lack of protection afforded to the people who actually inhabit the city. Sgt James is armoured, but his recklessness tends to make him (and others) more vulnerable; what he seeks, perhaps, in these moments is not a 'thrill' or a fix of adrenaline, but rather a moment of *contact* with the real, a means by which to rupture the encasing armour and experience human life, rather than war. Jonathan Rutherford, writing about T. E. Lawrence's final days hurtling along country lanes on a powerful motorbike, quotes Lawrence's letter to Lionel Curtis, in which he confesses: 'My nerves are jaded and gone near dead . . . so that nothing less than hours of voluntary danger will prick them into life' (Rutherford 1997: 96). Two potential readings of Sgt James's practice then suggest themselves: first, that he seeks, like Theweleit's *Freikorps* soldiers, to rupture the armour, to 'explode' beyond the limits of subjectivity in an ecstatic annihilation; or, second, that this is a kind of longing for *life*, not a drive towards quiescence (Freud's 'death drive', which will be explored in more detail in Chapter 11), not a yearning for annihilation and *nothingness*. If, as in *Apocalypse Now* or Lifton's *Home From the War*, the experience of war is absurd because it has no meaning, Sgt James's actions – placing himself in close proximity to death so that he may contact with life – provides it with a meaning that extends beyond contemporary geopolitics or the American mission in occupying Iraq. Although I agree with Hamilton Carroll's diagnosis in *Affirmative Reaction* (2011) of 'the generally reactionary and revisionist nature of post-September 11 constructions of masculine identity', *The Hurt Locker*'s Sgt James, with his ambiguous motivations and troubling behaviour, runs counter to this restitution of masculine heroism. The film's lack of resolution to the problem of Sgt James's behaviour – is he traumatized, or a retrograde masculine 'thrill-junkie', as articulated by his teammate Owen Eldridge (Brian Geraghty) as he is helicoptered out of the city – suggests, perhaps, that what James really desires is to throw off the armour of masculinity in its entirety.

4

The Special Relationship

In this chapter we will consider the figure of Tony Blair, and, in particular, a series of films scripted by Peter Morgan and starring Michael Sheen, which feature Blair as a central character; other films made around the same period feature the same writer/star combination and which, I will argue, offer a parallel representation of masculinity and homosociality; Robert Harris's book *The Ghost* (2007) and its film adaptation directed by Roman Polanski (2010), which have at their core a former British prime minister called Adam Lang, who is clearly modelled on Blair; and finally, with regard to reflecting the 'legacy' of Blair, a crucial concern for both *The Ghost* and *The Special Relationship* (2010), we will turn to the Chris Morris film *Four Lions* (2010), which articulates, in satirical form, the legacy of overseas intervention in Iraq and Afghanistan for British Muslim young men and the 'jihadi' masculinity they come to inhabit.

The key concept to foreground here is 'homosociality', because the masculinities investigated in this chapter are, in a sense, transactional, produced not in and of themselves but in relation to other men. Homosociality is the term foregrounded by the late critic and theorist of masculinities and gender, Eve Kosofsky Sedgwick, which she used in her book *Between Men* (1985). The word is 'homosocial'.

> 'Homosocial' is a word occasionally used in history and the social sciences, where it describes social bonds between persons of the same sex; it is a neologism, obviously formed by analogy with 'homosexual', and just as obviously meant to be distinguished from 'homosexuality'. In fact, it is applied to such activities as 'male bonding', which may, as in our society, be characterised by intense homophobia, fear and hatred of homosexuality. To draw the 'homosocial' back into the orbit of 'desire', of the potentially erotic, then, is to hypothesize the potential unbrokenness of a continuum between homosocial and homosexual – a continuum whose visibility, for men, in our society, is radically disrupted. (Sedgwick 1985: 1–2)

Homosociality is used within gender and particularly masculinity studies to locate the social and cultural practices that determine the kind of emotional and psychological relationships that are forged between men, often exclusive of women, and which are rigorously policed to place them in contradistinction to *desiring* relationships. The elements of sexuality, and by consequence emotion itself, are repressed in Sedgwick's diagnosis of male homosociality, the 'continuum' with heterosexuality disavowed. That homosocial relationships often devolve to rituals of 'male bonding' indicate both an anxiety about emotional closeness between men and an element of competitiveness or contestation that is built into homosociality to preserve an unproblematic emotional 'distance'. Many of the films I will analyse in this chapter are deeply homosocial environments – politics, football, a 'terrorist' cell – through which masculinities are performed.

Since the 2003 Granada/Channel 4 film, *The Deal*, Peter Morgan has written, and Michael Sheen has starred in several films which deal with crucial moments in the careers of well-known British men: in *The Deal* (Granada/Channel 4, 2003), *The Queen* (Granada, 2006) and *The Special Relationship* (HBO/BBC Films, 2010), Sheen plays former British Prime Minister Tony Blair; in *Frost/Nixon* (Universal, 2008) he played David Frost, whose successful career in the 1970s, 1980s and 1990s was cemented by his celebrated interviews with disgraced ex-President Richard M. Nixon; and in *The Damned United* (Columbia/BBC Films, 2009), the film focuses on the notorious '44 days' in which outspoken football manager Brian Clough (played by Sheen) was in charge of the club he had hated and previously sought to defeat, Leeds United. The so-called Blair trilogy of films is original screenplays by Morgan; *Frost/Nixon* was adapted by Morgan from his own, highly successful play; and *The Damned United* was adapted by Morgan from the novel of the same name by David Peace.

Sheen's portrayal of Tony Blair is crucial to the kind of masculinities repeatedly essayed by the Morgan/Sheen films. In an article published in 2008, Stephen Whitehead discussed the rise of Blair, and his legacy in terms of his successors as Prime Minister Gordon Brown and David Cameron, through the lens of 'metrosexuality', defined by Whitehead as 'a straight man, but one who cares for his appearance and grooming, is comfortable with diverse sexual and cultural identities, and is not in any way macho or overbearing. He is sensitive, reflexive and expressive. He has emotional intelligence' (Whitehead 2008: 237–8). This figure, a form of groomed, well-tailored, metropolitan 'soft' masculinity that gained media traction in the early years of the twenty-first century, found an emblem in Blair, who 'had an instinctive understanding' of the necessity for a certain kind of self-presentation as a powerful male, 'which is why he invested so much time and energy in maintaining the veracity of his identity as a "good bloke"' (Whitehead 2008: 236):

> The power of an individual, especially a politician, can only be attained, and maintained, through their discursive practices. No contemporary politician can afford to ignore their discursive performance and this means the totality of self-presentation: dress code, language, phraseology, physique, body posture, hairstyle, general grooming. In a media-driven global world, with a short attention span, power accrues to those who get this right. (Whitehead 2008: 236)

The metrosexual is a performative masculinity, presenting a particular idea of male subjectivity, while, in the texts we will see in this chapter, operating successfully in the often brutal arenas of politics, football and celebrity. In fact, this mode of performance enables success in that arena, and less successful 'traditional' masculinities – macho, overbearing, insensitive, incurious as to personal presentation or 'grooming' – are inhabited by the antagonist males such as Gordon Brown, Don Revie or Richard M. Nixon. This is acknowledged directly by David Frost in the introduction to *Frost/Nixon: Behind the Scenes of the Nixon Interviews* (2007), published prior to the film, where he meets Michael Sheen:

> When I interviewed Michael last December, shortly after the Broadway production and the film had been announced, Michael said, 'I'm going to be playing David Frost for the next year.'
> 'That's a coincidence,' I said. 'So am I.' (Frost 2007: 5)

Frost himself acknowledges the performativity at work in his own mediated subjectivity as 'David Frost'; he inhabits a 'character' as much as does Michael Sheen. Although, in the film, Sheen emphasizes the occasional brittleness in this performance, all the films discussed do not associate the traditional forms of masculinity with an 'authenticity' that is ultimately of more value than the Blair/Clough/Frost performance. Men like Brown or Nixon may feel themselves to be 'out of time' or step with the kind of imperatives towards overt performance identified by Whitehead above, but none of the films suggests that these are 'real' men compared with the Blair type; it is more that traditional forms of masculinity are a less successful performance. Although Adam Lang, in the film of *The Ghost*, complains that all the press talk about is his university career as an actor, implying that he is a kind of fake, mediation and so central to all of the texts studied in this chapter that a sense of a 'real' masculinity necessarily evaporates altogether.

An appreciation for, and skill in performing within the codes of contemporary mediation and performance is a recurrent concern. Tony Blair, in *The Deal* and *The Queen*, has to deal with a difficult and rather prickly person (Brown/the Queen) who does not see, or would rather reject, the necessity for communication with the public through television. In *The Deal*, former Labour Leader John Smith (Frank Kelly) suggests that Brown has 'presentational difficulties': 'politics is not always about higher matters; sometimes it is about the ugly business of making friends, keeping friends, being liked.' Brown's political integrity (and identity – his 'reticence' is discussed at one point in the film) causes him to be deeply suspicious of the kind of personality-politics that Blair uses as a strategy, in person and on television. Brown is in fact suspicious of *performance*, in the sense of presenting himself to be what he is not, because it transgresses his deeply felt social and political beliefs; he is entirely at home, it should be noted, on the stage of the House of Commons floor, however.

Sheen's face is a crucial performative tool in all of these films. The most obvious expression is the 'Cheshire Cat grin' (so-called by the Queen Mother (Sylvia Sims) in *The Queen*) which denotes performativeness, the 'on' public persona; at the end of the Granita discussion in *The Deal*, a close-up of a victorious but pensive Sheen gives way to a smiled 'Hi!' as Blair realizes his attention has been caught by someone, and the need for public performance reasserts itself. (It should be noted that Brown, The Queen and Nixon rarely smile in these films.) When Clough greets the Leeds United board in *The Damned United*, a medium close-up shows the same confident grin; Frost also wears a public smile with beaming confidence in *Frost/Nixon*. However, a recurrent facial tic is used by Sheen to reveal a disjunction between inner and outer, between public persona and a much more anxious masculine subject. Sheen often essays a kind of hesitant half-smile, particularly when in the presence of the powerful Other (Brown/Queen/Nixon/Revie/Clinton), signifying a self-doubt or anxiety about the role being performed. This, of course, is used to 'humanise', to make more sympathetic, the seemingly brash or arrogant younger man at the centre of the narrative. This suggestion of a much more troubled and anxious inner life is crucial to the narratives of triumph or redemption that are at work here, and provide psychological or emotional depth (once again expanding beyond the idea of the 'impersonation').

All the films use costume to great effect. Frost's self-regard is signified by his rather flashy, expensive clothing; Blair in *The Deal*'s domestic scenes wears jeans and chinos and casual Oxford shirts, in stark contrast to the always-besuited Brown (David Morrissey); in *The Queen*, Sheen generally wears a suit, even at 'home', but his personal informality is denoted throughout by his loosened tie and shirtsleeves. The semiotics of tie-wearing provide a nice joke in *The Deal*: on the 1983 election night on which both Brown and Blair enter Parliament, Brown arrives at his count with a food-stained necktie, and swaps it with his brother's tie in order to appear well groomed on television. Such a failure in terms of political performance is anathema to Blair. When he hears of John Smith's heart attack, his thought is whether he has time to go home and change into a darker suit before attending the Labour Party crisis-management meetings. (His second thought is to make a run at the party leadership.)

Dramatic structure

Across all of the Morgan/Sheen films (except *The Queen*), there is a recurring dramatic structure. Sheen plays a certain kind of masculine subject, a young, confident (even arrogant) man, personally charming and charismatic, sure of his abilities, yet beset by anxiety about his career and his ambitions, who is forced to confront a nemesis figure (Brown/Nixon/Revie/Clinton) in order to succeed. Each of these men is the Other, the self seen through a dark glass, a powerful and often brutal or brutalizing, physically imposing older man, either ruthless, cynical or corrupt (or all three). This homosocial relationship corresponds to that identified by David Frost between Nixon and Henry Kissinger: 'laden with dislike, distrust, disdain, and disgust on the one hand and, on the other, admiration, appreciation, respect, and mutual need' (Frost 2007: 37).

In *The Deal* and *The Damned United*, the character played by Sheen is something of a naïf at the beginning of the narrative. Blair is a bright young lawyer, displaced from his office into Brown's; Clough is the aspiring manager of the (then) Second Division Derby County, desperate to impress the visiting Revie, whose Leeds team come to the ramshackle Baseball Ground in Derby for an FA Cup tie. On the training ground before the match, Clough declares that he and Revie are 'like two peas in a pod': both from Middlesbrough, both having played for Sunderland and England, both centre forwards – and unspoken, both deeply ambitious, both content to be the public 'villain', both enmeshed in rumours of financial scandal later in their careers. As the film's coda reveals, both also suffer a final fall from grace: Revie in his England managerial failure and departure for the UAE, and in Clough's descent into alcoholism, which ultimately played a part in Nottingham Forest's relegation from the top division and his subsequent resignation in the early 1990s. Clough and Revie are two sides of the same coin, and Clough's resentment is symbolized in Revie's failure to shake Clough's hand or accept a glass of wine in Clough's office after the FA Cup game (which Leeds easily won).

The narrative of Clough's hatred of Revie and Leeds finds its origin point in the shot of two cut-glass wine goblets and an expensive bottle of French wine that remain unused on Clough's desk. It is revenge for being slighted, for failing to recognize similarity, which seems to drive Clough's overwhelming desire (or obsession) to defeat Leeds. When he is sacked from Derby County, he can no longer replace Leeds United and Revie at the top of the Division One table; instead he replaces Revie at Elland Road, and attempts to erase his predecessor's successful tenure by claiming that the trophies were won merely through 'bloody cheating.' Such revenge is a kind of self-negation for Clough; he is unhappy, at odds with the Leeds team, and can only be successful once again upon his departure from the club.

Both *The Deal* and *The Damned United* share a narratively doubled time frame through which the films organize the central confrontation, between the two men at the Granita restaurant in *The Deal*, and Clough's sacking from Leeds in *The Damned United*. *The Deal* begins on 31 May 1994, a title reveals: Blair phones Brown to arrange the meeting. Shots through the distortion of plate glass show Brown sitting in deep thought, before the film switches back to the 1983 General Election, when both Blair and Brown entered Parliament. *The Deal* then works its way back to the moment where Brown agrees to the meeting, in effect agreeing to stand aside and support Blair's run for the Labour Party leadership after John Smith's death. The 11-year span of the film roughly mirrors Blair's own premiership, when he finally stepped down in 2007 in order to allow Brown to take up the role as prime minister, a belated fulfilment of his end of 'the deal'. The film ends with a jokey title, 'Gordon is still waiting', as he was at the broadcast of *The Deal* in 2003. That year, of course, was in fact the beginning of the end game for Blair's premiership, precipitated by his leadership of Britain into war in Iraq; the film is full of prophetic and cautionary words, prompted by the fate of Margaret Thatcher, about 'going on too long', whereupon 'they' (the public) 'will hate you'.

We find a similar double time frame in David Peace's novel of *The Damned United* (2007), where the first-person narrative cuts back and forth between Clough and Taylor's appointment at Derby County, their success in gaining promotion to and eventually winning the First Division, and Clough's ultimate sacking from Derby; and the '44 days' of his time in charge of Leeds United: 5 years (1968–73) and 44 days (in the summer of 1974) run in parallel, so that Clough's sacking by Derby, and his sacking by Leeds United, are narrated very close together in the text. The first is thereby offered as the key to the second, the reason why he took the Leeds United job (for which he was a highly unsuitable candidate) in the first place, the enigma around which the text revolves.

The revelation of this motivation is in the desire for revenge, but neither homosociality nor the centrality of being slighted is as important in Peace's novel as it is in Morgan's screenplay and Tom Hooper's direction of *The Damned United*. The novel ends not in grovelling reconciliation with Taylor (see below), but with Clough celebrating the large financial pay-off and the new Mercedes he had extorted from the Leeds United board as the price of his termination. A plausible reading of the novel is that Clough had manipulated his way to a large financial windfall in the knowledge that he would find another job extremely quickly. The penultimate page of the novel ends thus:

> Down the motorway, their fingers and fists, their sticks and their stones, getting smaller and smaller; John at the wheel of my new blue Mercedes, Bill opening another bottle of champagne. But the sun is not shining, rain only falling; the blue sky is black, the yellow all purple, and I'm in the back with my two feet up and their cheque for £25,000 in my hands –
>
> > *I don't believe in God, I don't believe in luck, I believe in football –*
> > 'I've just come up on the pools,' I shout. 'The bloody pools!'
> > *I believe in family and I believe in me; Brian Howard Clough –*
> > It is Thursday 12 September 1974, and I wish you were here.
>
> (Peace 2007: 342)

Who does this 'you' refer to? To Taylor, to Revie, to the reader? It could be read, as the film suggests, as an acknowledgement that he needs Taylor, that he cannot operate effectively on his own, but melancholy works in conflict with triumphalism in this section of the novel. 'I wish you were here' plays against '*I believe in me*', partnership and individualism held in an unresolved tension; the anthropomorphic lowering sky stands in contrast to the euphoric shout 'I've just come up on the pools!' The ending of the film of *The Damned United* might be accused of a kind of strange sentimentality in its restoration of the Clough/Taylor partnership; in the novel, the last page attributes the winning of the 1979 European Cup to 'Nottingham Forest and Brian Howard Clough' (Peace 2007: 343): no mention of Taylor at all. In some ways, Peace's Clough is entirely unrepentant.

Television

In *The Queen*, Tony Blair has to 'manage' or advise the Queen (Helen Mirren) in the aftermath of the death of Princess Diana in 1997, some few weeks into Blair's premiership. Where the Queen insists on privacy, symbolized by the self-imposed withdrawal from the public performance of grief by staying in the royal enclave of the Balmoral estate, Blair understands that a public presentation of an emotional response – ultimately by live television address – is the only thing that will prevent the British public from turning away from the constitutional monarchy entirely. Blair, in both *The Deal* and *The Queen*, understands the temper of the times, and the means by which to address that public mood (itself in part constructed by newspapers and television. Both films are directed by Stephen Frears, who intercuts archive television broadcast footage throughout both films, to signify the mediated political landscape traversed successfully by Blair, and less so by Brown and the Queen).

The centrality of television to the *mise-en-scène* of *The Queen*, and the televisual personae investigated in the figures of Frost and Clough (who themselves perform a certain kind of brash, overconfident masculinity) indicates the extent to which that all of these films are embedded in a culture of celebrity at the same time as they are critiquing that very celebrity. Sheen's performances consistently signify the glossy, overbright projection of a persona on television, even when those personalities are off-screen, in 'real life'; indeed, it is the core of *The Deal*'s imagination of the Tony Blair/Gordon Brown relationship that Blair's 'time', his 1994 accession to the Labour Party leadership, comes to successful fruition because he understands the necessity for, in fact, the crucial nature of, interpersonal *and* media communications. In the key scene at the Islington restaurant Granita, where 'the deal' is struck for Brown to step aside, as Brown is exiting Blair encourages him to say hello to a young woman standing by the entrance. When asked why, Blair says that the young woman is a new actress on the popular BBC soap opera *EastEnders*, who reaches 15 million people per episode: 'Forget about politicians,' he says, 'that's real power.'

In *Frost/Nixon*, the narrative core of *The Deal* and *The Queen* – a brash and ambitious media-literate young man seeks to fulfil those ambitions by negotiating with a difficult and somewhat backward-looking heavyweight public figure – is varied so that the act of televisual communication is itself the end as well as the means. Nixon is interviewed by Frost not in pursuit of 'justice' for the crimes for which Nixon was pardoned, by his successor Gerald Ford, before the fact; nor to extract a confession or at least some expression of contrition, though it is clear that one of Frost's team, the writer James Reston (played by Sam Rockwell) does indeed seek such a thing. For Frost, however, the crucial element is money, rather than politics. By forcing Nixon into some kind of on-screen confrontation with the corruption and cover-up of the Watergate scandal, Frost is hoping that the interviews will be bought and shown worldwide, making him a wealthy man and securing his place in the media landscape of the United States. The act of media communication becomes a kind of redemption for Frost, rather than Nixon, and a validation of the kind of televisual literacy embodied by the 'Blair' male persona.

In *Frost/Nixon*, the late-night phone 'conversation about cheeseburgers' (a dramatic invention by Morgan) immediately precedes the climactic interview, where Frost finally defeats his antagonist, but here, the film plays this defeat as essentially *willed* by Nixon himself. A well-prepared Frost, leaning forward in his chair instead of back, corners Nixon into admitting that he believes that 'When the President does it [an illegal act], it's not illegal', at which point his *aide-de-camp* Jack Brennan (Kevin Bacon) intervenes and warns the president about 'unplanned emotional disclosures', a euphemism as telling as 'presentational difficulties' in *The Deal*. Nixon, however, determines to carry on, and it is here that pathos is generated. On re-entering the interview 'arena', the hulking Nixon, head bowed, is like a wounded former champion, losing his last fight; the crew and researchers watch his entrance with some sympathy, even the antagonistic Reston. When Frost declares that Nixon should make public confession, otherwise 'you're going to be haunted for the rest of your life', Nixon finds it hard to do so explicitly, but agrees he let down the American public and its system of government and regrets what he did. Pity and a kind of wonder is visible on the close-ups of Sheen's face: he has grappled with institutional power and laid it low, but the result is unexpectedly pitiable. Unlike the Queen's performance of (unfelt) emotion in *The Queen*, Mirren emphasizing in her acting a rather brittle, forced and mechanical to-camera speech by the Queen, there is a sense here of catharsis, of something that goes beyond performance towards revelation of the 'inner' Nixon, something that neither Brown nor Revie (still less the Queen) is afforded. Ironically enough, the emotion of the scene is transmitted not only through film, in the shot/reverse sequence of close-ups on the actors' faces, but also on the television monitors within the *mise-en-scène* that frame the close-up images of Frost and Nixon.

Two short scenes make-up the rest of *Frost/Nixon*; both are important. In the first, James Reston (Sam Rockwell) speaks to camera and makes explicit the importance of television to the Morgan/Sheen films. 'The first and greatest sin of television is that it simplifies,' he says; but eventually he 'understood the reductive power of the close-up'. In seeing Nixon's lonely, self-loathing face close-up on television, something other than political discourse is communicated: pathos, emotional truth. Once more, Morgan drives home his point, as in *The Deal*: 'forget about politicians, that's real power.' While critiquing the deformative power of television in particular and the mass media in general, these films pay homage to that power both in the *mise-en-scène* and in the figure of Blair/Frost/Clough, these televisual adepts who eventually triumph over less media-literate antagonists. In *Frost/Nixon*'s final interview, and in *The Deal*'s scene at Granita, the close-up (and even extreme close-up of eyes and mouth) predominates.

The last scene of *Frost/Nixon* compounds the pathos surrounding Nixon at the end of the film, when Frost and his girlfriend Caroline Cushing (Rebecca Hall) visit the former president in his San Clemente home before returning (in triumph) to London. Nixon is dressed, for the first time, in informal clothing – he jokes about his golf wear, but it signifies the finality of defeat, that he no longer seeks a return to power or influence. As in *The Deal* and the figure of Gordon Brown, the dark business suit is an index not just of power and authority, but also of a kind of superannuation, a masculinity located in the past. As the couple are about to leave, Nixon calls 'David' back for a private minute or two. Nixon asks whether Frost enjoys all the partying he does; the answer is yes. Nixon avers that Frost is lucky; 'Being liked, that charm. . . . I don't have it. Never had.' Nixon then suggests that Frost should have been the politician and he the investigative journalist.

This short dialogue confirms Frost as an avatar of the 'Blair' masculinity, where 'being liked' and televisual acuity are mutually implicated. Nixon, like Brown, is a man out of his time, a pre-television politician: it is part of the Nixon legend that he lost the 1960 presidential election to John F. Kennedy because viewers didn't like the way he looked in the televised presidential debates (while radio listeners to the same debates gave Nixon much higher approval ratings). Both Nixon and Brown go down to inevitable defeat. While, then, these films seem to encode a kind of nostalgia for a pre-televisual 'authentic' mode of political discourse, and diagnose the 'Blair' male figure and his success as an emblem of the problematic and engulfing power of the communication industries in contemporary British society, the Morgan/Sheen films reinforce the inescapable power of the visual by narrating the very triumph of media-communications man (Blair/Frost) and their mastery of the emotional power of the interpersonal close-up.

In Peace's *The Damned United*, the connection between television and successful masculinity is more ambiguous: Brian Clough's involvement with television at the same time as football is a double-edged sword. It is the source of friction between himself and the chairman of Derby County, the football team he took to promotion from the Second Division to Division One Champions in 1972. Clough appears as a television 'pundit' throughout his time at Derby, and is eventually sacked when he criticizes his chairman after a defeat in a European semi-final match. Clough uses television as a promotional weapon, and his verbal acuity, wit and charisma is ideally suited to the first era of colour television in Britain, the early 1970s; he becomes a 'television personality' as much as a person, the performance seeming to take over from, or mask, Clough the football manager.

In the film of *The Damned United*, when appointed Leeds United manager, Clough delays going to the Elland Road stadium in order to give an interview with Yorkshire Television; the *coup de grace* of his removal from this position is when, after the news of his sacking has been released, he agrees to be interviewed once more by the same regional television company. It is a trap, just as the Frost/Nixon interviews are a trap: Clough's predecessor and nemesis, Don Revie (Colm Meaney, a remarkable likeness) walks on to the set to pass judgement on the '44 days'. Clough, for once, is nearly lost for words. After the interview finishes, Revie, the interviewer and crew depart, leaving Clough still seated, on stage. The film uses close-ups of Sheen's face at this point to locate the psychological import of the scene, Clough's betrayal by the very medium of which he presumed himself the master. A similar scene can be found in *The Deal*, where Blair gives a television interview in which he loyally praises John Smith and deputy Margaret Beckett, then when off-air is captured close-up on a monitor with an expression of anger and self-loathing on his face. Blair storms off set, throwing down his lapel microphone away, and cursing 'Bollocks!' (a word repeated by Brown later in the Granita scene): the impatience of ambition is clearly represented. The difference between Blair and Clough is that, in Morgan's films, Blair never relinquishes his mastery of televisual communications.

Homosociality: The Special Relationship

For David Frost, his nemesis, Nixon, is an overt 'monster' to be overcome: Frank Langella's performance emphasizes a physically intimidating, as well as psychologically overbearing, personality. It is this bulldozing style that overmatches Frost in the scenes from the early part of the interviews: Frost is unable to cut Nixon off, allowing him to ramble, to dictate what is said, allowing pronouncements to go unchallenged. Sheen leans back defensively in his chair in these early interview scenes, as if physically cowed by Nixon's presence. It is towards the end of the film, when both Nixon and Frost (finally devoting his time to preparation rather than selling the broadcast rights) are gathering themselves to talk about Watergate and the cover-up, that the doubling self/other, protagonist/nemesis structure in *Frost/Nixon* reveals itself.

Frost, fearing that he has made a terrible mistake and is about to lose everything, receives a phone call. Sheen's face at this moment, in a close-up with the camera placed above and to the side, is stricken, the mouth open in something close to a rictus. When Frost answers, it is Nixon calling, who has had 'one or two' drinks. Nixon has been perusing a file on Frost (akin to the dossiers prepared by Revie on all of Leeds United's opponents), and from this, Nixon extrapolates a fundamental similarity between the two men that Frost, at first, finds difficult to accept. Nixon says: 'Methodist background, modest circumstances, then off to a grand university. . . . Did the snobs there look down on you too, Mr Frost? Of course they did. That's our tragedy. . . . No matter how high we get, they still look down on us.' The scene cuts between Frost and Nixon. Sheen is usually shot in close-up, the camera sometimes tracking slowly around his face, lit by warm ambient light; Langella is generally framed in medium shot, looking out of the French windows, talking on the speakerphone in semi-darkness. Nixon reveals the centrality of ambition or aspiration to these narratives: they are both 'looking for a way back, into the sun, into the limelight'; but then anxiety gives way to rage: 'We could feel it slipping away. . . . We are going to make these motherfuckers *choke*.' 'Yes,' agrees Frost, 'but only one of us can win.' Blair, Frost and Clough share with their nemeses a worldview in which competition is a zero-sum game. Not only is there is a winner and a loser: their ambition *must* be at the cost of the defeat of the Other. For *The Damned United*, the competition that takes place on the football field – where Derby could play and beat Leeds United – could stand as an emblem of this particular worldview, but is complicated by Clough's desire to supplant

Revie and erase his history of success. Clough attempts not just to beat Leeds United, but to *become* them as well; or rather, transform them into his own image, thereby eradicating the past.

In *The Special Relationship*, the narrative is punctuated by telephone conversations between Blair and President Bill Clinton (Dennis Quaid). These often act as 'chapter' markers, sections of the film ending on a fade to black before the next sequence begins with a further telephone conversation. The telephone is at once public and private: Blair first meets the president, hesitantly entering as a schoolboy called to the headmaster's study, to find Clinton on the telephone to someone else, and many of Clinton's conversations take place interstitially both spatially and politically, with Clinton speaking to Blair (and sometimes cutting him off) between conversations that he is conducting with advisors in the White House. The protocols of the conversation shift over the time of the film (from 1992, when Blair arrives unheralded as a member of the Opposition to learn from the Democrats electoral success) to 2000, when Clinton departs the presidency. In the beginning, it is Clinton who controls the timing and duration of the conversations. Arriving at Number 10 Downing Street, Blair takes a congratulatory call from French president Chirac, who he then cuts off to take the call from Clinton. After a short conversation, Clinton hangs up; he does so again in a later conversation, when Blair speaks his thanks ('And if there is anything we can do for you') to a dead line. After Clinton becomes embroiled in the Lewinsky scandal, Blair's public show of solidarity results in his growing confidence and Clinton's weakness; when discussing the possibility of military intervention in Kosovo, Blair interrupts Clinton, a significant reversal of the power relationship established through telephone protocols.

Blair throws off Clinton's patronage over this issue, and ultimately forces the president's hand not through the private appeal down the telephone line, but through a mediated address on the television screen. In a speech made in Chicago, where Blair instructs his aides to make sure that right-wing foreign policy 'hawks' are prominent in the audience, Blair addresses the anxieties of the American public about overseas intervention in declaring the need for such 'moral' action to preserve humanitarian, and in fact 'human' values. Clinton watches this on television (he is recurrently seen with a small portable television propped up nearby), and the film focuses on Sheen's face in close-up on the television screen, as though Blair is addressing Clinton himself, not the Chicago or television audience. This is a thoughtfully staged scene, in which the centrality of mediation in the *mise-en-scène* of the

Sheen/Morgan films is represented as a personal communication by other means, where television trumps the telephone. This also heralds Blair's accession to a role that is more than that of a 'junior partner', or his refusal of the terms Clinton explicitly uses on another phone call: 'look at you, baby brother, stepping up to the big roulette table'. Younger brother no more, this scene is followed by one in which Blair gives a speech to Parliament, in which he sets out the 'moral justification for invading another country for humanitarian ends', followed by a rapturous ovation. The filial relationship becomes one in which power is increasingly and explicitly present, a personal relationship which finds its analogue in the 'special relationship' between the United States and the United Kingdom.

The 'special relationship', the title of the final Sheen/Morgan film focusing on Tony Blair, makes manifest the underlying connection between private and emotional 'friendship' and public and political connection in a way that is a structuring device for all the other films. When aide Jonathan Powell (Adam Godley) tells Blair that 'all political friendship is strategic', the struggle underpinning male relationships between Blair and Brown, Blair and Clinton, Frost and Nixon, and Clough and Revie is exposed. It is no coincidence that personal betrayal is a significant motif in all the films discussed in this chapter. Homosocial relationships, the films suggest, are striated by contestation and struggles for power. Blair and Brown, Blair and Clinton and Clough and Taylor are clearly homosocial 'couples', caught in 'romantic' partnerships that are privileged over their heterosexual marriages, and ultimately their wives are excluded from the narrative diegesis. In *The Queen*, Cherie Blair (Helen McCrory), and in *Frost/Nixon* Caroline Cushing (Rebecca Hall) are more narratively prominent, but this is almost certainly an effect of the lesser importance of the homosocial partnership: Frost's relationship to Nixon is one where underlying likeness must be acknowledged and the antagonist defeated, but it is only *after* the crucial confrontation that a kind of friendship can be established; in *The Queen*, the relationship between the Queen and Tony Blair clearly operates very differently from homosociality. In *The Queen*, in fact, the relationship between Blair and the monarch is largely conducted (once again) by telephone, when the Queen is sequestered in Balmoral, with two personal meetings bookending the narrative, and this central pairing is played against an array of heterosexual marriages of differing qualities: that between the Queen and Prince Philip (James Cromwell), Prince Charles and Princess Diana and between Tony Blair and his wife Cherie, who consistently pokes (rather pointed) fun at her husband's growing respect for the monarchy, as an institution and in its female embodiment: 'All Labour Prime Ministers fall for her', Cherie says.

The emotional depths that are usually repressed in the homosocial pair is explored in *The Damned United*. I noted above that the shot of the two unused cut-glass goblets is used in the film as a sign of the origin point of Clough's hatred of Revie and Leeds United. When the shot is reversed, so it is not Clough but his friend and assistant Peter Taylor (Timothy Spall) who is seen looking at the glasses, the significance is altered. Here, Spall's uncomfortable facial gestures indicate his own wounded feelings, that Clough would exclude him to have an audience with Revie. That there are two glasses, not three, indicates a fundamental problem in the outwardly successful Clough/Taylor partnership: until the end of the film, when Clough has failed (without Taylor's support and guidance) at Leeds United, he is unable to acknowledge Taylor's importance as friend, and as more-than-friend. When Clough drives to Brighton after his sacking from Leeds to meet Taylor and apologize, a curious scene takes place. Before accepting the apology, Taylor forces Clough to kneel on his driveway and plead for forgiveness, prompting Clough to say the words 'I want you back, baby.' Clough balks at first, then relents and repeats the phrase. While clearly a parody of a romantic break-up and reconciliation, what renders this scene uncomfortable is the overt power Taylor is able to wield, forcing a particular performance from Clough that not only reveals the centrality of the homosocial 'love story' to *The Damned United*'s narrative (as it is in *The Deal* and *The Special Relationship*) but also violently ruptures the (televisual) Clough persona/performance that had already been undermined by the interview scene with Revie immediately preceding it in the film. Once forgiven, Clough rises and embraces Taylor, saying softly in his ear, 'I love you, you know.' As the coda reveals, it is this reconciliation with Taylor, the restoration of the homosocial 'buddy' pairing and the rejection of individual ambition, which leads to Clough's greatest footballing triumph: winning and retaining the European Cup with Nottingham Forest in 1979 and 1980, a feat that Revie himself was never able to achieve.

The legacy of Tony Blair

The Special Relationship is particularly concerned with issues of 'legacy', not least because the time frame of the narrative (1992–2000), and in particular the cause of 'liberal intervention' that becomes associated with Blair after Kosovo, plays against what we know will come post-9/11: military interventions in Iraq and Afghanistan, the political furore about 'WMDs' and the lack thereof found in Iraq, the ongoing instability in both countries and the failure of the 'War on Terror' to bring about a 'defeat' of terrorism. The personal legacy for Tony Blair, at least in Britain, is vilification and an absence from the political landscape; Blair and Clinton's talk of permanently changing the global political landscape towards a centre-left 'progressive' politics is revealed in *The Special Relationship* to be hollow indeed. This resolves itself partly through Clinton's own denunciation of Blair in his final visit to Chequers after the 2000 election, in which he asks whether Blair will try to find a similar position of political and emotional proximity to the incoming George W. Bush, or whether he will 'turn for home'. Clinton wonders aloud whether Blair was ever a 'centre left progressive politician', and the end-credits sequence is overlaid pointedly with Conway Twitty's 'Lonely Blue Boy', deftly suggesting, in British political terms, Blair's conservatism, and in American terms, Clinton's Democratic isolation. The film's narrative, with Blair's increasing feeling of being lied to by Clinton over the Lewinski scandal, ironizes this Clintonian condemnation: the president's own political legacy is tarnished, if not outright evacuated, by the troubles of his second term (leading to Al Gore's failed presidential campaign in 2000). In *The Special Relationship*, Blair's (and Clinton's) legacy is one of discord, war and the defeat of 'progressive' politics.

In Robert Harris's *The Ghost* (2007), Blair is recast as 'Adam Lang', the former British prime minister whose memoirs the 'ghost' (writer) of the title attempts to pull into shape during the narrative. Lang is the performer *par excellence*, but one whose performance masks a fundamental absence or lack:

> That was when I realised I had a fundamental problem with our former prime minister. He was not a psychologically credible character. In the flesh, or on the screen, playing the part of a statesman, he seemed to have a string personality. But somehow, when one sat down to think about him, he vanished. (Harris 2010: 192)

Lang simply is not there. This is an extension of the revealing way in which Tony Blair, in his political memoir *My Journey* (2010), writes about speechmaking as a political performance. When hearing the left-wing Tony Benn, Blair writes:

> I sat enraptured, absolutely captivated and inspired. I thought: If only I could speak like that. What impressed me was not so much the content – actually

I didn't agree with a lot of it – but the power of it, the ability to use words to move people, not simply to persuade but to propel. (Blair 2010: loc914)

This moment is revealing in its admiration for the techniques of rhetoric rather than the left-wing 'content', which Blair explicitly rejects; in fact, in the book's introduction, he explicitly characterizes himself 'not so much a politician of traditional left or right, but a moderniser' (Blair 2010: loc187). The admiration for the power of the spoken word 'not simply to persuade but to propel' finds its analogue in the insistent mediation, particularly the use of television as a tool of mass communication, which we have seen in the films analysed in this chapter. Blair quotes (the real) Bill Clinton as saying: 'Don't forget: communication is fifty per cent of the battle in the information age. Say it once, say it twice and keep on saying it, and when you've finished, you'll know you've still not said enough' (Blair 2010: loc746). Blair's political masculinity is, in effect, a linguistic act; not simply transactional, performed in relation to another masculine subject, but physically enacted in the speech act itself.

In *The Ghost*, Lang is pursued by an international court for war crimes; he had allowed 'enemy' combatants to be seized and 'rendered' for questioning under torture. In a late conversation with the ghost, directly before Lang's assassination, he blithely sets out his rationale for these acts:

'Look', said Lang. 'I don't condone torture, but let me say this to you. First, it actually does produce results – I've seen the intelligence. Second, having power, in the end, is all about balancing evils, and when you think about it, what are a couple of minutes of suffering for a few individuals compared to the deaths – the *deaths*, mark you – of thousands. Third, don't try telling me this is something unique to the War on Terror. Torture's always been a part of warfare. The only difference is that in the past there were no fucking media around to report it.' (Harris 2010: 351)

The rationales slip from defending its utility, to a moral justification, to one which implies that everyone has always done it anyway, mediation being the only difference. The hollowness of Lang's discourse mirrors his own ethical vacuity. When, early in the film, in response to questions about how Lang should present his emotional state, the ghost says 'what exactly are you?', the question resonates across the film both ethically and psychologically. Because all of Lang's decisions in office have been in the interests of the United States, he is suspected as a CIA agent. When it is revealed that the agent is in fact his wife, the idea that Lang may have been a puppet of an external espionage agency is more comforting than what is revealed to be the truth: in Lang's words, 'that everything I did, both as a party leader and as prime minister – everything – I did out of conviction, because I believed it was right' (Harris 2007: 355). This becomes the rationale that trumps all others: not that Lang was a political marionette, not that he was a cynical strategist, not even that he was engaged in a homosocial conflict with a powerful masculine antagonist: rather, that he *believed* it was the right thing to do, and thereby he was ethically in the right.

To end this chapter, and also the first section of the book, I would like to turn to the film *Four Lions*, directed by Chris Morris and released in 2010. Concerning the jihadist activities of five young male Muslims living in Sheffield, *Four Lions* is, as well as being a satirical comedy of the darkest kind, also a meditation upon the fabric of contemporary Britain, particularly in the wake of the 9/11 and 7/7 bombings. Omar (Riz Ahmed) is the leader of the jihadist cell, and seemingly the most capable of the group; he is the only one who is portrayed as having a family life (he has a wife and son who are fully supportive of his jihadist ambitions), and seems most intelligent. We see him, at the beginning of the film, working as a security guard in a Sheffield shopping mall, watching the security monitors while checking his email inbox for an invitation to a Pakistan-based training camp and talking to his colleague Matt (Craig Parkinson). While the most articulate of the group in his criticism of the consumerist imperatives of the society in which he lives – home-made jihadist videos made by the group are a recurrent motif in the film, and the narrative begins with the filming of one – he is as invested in a delusive sense of agency as much as his friend (and increasingly antagonist), the 'loose cannon' Barry (Nigel Lindsay), a white convert from Folkestone who is the most belligerent of all the men ('I'm the most Al-Qaeda one,' he tells Omar when they argue about who will go to the training camp in Pakistan). Omar is also the most Westernized in terms of dress, not just in his security guard uniform but in the T-shirts and tracksuit bottoms he continually wears, in direct contrast both to Barry and to the simple Faisal (Adeel Akhtar) who wear more traditional Muslim dress. Omar is particularly antipathetic to his brother, a devout Muslim who refuses to enter the same room as Omar's wife Sofia (Preeya Kalidas) and who inhabits a rather pompous and sanctimonious form of 'traditional' Muslim masculinity: encountering his brother playing football under umbrellas in the rain, Omar is drawn to confide in him, but when his brother puts on 'that face' (one of exaggerated piety) he flees. Towards the end of the film, Omar's brother is the subject of a police raid on his house and is 'rendered' to a hangar in RAF

Mildenhall, which is designated to have Egyptian sovereignty, his overt display of Muslim identity making him visible to the (white) authorities in a way that Omar is not.

Omar is failed both by traditional articulations of Muslim communal authority (in the shape of his brother) and by the mores and imperatives of a late-capitalist socioeconomic system that he rejects and would like to confront directly. There is little trace of the directly political in *Four Lions* except in the shape of the 'radicalized' cell of jihadists, for whom a martyr's death in a terrorist act is proposed as the only form of protest that remains available. The civic and political structures that should provide a means by which the alienated citizen can dissent and protest have been erased by the matrices of surveillance that characterize the security state. Waj (Kayvan Novak), whom Omar calls 'our kid' and who is presented as somewhat dim-witted, finds himself at the end of the film in a kebab shop, surrounded by fellow Muslims, ready to detonate a suicide bomb. His phone is called by a police negotiator (Benedict Cumberbatch), who fails to engage Waj in negotiations; comically, Waj asks whether the police have agents inside the Orange network, and declares that he should have joined a different one. While absurd, this moment does indicate that such technological networks do exist, and perhaps that Waj has been tracked for some time.

By the end of the film, all five men have died in explosions, by accident, in confusion, by the hand of another, or on purpose, like Omar. He is the last, having heard and seen Waj detonate his own bomb, knowing that Waj's own heart has told him, 'it's wrong, Waj, don't do it', and that he has convinced his friend to go to his death. Omar enters a chemist's shop (previously dismissed as an unworthy target) and blows himself up no longer for a cause, but in despair: he had, seconds before, told Waj that he was giving himself up. The final moments, for Omar, are ones that signify the failure of communal and homosocial bonds. Barry's gloating accusation – 'you tomatoed your friend. You killed the special needs donkey' – strikes home, but not in the way that Barry intends; rather than articulating Omar's failure in terms of jihadist purpose, it indicates his failure as a friend. The shots that follow Omar's death, showing the fate of his brother, satellite images of Omar and Waj inadvertently destroying a jihadist base and even killing Osama Bin Laden, and Omar's white colleague Matt refusing to believe Omar was part of the bombing, indicates how little effect the activities of the 'four lions' have on the world they intend to change. They are re-inscribed into ideological media narratives that render their resistance futile or, worse, laughable. *Four Lions* escapes this accusation itself in the detailed interaction between the men, and in particular, Omar's relationships with his wife and son, with his brother, and with Waj. Their failures are absurd, but also arouse pathos, in that none of the men have truly developed a mature and sophisticated way of processing, and resisting, the world that repulses them. As we will see in Chapter 13, a visceral reaction to the moral or ideological fabric of post-war Britain (in particular, two cities in Yorkshire) can all too easily turn into an apocalyptic, 'cleansing' violence that simply recapitulates the most retrograde masculinist fantasies of 'heroic' agency. Omar and his friends are not the hyper-mobile terrorist subjects that haunt the world of globalized mobility that is represented in the Bond films, nor yet the 'bad men' that stalk the streets of Leeds in David Peace's Red Riding Quartet (from corrupt and violent policemen to the figure of the Yorkshire Ripper); the failure of masculine heroism, even as they complete their 'mission' to bomb the London Marathon, is all too apparent in their ends.

Part Two

Science Fiction

5

The Enclave

Steven Soderbergh's *Contagion* (2011) opens with a shot of Gwyneth Paltrow, clearly unwell, lit in acid yellow tones, making a cell phone call at an airport arrivals hall. As the film progresses, it appears that Paltrow is 'Patient Zero', the carrier of a particularly virulent influenza virus, and the film narrates both forwards as the pandemic spreads, and backwards to the 'origin' of transmission, with the film showing the transmission of animal flu to Paltrow via infected food on 'Day 1'. While the film downplays the generic markers of science fiction, its scenes of empty streets, looted shops and displaced population clearly indicate post-catastrophic SF scenarios, and *Contagion* can be read as part of a cycle of contemporary films that place *transmission* at the centre of the narrative: transmission in terms of disease and its spread, in terms of global communications networks and the internet and in terms of the physical hyper-mobility of global air travel and tourism (and its attendant spectre, the terrorist). At the beginning of *Contagion*, the multiple discourses of transmission-anxiety are visually engaged, from the airport location (spatial paradigm of globalized mobility), to viruses and disease vectors, to global cell phone networks. *Contagion* asserts parallels between the spread of actual disease and the global flows of (mis-)information, through news media, the internet, blogs and vlogs, particularly in the malignant shape of Jude Law's Alan Krumwiede, a high-profile blogger who attempts to characterize the discourses surrounding the contagion as a conspiracy abetted by the pharmaceutical industry. Not only must the biologists in the film isolate and find effective medical treatments for the virus, but Homeland Security agencies are engaged to distribute the virus, manage panicked populations and also, problematically, silence Krumwiede as the disseminator of false information. The spread of the virus is explicitly connected to the spreading of rumour; careless talk does indeed cost lives. This engagement of wartime discourses engages the cultural and political contexts of the 'War on Terror' post-9/11, but somewhat fudges its critique in presenting

Krumwiede as either delusional or mendacious, and various other characters in its ensemble cast as paranoid (in particular, the widowed father played by Matt Damon). Heroic scientists Laurence Fishburne and Jennifer Ehle finally help produce a vaccine, but this only becomes available, through limited initial stocks, through a lottery based on birth date. The motif of the lottery again returns the film to its own ground zero, 'Day 1', where Paltrow consumes infected food and drink in a Hong Kong casino. The casino and the lottery are figures of the global financial flows that characterize a late capitalism haunted by the possibility of over-extension and collapse, just as the enhanced mobility of travellers from the developed world through air travel infrastructures is haunted by the potential for disease pandemics or the actions of the hyper-mobile 'terrorist'. *Contagion*, a film dominated by images of automobiles, cars, buses, bridges, airports, mobile phones, laptop computers, the internet and digital media, at once critiques and inhabits contemporary anxiety about borders, mobility and transmission (and is, thereby, a loose sequel to the 2000 film *Traffic*).

Globalized networks of mobility (particularly, air travel) have been haunted by the figure of the globally mobile 'terrorist' (as we saw in Chapter 1) and by the possibility of global pandemics, such as the SARS epidemic of 2002–03 or the H1N1 'swine flu' panic of 2009, which resulted in the UK government stockpiling antiviral drugs in case of the spread of a 'killer virus'. In an increasingly mobilized world, anxieties about movement of people, transmission of data and disease, or terrorism, produce systems for policing and regulating mobility. The seeming 'freedoms' of financialized capitalism and its technologies of global travel and digital networking do not simply create anxiety through massive dislocation or destabilization, however; they are *foundationally* implicated in systems of policing and control, and these systems themselves call up fears of a dystopian or catastrophic future. As Ginette Verstraete wrote of the increasing control of external borders in the development in the EU (at the same time as internal borders were becoming more porous): 'the freedom of mobility for some (citizens, tourists, business people) could only be made possible through the organised exclusion of others forced to move around as illegal "aliens", migrants, or refugees' (Verstraete 2001: 29).

Homeland Security, Sky Marshalls, the terrorist: mobility, as the first decade of the twenty-first century passed, has become increasingly problematic and subject to policing (physical and biometric), militarization (at airports, in aircraft) and the involvement of intelligence agencies. It is also shadowed, of course, by another kind of mobilization: that of the projection of US military power on a global scale in the 'War on Terror', in Iraq, Afghanistan and Libya. While several Hollywood SF movies in the decade offered alien-invasion tropes – notably *Cloverfield* (2008), *War of the Worlds* (2005) and the *Transformers* franchise – that have greater or lesser explicit connection to 9/11 (as we shall investigate further in Chapter 7), these films are less concerned with borders and migration, and do not have the same emphasis on biological transmission that we find in transmission-anxiety texts. Their recurrent concerns with borders, migration, enclaves, transmission of disease and the failures of political and particularly military authority present estranged versions of globalized (and militarized) late capitalism. Until the events of 2008, the 'credit crunch' (liquidity crisis) and subsequent global economic recession, the dominant model of free-market capitalism stressed liquidity and mobility of both finance and data. The over-extension of credit, as an engine of economic growth, ultimately led to the 'freezing' of lending between banks, which precipitated the crisis of economic institutions and national economies that still unwinds 4 years later. The flows of data and finance, however, were not accompanied by corresponding flows of economic migration, except within economic and political blocs whose external borders were closed. The primary example of this is the EU, as we saw in Chapter 1. The abolition of *internal* barriers, as we saw in Chapter 1, found its correlative in 'the introduction of firm external frontiers to keep illegal immigrants, terrorists and drug-dealers out, and guarantee internal security and stability' (Verstraete 29). While the Schengen space *enabled* greater mobility for white Europeans, this was predicated on the policing and exclusion of non-European others.

Code 46

Michael Winterbottom's *Code 46* (2003) is a near-future dystopia located in just such a world of late-capital globalization and of securitized borders. *Code 46* begins with shots of the desert taken from a plane, overflying the zones of exclusion; a title indicates the prohibitive 'code 46' itself, which prevents sexual relations and reproduction in people with too-similar DNA profiles. This, then, is a world of clones and gene splicing, a world in which the conception of a genetic 'family' is dispersed so widely (globally, in fact) that laws and prohibitions are in place to prevent accidental incest. There is little sense in *Code 46* of a dystopian principle of the protection of genetic (or, more problematically, racial) 'purity', however, and the film does not overdetermine the spatial exclusion of certain people along ethnic lines: 'inside' Shanghai is culturally plural and polyglot, although the casting of the very tall Tim Robbins, as the investigator William, marks his difference overtly from the crowds that populate the night-time city. When being driven from the airport at the beginning of the film, William comments, 'A lot of people live out here', to which his driver replies, 'It's not living, it's existing.' Here we can turn to the work of Giorgio Agamben, in particular *Homo Sacer* (1998), as a means by which we can diagnose *Code 46*'s distinction between 'life' (inside the city) and 'existing' (outside, *afuera*). Michel Foucault, in his lectures to the Collège de France and in the first volume of *The History Of Sexuality*, suggested that a decisive transition in modernity can be said to come at the point at which 'bare life', *zoē*, previously excluded from 'political life', was drawn into the sphere of the political. Agamben, in *Homo Sacer*, suggested that the implication of *zoē* and *bios* is actually foundational to sovereign power: 'Western politics first constitutes itself through an exclusion (which is an inclusion) of bare life' (Agamben 1998: 11). Sovereign power, according to Agamben, is identified with 'he who decides the exception' (both *homo sacer*, the figure excluded from law, and therefore both prohibited from being sacrificed but who may be murdered without punishment; and that the sovereign himself, who is both within and outside the law). In deciding the exception, that which is excluded (*homo sacer*), the sovereign re-includes the excluded. It is at this point that politics comes into being. Agamben writes:

[t]he fundamental categorical pair of Western politics is not that of friend/enemy but that of bare life/political existence, *zoē/bios*, exclusion/inclusion. There is politics because man is a living being who, in language, separates and opposes himself to his own their life and, at the same time, maintains himself to the their life in an inclusive exclusion. (12)

Modern democracy, then, 'is constantly trying to transform its own bare life into a way of life and to find, so to speak, the *bios* of *zoē*' (Agamben 1998. 13). The world of *Code 46* is structured by a radical division between *zoē* and *bios*, between the 'bare life' of those *afuera* and the 'political existence' of those within the city. While seeming to critique the construction of boundaries, *Code 46* internally replicates the ideology of exclusion: it seems that there is no 'life' in the favelas 'outside', and the final shot of his excluded lover, Maria (Samantha Morton), facing away from the camera, indicates a yearning for inclusion which seems to preclude the forging of a meaningful life outside Shanghai, even though it is revealed in the film that she has already spent 10 years of her life 'outside'.

The last words of the film are 'I miss you'; spatial exclusion becomes not just emotional lack, but also a *lack of amnesia* or anamnesis, the forgetting that is granted to the erring William.

In *Code 46*, the inhabitants of Shanghai fear and shun daylight, believing it to have some kind of malign property. The *mise-en-scène* of bleached-out desert highways and empty city streets place it in a continuum with SF disaster scenarios (images found in *Contagion* and *28 Days Later*, for instance), though the nocturnal world is as busy as our own. Just as Maria is a version of the double (with perhaps an aside to *Metropolis*), a destabilizing and ultimately tabooed self/other, Shanghai is itself doubled, day/night, dead/alive, empty/over full. Shanghai in *Code 46* is itself post-national. It is ethnically diverse (and one of its denizens, Maria Gonzalez, is played by Samantha Morton, an actress who is notably not Hispanic), and Chinese; it is modern, a city of glass and neon signage, yet it is a kind of enclave in a world of other enclaves. Signs of hyper-mobility – airports, express highways, the subway – are prominent in the visual fabric, but the world of the film is predicated upon the strict delimitation of mobility, and the narrative 'Macguffin' of the text is the 'papelle', the item that enables mobility (even if, as occurs in the film, circumventing prohibited travel leads to the death of one of Maria's customers). The papelles are travel papers, but the idiomatic word for them within the film is 'cover', a word derived from the financial world of insurance. 'If people can't get cover, there must be a reason' is a line delivered twice during the film, and the death in India of the researcher into bats, recipient of one of Maria's forged papelles, seems to indicate that the system, if exclusionary, is at least based on reasonable principles. Unlike other films considered here, except *District 9*, the securitized borders of *Code 46* are not run by government agencies or the military: William works for 'the Sphinx', a corporation that controls the production and use of papelles. *Code 46* is a world where some form of catastrophe has occurred, but the future is privatized as well as securitized, run by corporations rather than dysfunctional or dystopian governments.

This vision of the carceral city, urban space characterized by securitization and enclosure, was diagnosed in Los Angeles by Mike Davis in *City Of Quartz* (1990), where Davis catalogued the privatization of public space, especially downtown, in the creation of shopping malls and gated communities, and the forced displacement of 'economic undesirables' (the homeless, the poor). More recently, Wendy Brown investigated this securitization as an effect of globalized capital. Brown, in *Walled States, Waning Sovereignty* (2010), argues that the 'new nation-state walls [along the Rio Grande, separating Israeli and Palestinian] are iconographic of [the] predicament of state power. Counter-intuitively, perhaps, it is the weakening of state sovereignty, and more precisely, the detachment of sovereignty from the nation-state, that is generating much of the frenzy of nation-state wall-building today' (Brown 2010: 24). For Brown, the 'global landscape of flows and barriers' (Brown 2010: 23) is foundationally interconnected; in the seeming paradox, the political fantasy of a 'world without borders' and of a hyper-mobilized global migration is always accompanied by physical barriers, 'exclusion and stratification' of populations and 'network to and virtual power met by physical barricades' (Brown 2010: 20). As Brown notes, however, in contemporary globalized capital, the 'threats' to the nation-state come not from other nation-states, but from 'nonstate transnational actors – individuals, groups, movements, organisations, and industries' (Brown 2010: 21). The walls are in fact 'icons of erosion' (Brown 2010: 24), indices of the waning sovereignty of the state, and an 'increasingly blurred the distinction between the inside and the outside of the nation itself' marked by 'eroding lines between the police and the military, subject and *patria*, vigilante and state, law and lawlessness' (Brown 2010: 25). The *physical* walls of *Code 46* actually prove effective barriers to migration (though how the porous desert boundaries are policed, rather than the road-blocking checkpoints, is left unexamined) partly through the film's insistence on mobility as mass transportation: William and Maria (Samantha Morton) travel by car, plane, metro and riverboat at key points in the film. Still more effective, of course, is the system of *genetic* profiling and control that itself relies upon strongly maintained *physical* barriers to mobility through nodal points such as airports or road checkpoints. *Code 46*'s walls are virtual as well as physical, even though the nation-state appears to have withered away.

A signature space in *Code 46* is the airport, William's entry and departure point (and location of a deeply ironic scene where he himself is not allowed to leave Shanghai, his temporary 'cover' having run out). The border crossing, the airport departure lounge, passport and immigration controls are the visible site of the problematic logics of Schengen space and financialized capital that forms the economic base of the world of *Code 46*. Tim Cresswell writes that 'the airport lounge, once seen as a reprehensible site of placelessness, becomes a contemporary symbol of flow, dynamism, and mobility' (Cresswell 2006: 44–5). Where the anthropologist Marc Augé, in *Non-Places* (1995), lamented the erasure of local practices of lived space in supermodernity's 'airports and railway stations, hotel chains, leisure parks, large retail outlets' (Augé 1995: 79), signature 'non-places' of contemporary capitalism, the sociologist Manuel Castells instead saw the first-class departure lounge as a paradigmatic contemporary 'space of flows', a system or network that allowed the free passage of travellers (if, of course, one has the right documentation). In the year 2000, Castells proposed a coming 'network society' characterized by a 'space of flows' in which people, finance, information existed in a state of radical and enabling flux. He outlined several characteristics of the new formation: (1) a new technological paradigm, based on advances in IT and genetic engineering; (2) economic globalization; (3) the dominance of electronic hypertext in cultural production; (4) the demise of the sovereign nation-state; (5) a crisis in patriarchy; (6) popularization of advances in scientific understanding, leading to the growth of ecological, neurological and other discourses in political and ethical thought (Castells 2000: 693–4). Clearly, Castells understood the rapidly developing forms of social and techno-logical change visible on the horizon in 2000, but his analysis of the 'networked space of flows' partakes of what Cresswell criticizes as 'nomad thought', which is 'symptomatic of postmodernity' (Cresswell 2006: 45). Cresswell points out that 'words associated with mobility are unremittingly positive' (Cresswell 2006: 25): flux, fluidity, dynamic, mobile, all words that seem to offer the possibility of disrupting the ideological landscape, to resist or destabilize hegemonic forms of subjectivity, cultural representation or everyday life. Rather than celebrating the 'networked space of flows' or the airport as a 'simulated metropolis . . . inhabited by a community of nomads' (Cresswell 2006, quoting Iain Chambers: 45) as a space of untrammelled freedom, analysis of the potentialities of contemporary mobility for 'new social formations' must be balanced by analysis of the disrup-tive, dislocating effects of globalized mobility. If the 'network' society has been acknowledged as a new cultural and social formation, the implicit neutrality of its conceptualization towards a neoliberal, free-market capitalism as a natural-ized or 'unseen' structure which enables these flows is deeply problematic. Films such as *Code 46* bring these structures into view by positing futures where con-trol of population movement, and ideologies of inclusion and exclusion, have become much more explicit.

Code 46 offers a rather conflicted critique of a global system of spatial exclusion, albeit one that is clearly proximate to our own. When the spiky attendant of the 'Westerfields' clinic that Maria is sent to for her code 46 termination severely remarks to William that 'here on the outside, we do not have access to pleasures freely available in the city', it at once uncomfortably skewers William's privileged position (and his assumptions of authority) and validates the assumption that life only exists in the city itself. *Code 46* itself encodes a liberal, developed-world guilt about the privileges of global mobility and the 'pleasures' of contemporary capital while itself excluding the possibility that life may be possible *'afuera'.* When William and Maria travel to the Middle Eastern city state of Jebel Ali (actually in Dubai), this represents a kind of Orientalist fantasy of escape, a temporary holiday from the 'real' to which the couple are inevitably returned. Life does indeed exist here, in teeming abundance; but we only see it from the point of view of the 'outlaw' Western tourists, for whom it figures as a backdrop to their romantic intoxication. This Orientalism is deeply ironic, considering that *Code 46*'s conception of the future city is based on Shanghai and the density and energy of East Asian capitalism (and, it should be remembered, *Contagion* places its own viral 'ground zero' in Hong Kong). It 'is not insignificant', suggests Jackie Stacey in *The Cinematic Life of the* Gene (2010), that it is Shanghai that figures in *Code 46* as the future urban zone, 'the location for a story about the regulation of highly dispersed populations through rigid, centralised modes of genetic and surveillance technologies' (Stacey 2010: 146). Shanghai, Stacey suggests, 'condenses the tensions between fluidity and mobility on one hand, and restriction and state control on the other hand' (Stacey 2010: 146). The future of US/European societies, corralled in 'Schengen space' and protected by Homeland Security, is itself haunted by the uncontrollable dynamism of the East Asian city and its people.

Both *Code 46* and an earlier film whose future is predicated on genetic profiling and exclusion, Andrew Niccol's *Gattaca* (1997), are dealt with in detail by Jackie Stacey in *The Cinematic Life of the Gene* (2010). Stacey notes that *Gattaca* first shows Jerome Morrow (Jude Law), a genetically 'Valid' subject who was once an Olympic swimmer, but now is wheelchair-bound after an accident, moving 'from behind a concrete pillar in his wheelchair, in long shot, moving to share the center of the frame with the base of an imposing spiral staircase. The design of the spiral plays upon an association with the now familiar twisted structure of DNA: the double helix' (Stacey 2010: 1). Stacey reads the image of the wheelchair combined with the helix as articulating 'anxieties about the violence of genetic selection with fantasies about engineering improved human beings' (Stacey 2010: 2). While this is certainly true, *Gattaca* also investigates problems of mobility, in the social and physical sense. While Jerome cannot use the stairs with which he is visually associated (except in one scene, where he physically manhandles himself to the upper level), Vincent Freeman (Ethan Hawke), who is abetted by Jerome to impersonate him and enter the Gattaca space centre, is an 'Invalid', a subject born by 'natural' (i.e. non-technological) means, and thereby subject to hereditary physical impairments that are coded out of the 'Valids'; namely, myopia and a heart problem, likely to result in early death. As an 'Invalid', Freeman is socially and economically excluded from legally entering Gattaca as a prospective voyager to Titan, instead forced into employment as a cleaner. Stacey calls Freeman an 'imitator of that lost perfection' (Stacey 2010: 2), a kind of copying or 'cloning' done without genetic biotechnology. This deception is, in fact, a version of what became known in the United States during the early twentieth century as 'passing', where light-skinned African-Americans 'passed' socially as white. This mobility of ethnic categorization, or double subjectivity, is of course the product of legal and economic systems of exclusion, and its consequences can be dislocation or dissolution of the subject itself. Jerome reveals that his damaged spine was caused by deliberately stepping out in front of an automobile; and at the end of the film, he enters the chamber in which Vincent scrubs and depilates himself (to remove dead skin, possible traces or DNA evidence of who he 'really' is) and immolates himself. Vincent, close to being discovered, in one scene later in the film is found naked on a beach, rubbing himself compulsively with a stone, repeating his ritual of cleansing, but here becoming a marker of psychological damage. His compulsion to repeat here suggests trauma, as Freud argued in *Beyond the Pleasure Principle* (see Chapter 11), a trauma to do with fundamental problems with his sense of self. Vincent, already marked as deficient in relation to a younger sibling, the product of a technologized birth, is not remade in his process of disguise or 'cloning'; instead, as we will see with the transcendental space fictions that are the subject of Chapter 9, his masculinity risks dissolution in a willed trajectory to the stars.

Science fictions such as *Blade Runner* (1982/1991/2008), or the *Alien* films, in particular, connect the presence of 'artificial persons' with the transcendental experience of outer space: Roy Baty tells Deckard, in *Blade Runner*, that 'I've seen things you people would not believe. Attack ships on fire off the shoulder of Orion. I've seen sea-beams glitter by the Tannhauser Gates'. As we will see in Chapter 9, the *dissolution* of the subject (often desired, a product of the death drive) is mirrored in oceanic imagery, from the ocean world of *Solaris* (1973 and 2002) to the Stargate sequence of *2001: A Space Odyssey* (1968). Androids or replicants or clones are Others, often posited as a threat to the humans in the film, or at least a shadow of their own problematic sense of integrity and purpose. *Moon* (2009), directed by Duncan Jones, features the American actor

Sam Rockwell as Sam Bell, who it appears is the sole inhabitant of a mining-operation moonbase, descending into eccentricity at the end of a 3-year tour. After an accident in a moon rover vehicle, a clean and shaven Sam awakes in the medical facility, but soon realizes that the moon rover still outside the base. When reached, Sam discovers the 'first', original Sam, unconscious within it. The scenario is partly dystopian and is familiar from films such as *Alien* (1979) and *Outland* (1981), or the Tyrell Corporation in *Blade Runner*. The mining company has produced a series of clones illegally, implanted memories from the 'original' Sam, and disposes of each clone as it comes to the end of its 3-year 'tour', in fact, revealed to be its life span. Where *Blade Runner* asserts, through the character of Baty, the fallibility of assumptions of 'human' superiority over replicant, 'original' over 'copy', the fact that *Moon* is largely a two-hander where both protagonists are clones of an absent 'original', though in markedly different states, lends a poignancy to their condition. Sam Bell is no Baty, no Blakean rebel demanding 'more life, fucker/father'; in a wonderfully underplayed scene, the dying 'first' Sam eventually manages to contact what he believes to have been his home, only to discover that his 'daughter' Eve is now 15, and his 'wife' has been dead a number of years. We even hear the 'original' Sam Bell asking Eve who is phoning. She does not know, because, in a subtle and unemphasized gesture, the dying 'first' Sam covers the camera of the videophone with his hand so that Eve cannot see who it is, or perhaps, who Sam looks like. Where *Blade Runner* is able to suggest the difference (not inferiority) of replicant subjectivity through the power of Baty's (heroic/Satanic) agency, *Moon* offers instead a kind of tragic hollowness: life is indeed elsewhere. Although the 'second' Sam escapes to earth, and we hear at the close of the film Congressional hearings into the company's activities, it would seem that the 3 years of the second Sam's life on earth might be taken up in courtrooms rather than in roaming mountain ranges.

Never Let Me Go

Kashuo Ishiguro's *Never Let Me Go* (2005), adapted for the screen in a 2009 film directed by Mark Romanek, offers a different kind of negotiation of the figure of the patient and the themes of genetics or cloning. In this narrative, a medical 'breakthrough' occurs in early 1950s Britain, after which human longevity is extended, so that most people now live to over 100. This necessitates the inauguration of a 'National Donor Programme', the creation of cloned human beings whose sole purpose is to act as donors for the population of 'originals'. The film is narrated from the point of view of Kathy H. (Carey Mulligan), who is first shown watching as a young man is prepped for a medical procedure. As the film progresses, it is revealed that both she and the man are clones, brought up in the same 'boarding school' of Hailsham, though their paths have diverged: she is now a 'carer' (a clone who acts as a kind of helper, friend and next of kin for other clones, who otherwise have none of these), while the young man Tommy (Andrew Garfield) is undergoing his third (and last) 'donation' of a vital organ. While 'we aren't machines', Kathy asserts in her voice-over, the 'donors' are constructed as dispensable commodities in a medico-bureaucratic system; if not machines, then organic growth media for transplantable organs.

The first third of the film takes place in 1978, an inter-title declares, at Hailsham, which is presented as a kind of British boarding school familiar from British children's literature (and popularized by the Harry Potter books and films). This is a rather dowdy, run-down place, an imposing edifice of red brick, but where the children wear hand-me-down clothes and whose main source of personal belongings are the occasional 'sales' held in the school hall: broken toys, old audio tapes, the detritus of a commodity culture that exists on the borders of the film, just as these children (and carers/donors) exist on the margins of mainstream society. Though this is '1978', it looks much more like the British 1950s: a time of austerity, prior to the late 1950s/early 1960s consumer boom (of Harold Macmillan's famous boast 'You've never had it so good'), almost a place *out* of time. The physical fabric of the film insists upon the built environment of post-war British civic and municipal architecture: Hailsham itself, the brick-built hospitals, 'centres' and clinics that Kathy visits later in the film in her role as a 'carer', the concrete tower block (in an unnamed city) in which she is shown in 1994. *Never Let Me Go* astutely ties in the architectural fabric of the Welfare State, and in particular the 'cradle to grave' medical system of the National Health Service, to the system of 'donation' which provides health for the general population of Britain at the cost of the health, and ultimately the lives, of the 'donors' who are created only for this purpose.

At the end of the film, Kathy and Tommy travel to a seaside town to talk to 'Madame', a former art teacher at Hailsham who they believe has the ability to grant them a 'deferral' from donating if they can prove to her, through their art, that they are truly in love. While there, they also encounter their former headmistress (Charlotte Rampling), who disabuses them of this notion, not unkindly, but who reveals the true nature of why the children's art was examined.

'Hailsham', she says, 'was the last place to consider the ethics of donation' (Tommy has already referred to Hailsham's closure, and that 'the only schools left are like battery farms'); to assess whether the clones were 'almost human', the art gallery was used as a means by which 'to see if you have souls at all'. Tommy's and Kathy's art, of course, suggest that they have; and this scene is a moment of estrangement, where the ethical problematic of the 'National Donor Programme' is put into sharp relief. The headmistress tells Kathy and Tommy that because serious illnesses have been 'cured' in the general population through donation, 'no-one' would agree to ethically interrogate the system any more. An ethical instrumentality has triumphed, and questions of the 'humanity' of the clones are no longer alive. In a sense, the film problematizes the ontological status of the clones through suggesting that they are, in some ways, different from the general population. They remain childlike, unworldly, even when they have entered adulthood; they naively believe stories to do with 'deferral' of donation as a form of wish-fulfilment, and when told otherwise, Kathy in particular accepts this information with resignation. Only later, as Kathy drives Tommy home, does he ask her to stop the car, whereupon he lets out screams of anguish and anger into the dark country night. Whether this childishness is innate, an ontological marker of their difference from humanity, or whether it is a product of the educational and social systems which raise them to accept their roles as carers and donors, is undecided. At the least, however, this ambiguity allows the possibility that they are indeed different, even deficient, as 'humans'.

Tommy's difference is marked as social as well as biological; in a scene at the school, he is last to be picked for a game of football, leading the other children to tease him. In shots that foreshadow his later outburst in the country lane, he stands alone on the playing field and shouts his frustration. The three main protagonists, Kathy, Tommy and Ruth (Keira Knightley) are recurrently presented in emptied-out *mise-en-scène*, from Tommy in the playing field to the shot of Ruth's dead body, prostrate on an operating table, after her final donation, whereupon no effort is made by the medical team to save her, and after the organ is removed, the doctors and nurses turn off the light and leave her corpse behind (presumably for disposal). This sense of aloneness, an existential isolation that is prior to and countermands the communal social spaces of the school or the 'Cottages' that the teenage Kathy, Tommy and Ruth depart for when too old to stay at Hailsham, extends even to the scenes in which the clones visit the 'real' world. In search of Ruth's 'original', the three clones and two (older) others drive to a Norfolk seaside town. There, they discover that the rumoured 'original' is nothing of the sort, and Ruth tells the others that they will never find their 'originals' because they are copies of 'trash', people of the 'gutter'. This is an index of Ruth's (and the other clones') self-alienation and exclusion, of course, but this sequence reveals the donors' need to construct some kind of primal scene, some kind of traumatic confrontation with the 'real', that they have been consistently denied in their lives. (When a new 'guardian' at the school, Miss Lucy, tells them the truth of their condition, and that they will 'live the life that has already been set out for you', she is swiftly removed.) Even their journeys to the 'real' world (recurrently, British seaside towns) result in the navigation of deserted country lanes, empty streets, and ultimately at the arrival at a beach where a small trawler has been washed up and abandoned. This symbolic craft, isolated and ruined, connects the clones with the refuse that becomes their toys. Mobility is the traversal of a featureless, dematerialized space, 'shuttling from centre to centre, hospital to hospital' in Kathy's words, but these are fundamentally displaced persons. When the nurse tells Kathy that 'it's always better to wake at home', the ironies of the scene – that the nurse is an 'original' and Kathy a carer/donor, and that Kathy has no 'home' to return to – are all too apparent.

The spatial motif of displacement and exclusion, just as in *Code 46*, suggests a radical division in Agamben's terms between those to whom 'human rights' are extended – the 'originals' who are the recipients of donation – and the 'bare life' that is the condition of the clones. Hailsham acts as a kind of enclave, an ideologically constructed 'safe space' in which the children grow – a key scene early in the film is when the children repeat to Miss Lucy the stories that have been circulated about what happens to those who leave the school grounds, all involving physical violence and/or death – but the reactions of the 'human' visitors to the children, or to the donors as adults, indicate that the true boundaries are ethical or ideological. Madame, when Kathy and Tommy depart the house shared with the headmistress, tells them: 'You poor creatures. I wish I could help you.' Delivery men, nurses, the workers who help operate the National Donor Service system, are kind but keep a distance, are wary of otherness, perhaps too aware of their fates: that these children are future sacrifices, *homines sacri* in Agamben's terms, raised for the welfare of the 'originals'. Just as the system of *Code 46* returns the insider William to an anaesthetic grace of forgetting, back home in Seattle, the Sphinx seemingly undisturbed by the attempted subversion/refusal of William and Maria, so the National Donor Service goes on in a maintained system of ethical blindness that leaves Kathy, Tommy and Ruth unable to refuse their 'fate'. In fact, their conditioning (biological or ideological) is so pronounced that they do not even think of rebelling, and seem to accept the denial of their hopes with resignation.

Ultimately, *Never Let Me Go* is a world without agency, particularly on the part of the donors/carers. Where, as we will see in the next chapter, the protagonist Theo of *Children of Men* (2006) is afforded a recovered agency in terms of his political attempts to work against a dystopian system, Tommy, who is marked as the potential dystopian 'rebel', finally accepts his role with equanimity: 'I wouldn't have made a good carer,' he says, 'but I think I've made a good donor.' Tommy is a sensitive misfit who, like his friends, is never able to grow fully into adulthood, emotionally, intellectually and physically, even though he shares moments of insight into his condition that are only fitfully articulated in the film. (Ruth, the least sympathetic of the characters, is actually the one who is able to express some kind of deeper thought about their lives, and asks Tommy and Kathy for forgiveness for what she has done before her final donation.) The lack of communication, which extends to Kathy, whose point of view the film articulates and who is given the privileged role of first-person speaker (the voice-over), again expresses a kind of deficiency: that they cannot understand and articulate their own condition, much unlike the replicants of *Blade Runner*, seems itself to express something about them. When, at the end of the film, once again alone in the landscape and having lost both her friends, Kathy speculates that the donors are like anyone else – everyone 'completes' (dies), and wonders about the life they have left – the banality of this simple parallel somewhat belies the rather subtle markers of differentiation that have been present in the rest of the film, and perhaps overstates the metaphorical reading of the film. As we will see in Chapter 9 and the film *Solaris* (2002), the expression of the point of view of the excluded other (there, the visitor Rheya) signifies *unknowing* as much as it does insight. That the clones/visitors *do not* know their own condition, and are unable to articulate it, however, enhances the film's poignancy.

28 Days Later and *28 Weeks Later*

Both *Contagion* and *Code 46* extrapolate from biologically motivated anxieties about transmission, whether this is the viral agent that causes near-collapse in the United States (*Contagion*'s mapping of biological and civic body) or the problematics of DNA transmission in procreative sex between unknowing kin (the 'Code 46' infractions produced by cloning). The 'Patient Zero' of the transmission-anxiety cycle is *28 Days Later* (2002), which was released in the immediate aftermath of the September 11, 2001 attacks and bears the traces of the changing discourses of securitization and of dangerous mobility that were to haunt the rest of the decade. At the beginning of *28 Days Later*, we are shown a sequence of images from global news outlets, of angry crowds, civil disturbance, violence, beaten protestors, explosions. These are hand-held, *verité*, video rather than film, offered to the viewer without a frame, or title. As the scene unfolds, a diegetic viewer is revealed to us: a higher primate, physically 'wired up' to the contemporary flow of media images. Fred Botting argues that the chimpanzee reveals to us that we, too, are 'rats in a lab': that the opening montage 'speaks to a generalized subject of global news media' (2010: 177), to *us*, pinioned to an ideological gurney. These shots are repeated a few minutes into the movie when Jim (Cillian Murphy) awakens in a hospital bed; like the primate, he is 'wired up' with catheter tubes. In the interim, a catastrophic pandemic has overtaken Britain, a viral incubation of a violent, murderous and hyper-mobile subjectivity that makes the infected subject *run*. Although *28 Days Later* has been characterized as a 'zombie' film, the characterization of 'Rage' points towards viral infection as the crucial point of extrapolation: in particular, long-standing British cultural anxieties about rabies. In *28 Days Later* and its sequel, the Rage-infected humans (ultra-mobile 'zoombies', rather than the traditional shambling 'zombie', in Fred Botting's coinage (2010: 188)) consistently rupture the physical containments which are meant to prevent infection, be they medical or, ultimately, military. These dangerous subjects inhabit a mobility which is non-containable, which is excessive, which exceeds all boundaries: as Botting writes, *28 Days Later* offers a spectacle of 'violence without borders', where 'global rage is repeated – perhaps induced – in the laboratory' (2010: 178).

The failure of civic, political and limitary hierarchies to deal successfully with the virus, to contain it within biomedical and social limits, is represented by the military compound constructed by Major West (Christopher Ecclestone), a figure who is presented as offering the possibility of security and survival but whose leadership is revealed to be ethically deficient. The motif of spatial security and exclusion that is common to the films discussed in this chapter, and to post-catastrophic narratives in general (see Chapter 6), is presented in *28 Days Later* as a country house and grounds that have been commandeered by Major West's soldiers. West attempts to retain control over his small group of men by forcing the two central female characters in the film into sexual servitude. (One of the young women is 14 or 15.) West explains: 'Survival – I understand. I promised them women. . . . Women mean the future.' West inhabits an instrumental morality where the maintenance of the homosocial group, and his own authority over it, is dependent on the subjugation of sexually available women. There is no 'survival of civilization' that one finds in the enclaves of post-catastrophic fiction, only a kind of microcosmic dystopia inset in the post-apocalyptic world. West's failure as a quasi-paternal authority figure is underlined just before his death at the hands of one of his own infected soldiers: before he shoots the protagonist Jim, he says, 'you killed all my boys'. West's militarized future is ultimately cancelled by Jim's own recourse to violence, one that is validated by the film as a necessary strategy to free both himself and the women from oppression and, ultimately, destruction.

The 'ideal' father figure in *28 Days Later* is the taxi driver Frank (Brendan Gleeson), who not only protects his daughter Hannah, but also comforts the protagonist Jim (Cillian Murphy) when he dreams of being abandoned, of waking alone again: 'Thanks, Dad,' says Jim to Frank. Frank's last act as a father, becoming instantly aware that he has become infected with the Rage virus that is the catastrophic *novum*, pushes his daughter away from him so that she may not be hurt. Jim must ultimately protect/rescue Hannah and the other young woman, Selena, from the violent desires of the soldiers, and it is he who emerges, in contradistinction to Major West, as the male figure in which heroic agency and physical violence is not placed in the service of subjugation or violation. Near the beginning of the film, Jim tells Selena that he would not abandon Hannah and Frank if they were all in danger – Selena has to learn the importance of such empathic and self-sacrificing feelings – and it is in him that the survival of an ethical schema, the trace of the cosy catastrophe, can be found.

28 Days Later exhibits what Fred Botting has diagnosed as a 'Romantic arc' from city to countryside, where the surviving characters do reach such a safe space, right at the end of the film. After he has been shot by Major West, Jim wakes in bed, again '28 days later'. He emerges into a bucolic idyll, an upland farm cottage where Selena and Hannah await the fly-by of a military jet that they greet with a huge banner laid out on the ground: 'HELLO'. Even this enclave is temporary: Jim had previously seen the contrails of overflying jets in the sky, suggesting that the world has waited while the Rage virus burns itself out, the victims dying of starvation (significantly, on the road). The sequel, *28 Weeks Later* (2006) directed by Juan Carlos Fresnadillo, inverts this trajectory, beginning with six survivors barricaded into a rural cottage, in a perpetual darkness lit by candles. After a child comes to the door, escaping from

Rage-infected parents, the enclave is discovered and breached, and all but Don (and later, we discover his wife) are bitten and infected. *28 Weeks Later* narrates a trajectory from rural space back to the urban, to London and the Green Zone of Canary Wharf: but these boundaries too are breached. What is striking in the later film is that it is the very thing that marks human beings' difference from Rage-infected zoombies – a sense of empathy, the love for and wish to protect others – is consistently their weakness. Don allows the young boy into the house, causing it to be targeted by the hordes; the children escape the Green Zone in search of home; their mother is brought back into the secure zone, where a kiss infects Don and causes an outbreak; and at the end of the film, the empathy of the helicopter pilot Flynn (Harold Perrineau) for the children motivates him to fly them to France, not knowing that the boy is, like his mother before him, now an asymptomatic carrier. The last shots are of zombies emerging from the Trocadero Metro station in Paris. Jim, in *28 Days Later*, must recover an ethical masculinity that opposes and eventually supersedes Major West's instrumental amorality. In *28 Weeks Later*, the opposite is true: to allow ethical scruples or emotional responses to cloud absolute principles of self-preservation leads to disaster.

Both *28 Days Later* and *28 Weeks Later* contain a sequence where central characters return 'home' to the house in which they once lived, as an attempt to come to terms with or to reconstitute the world that has been lost. Jim (Cillian Murphy), the protagonist of *28 Days Later*, had found the bodies of his own parents in peaceful death, side by side in bed having committed suicide, but the children in *28 Weeks Later*, escaping from the uninfected 'Green Zone' to wander uninhabited London, find their bedraggled mother still alive in their former home. She is an asymptomatic carrier of the virus, whose removal *inside* the securitized zone ultimately leads to a new outbreak. This *unheimlich* discovery is the fulfilment (but ultimate destruction) of a sentimental fantasy of recuperation of the past, and is the beginning of a much more violent, and violently mobile, narrative journey. Jim leaves the past, and his parents' bodies behind; the children take their mother, and the dangers associated with past, with them. For the children in *28 Weeks Later*, a mobile estrangement is partly predicated on the knowledge of a morally troubling act of cowardice by their father (now a civilian involved in the technical running of the Green Zone): earlier in the film, we had seen Don (Robert Carlyle) close the door on his wife when she is about to be attacked by zombies, saving himself by running away. He tells the children upon their return, however, that he had seen his wife die: his deception (and self-torment) turns to murderous rage when he himself is infected, with a kiss. Don's rage is, then, psychologically motivated, unlike the unmotivated and viral Rage of *28 Days Later*'s zoombies: cut-aways suggest that his violence is an expression of the guilt he felt in abandoning his wife, and she and the children become the focus of his rage. No wonder, then, that the denouement of the film takes place in the London Underground, symbolic of depth psychology, where Don's daughter resolves the conflict with the father by shooting him dead. This *location* of Rage within psychology is, in a sense, comforting, because it displaces the free-floating (free running), mobile and virulent psychosis inhabiting the zoombies onto something much more comprehensible, an expression of human emotions, albeit repellent ones.

The importance of the London '7/7' events to *28 Weeks Later* indicates a particular British context to consider with regard to its imagination of borders, the nation-state and militarized security. While *Code 46* translates these anxieties to a global locale and context, the *28 . . .* films insist on a specifically British response to the conditions of a 'War on Terror' that is returned to the once-Imperial centre, just as we saw in *Skyfall* in Chapter 1. Their dystopian and catastrophic scenarios are largely focused upon London itself, and all three narrate increasingly problematic attempts to escape the confines of the city, a space which materializes the violence experienced by the populations of Iraq and Afghanistan post-9/11. The indictment of militarism is expressed not only in these films but, according to Linnie Blake, are also at the heart of British *horror* film in the twenty-first century, not only in *28 Days Later* and its sequel but also the werewolf horror film, *Dog Soldiers* (2002). These display, Blake argues, 'a profound discomfort with Britain's imperial past and with the ways in which "warfare and the militaristic masculinity integral to combat" have been historically used "as a means by which young men are socialised into the essential ingredients of contemporary manliness"' (Blake 2008: 173). The revisions of masculinity are particularly ironized in *28 Days Later* and its sequel, because Rage-infected subjects inhabit *to excess* traits that might be deemed important to the formation of the soldier-subject: a capacity for violence, physical imperviousness to danger, hyper-mobility and the suppression of the individual to the dynamic of the group. The soldier-subject itself incubates 'rage', a violence that exceeds the bounds of law or ethics and ultimately returns to haunt the polis that projects them across the global stage. It is an index of the problematic role of masculinity in the films under discussion that the excessive, violent and *violating* potentialities of the soldier-subject, a (partly) restrained reflection of the Rage-infected zombie, is itself countermanded by the near-heroic masculinity and agency afforded to *28 Days Later*'s Jim.

As Mark Dery notes in his essay 'Dead Man Walking', the rise of the zombie film in the past decade has shifted the significance of that particular sub-genre of horror to articulate 'free-floating anxieties about viral plagues and bioengineered outbreaks [and] look a lot like the troubled dreams of an age of terrorism, avian flu, and H1N1, when viruses leap the species barrier and spread, via jet travel, into global pandemics seemingly overnight' (Dery 2012: 11). Where the contemporary zombie film, as Botting or Dery argue, offers the means by which to articulate critique of contemporary capital's consumerist and post-industrial Western economies, the SF films I have analysed here articulate anxieties about the unstable and porous borders of both the nation-state and its subjects/citizens. The anxieties about boundaries and the destructive effect of the 'space of flows' encoded in the films discussed in this essay may acquire greater, even political, urgency in the decade to come. What William Brown diagnosed as the signs of a 'post-British' cinema in the first decade of the twenty-first century has already been transmitted across national and generic cinematic boundaries.

6

Dystopia and the Apocalyptic Scene

In 'Not Flagwaving but Flagdrowning, or Postcards from Post-Britain', the final chapter proper of the third edition of *The British Cinema Book* (2008), William Brown proposed a set of mainly twenty-first-century films that, 'whether through their content, their form and/or their production history, can be simultaneously be classified as "post-British"'. These films, Brown asserted, were forerunners of a 'post-national (or, particularly and paradoxically, post-British) cinema'. Two of the films cited were *V for Vendetta* (2006) and *Children of Men* (2006), both of which we will consider in this chapter. These films, Brown argued, employed catastrophic scenarios to imagine 'a new world order in the aftermath of apocalypse', a new world where the survivors 'belong to minority national and ethnic groups within Britain' (Brown 2008: 409–10). The imagination of catastrophe and the importance of national borders, mobility and transmission is not simply a concern of British science fiction film, as we saw in the previous chapter, but one that inflects the science fiction imaginary in a hyper-mobile contemporary global capitalism, particularly in the time of the 'War on Terror'. William Brown's argument is that such films are 'British, but . . . whether through their content, their form and/or through their production history, can simultaneously be classified as "post-British"' (Brown 2008: 408). British and post-British are almost coterminous here: it is as if the very imagination of the end of Britain is peculiarly British.

Catastrophe or disaster is of course a familiar motif in British science fiction literature. In the immediate post-war period, the characteristic mode of British science fiction was the 'disaster novel', including the works of Wyndham, John Christopher (*The Death of Grass* (1956) and *The World in Winter* (1962)) and even, in an altered form, J. G. Ballard's early fiction, such as *The Drowned World* (1963). In *Billion Year Spree* (1973), a history of science fiction, Brian Aldiss calls the work of Wyndham and Christopher, rather dismissively, the 'cosy catastrophe'. 'The essence of the cosy catastrophe,' writes Aldiss, 'is that the hero should have a pretty good time (a girl, free suites at the Savoy, automobiles for the taking) while everyone else is dying off' (Aldiss 1973: 294). These texts are 'anxiety fantasies', avers Aldiss, and explains their popularity by suggesting 'either that it was something to do with the collapse of the British Empire, or the back-to-nature movement, or a general feeling that industrialization had gone too far, or all three' (Aldiss 1973: 294). In a somewhat less dismissive article from 2005, Jo Walton enumerates six characteristics of the cosy catastrophe: 'the catastrophes are British, written in their heyday of 1951-1977 by people who were adult before the Second World War' (Walton 2005: 34); 'the catastrophe in a cosy catastrophe need have no worries about plausibility', and 'nothing really happens' (Walton 2005: 34); 'despite being written during the Cold War, nuclear wars are quite specifically a banned topic in cosy catastrophes'; 'cosy catastrophes focus on one small group of people' and 'cosy catastrophes are structured in a very interesting way. They spend hardly any time on the catastrophe itself' (Walton 2005: 35).

Walton locates specific class and gender imperatives at work in the cosy catastrophe: that the texts articulate a particularly male, bourgeois hegemonic worldview. The protagonists are usually in the mid-30s, professional, secular and educated. The disaster impels them not to change (as it would do in a Ballard novel), but to preserve the 'civilization' that has come under threat, often within spatially delimited zones (such as 'the Pale' in Christopher's *The World in Winter*). Walton writes:

> These nice middle-class men survive disaster after disaster. They find themselves again and again, surviving a terrible catastrophe by blind chance, and looking around a clean and empty Britain. Cosy catastrophes tend to be very clean, with a distinct lack of bodies. Where messy events do occur they are not described. You may see people walking out of a window, but never see them hit the ground. The heroes look around the emptiness and make a definite decision to rebuild, to preserve what was good and to forget what was bad about the world they came from. They do this generally in a very organized and scientific way, and while they certainly make use of things people have no use for any more, they'd certainly never stoop to wanton looting. As for the victims, well, it's a pity, but. . . . (Walton 2005: 37)

If we turn to I. Q. Hunter's characterization of the recurrent concerns of post-war British science fiction cinema, we can diagnose a fair degree of overlap with the cosy catastrophe. The SF films 'privilege male know-how and scientific rationality'; 'women are either absent, marginalised or ruthlessly objectified';

the films 'treat their monsters . . . with rationalistic disgust rather than barely repressed fascination' (Hunter 1999: 6); and he finds a recurrent ideological underpinning of 'conservatism . . . and staunch but worried defence of the patriarchal order' (Hunter 1999: 13). It is through the mode of the post-war British disaster novel that an articulation of anxieties about social order takes place, in imagining fantasies of the erasure of social diversity and the reconstruction of a community based upon codes of social restraint, hierarchy and exclusion. The narratives encode an articulation of anxieties about patriarchal dominance in the threatened displacement of, but subsequent elevation to the heroic of the middle-class professional man, and end-of-Empire white racial or ethnic anxieties about invasion and the 'end of our way of life' (ultimately preserved).

Anxieties about nation and the (patriarchal) subject are often, in the disaster novel, enunciated though biological, ecological or evolutionary motifs. The cause of the disaster in Christopher's *The Death of Grass* or Ballard's *The Wind from Nowhere* (1962) is self-explanatory; in Wyndham's *The Day of the Triffids* (1951), giant perambulatory bioengineered plants take advantage of the mass blinding of the human race after a meteor shower to 'take over' the Earth, and the novel narrates the efforts of small groups of human beings to construct viable communities after this catastrophe. More recent dystopian or post-apocalyptic films, such as *Children of Men* or *28 Days Later* (2002), which articulate contemporary variants on the concerns of the 'cosy catastrophe', are considerably less cosy.

Children of Men

Children of Men (2006), directed by Alfonso Cuaron and loosely adapted from P. D. James's dystopian 1992 novel *The Children of Men*, negotiated the motifs of space and mobility derived from the disaster novel. In James's novel, the last generation, known as 'Omegas', are physically beautiful but violent and cruel. In this, the text seems to echo other 'disaster' fictions that reveal anxieties about generational conflict, in particular, the *mise-en-scène* of the early 1980s' television Quatermass series *The Quatermass Conclusion* (starring John Mills in the title role), which featured roaming gangs of violent youths predating upon the weak and the old. Anxieties about social order, so clearly manifest in the cosy catastrophe, are represented by ruined and burnt-out buildings, favelas, bonfires on street corners and dangerously mobile groups of marginalized subjects (in terms of ethnicity or age) or in more estranged fashion, 'alien' entities such as the Triffids. The film was a major Hollywood studio production, made with a Mexican director and largely British cast and crew, and was based on a British novel and set in a near-future dystopian British state. The protagonist of James's novel is Theo Faron, an Oxford history don, the cousin of a dictatorial 'Warden' of a near-future Britain who rules in a world where no children have been born for nearly 30 years. The novel outlines a world of dissipation and ennui, a world without a future, without meaning. Faron is drawn into a narrative where a new child is born, offering hope that the entropic decline may be halted or reversed. In the film adaptation, Theo (Clive Owen) becomes a former political activist who, after the death of his son Dylan in the '2008 flu pandemic', drifts into a minor bureaucratic role at the Ministry of Energy. The opening scenes of the film indicate its divergence from the novel: after visiting a shop, Theo is almost killed when a 'terrorist' bomb destroys it, and as he walks down the streets of London, he is menaced by black-clad soldiers who round up 'fugees' (refugees) and hold them in on-street cages. A news report on the soundtrack at the film's beginning (the *mise-en-scène* is also filled with screens bearing broadcast news and text) informs the viewer that 'After 8 years, British borders will remain closed. Illegal immigrants will be deported', and a television screen on board a bus declares 'The world has collapsed – only Britain soldiers on.' Here, nation-state and closed borders are expressly connected to xenophobia, to state violence against civilian populations, and to totalitarianism.

Children of Men clearly bears the traces of the 'terrorist' attacks on London on 7 July 2005, and it is this New World Order, of violence projected onto the streets of London rather than Baghdad, that forms the cultural context for the film (rather than its diegetic motivation of a 'flu pandemic). Mark Fisher, in *Capitalist Realism* (2009), suggests that 'the dystopia in *Children of Men* is specific to late capitalism . . . [involving] the stripping back of the state to its core military and police functions' (Fisher 2009: 1, 2). The fabric of the city is ruinous, rubbish sacks line the street, buses are a smeared ochre rather than red; the colour palette is grey/brown and washed-out. The streets are militarized, patrolled by black-clad police/soldiery with automatic weapons clearly displayed; the horror is that the civilian population ignores both the military and the caged 'fugees': dystopia has become normalized. As Fisher states, 'the catastrophe in *Children of Men* is neither waiting down the road, nor has it already happened. Rather, it is being lived through' (Fisher 2009: 2).

In *Children of Men*, mobility is politicized and controlled. Theo is asked by his estranged wife to source papers to allow the young woman Kee (Clare-Hope Ashitey) to travel to the south coast of England (and we see early in the film a scene where Theo arrives at a train station where a sign commands that 'Identity card and transit papers' must be shown); as the narrative progresses, the possibility of mobility is constantly imperilled by operatives of the state, loosely organized gangs (themselves dangerously mobile) and by other political activists. Where Michael Winterbottom's *Code 46* (2003) imagines a world of securitized city-enclaves, restricting the movement of populations on genetic grounds (see Chapter 5), in *Children of Men* the dynamics of spatial exclusion are much more troublesome: that exclusion is informed by racism, and reveals the violence the nation-state uses to keep itself going at the point of collapse.

In terms of the disaster narrative, *Children of Men* overturns some of the recurrent tropes of the cosy catastrophe. In the film, the countryside offers no respite from the horrors of the city: it too is ravaged, depopulated, prey to roaming gangs of desperate survivors and violently aggressive police units. The one enclave that is offered is the concealed cabin of Theo's friend Jasper (played as a hippy throwback by Michael Caine), but this only offers temporary respite, and is ultimately violated by the 'terrorist'/revolutionary group that Theo and Kee flee from. Order and safety is dislocated from 'security', and cannot be maintained against the forces of violent oppression and resistance at work in this dystopian Britain. There is, however, a space 'outside', but this is only achieved at the point of Theo's death, when he rows Kee and her child into the English Channel at the end of the film to rendezvous with the shadowy 'Human Project', who are rumoured to have their own secure enclave in the Azores. Like many another dystopian narrative, the text ends at the point of possibility, rather than the achievement of some kind of alternative space or mode of life to that of the ruined fabric of the dying nation-state. In a final (and unconscious) return to the gender politics of the cosy catastrophe, we can diagnose the traces of the heroic middle-class white male in *Children of Men*; although Theo presumably dies at the end of the film, it is by his agency and sacrifice that the escape of Kee and her daughter is achieved.

Heather Latimer's reading of *Children of Men* interrogates the film in terms of biopolitics, and in particular the work of Giorgio Agamben, whose work we have encountered in Chapter 5. Latimer follows feminist theorists who 'have noted a critical absence in [Giorgio] Agamben's work when it comes to women and gender, and have argued that we are not all subject to bare life in the same ways' (Latimer 2011: 51). She argues that 'the reproductive body is a blank spot in Agamben's definition of bare life' (Latimer 2011: 53), and reads the film through the centrality of the female refugee: Kee focalizes a 'direct correlation between infertility and terror, and pregnancy and hope' (Latimer 2011: 60). Latimer argues that the film 'critiques the politics of bare life: it is *only* through Kee's ability to carry the "super-person" or "unborn citizen" . . . that Kee is able to access any type of political agency' (68). The refugee (*homo sacer*) and the 'fetal citizen' (the as-yet-unborn child whose subjectivity throws into biopolitical relief that of its mother and of citizen 'terrorists' who try to claim them both for political ends) are limit cases of what is considered to be 'living', and it is in that, Latimer argues, that the film 'highlights how it is often on the level of reproductive policy that bare life takes on its gendered and racialized dimensions' (Latimer 2011: 68). Nation-state and closed borders are expressly connected to xenophobia in *Children of Men*, to state violence against civilian populations, and to totalitarianism, even Nazism. When the protagonist Faron and the young pregnant woman Kee journey to 'Bexhill refugee camp', attempting to contact a resistance group that might protect the newborn infant, they witness scenes of violence, torture and murder of refugees. If Britain is the only surviving nation-state, it barely keeps back the forces of social catastrophe that have engulfed the rest of the world, and the price to be paid is far too high. Clearly in these scenes we find estranged reference to Guantanamo and Abu Ghraib, but here the war takes place on the streets of London and Bexhill rather than Iraq (or another visual point of reference, the wars in the former Yugoslavia in the 1990s). The violence visited upon the developing world's 'others' is returned to the (post-imperial) centre.

V for Vendetta

Children of Men is, like both the graphic novel and film of *V for Vendetta*, in part a London fiction. The streets of the capital are recognizable and their near-future dystopian scenarios largely take place on streets that are unchanged from those that existed at the time of production. There are no additional skyscrapers or enhanced modes of mobility; in the film of *V for Vendetta*, in fact, the London Underground has been closed for some time after a biological 'terrorist' attack on an Underground station. What connects both films in terms of *mise-en-scène* is the presence of television screens, and in particular, rolling 24-hour news channels, whose feeds command the attention of the populace. In *Children of Men*, these screen are ubiquitous, found in shops, public transport and on the street itself; in *V for Vendetta*, apart from a large screen at Piccadilly Circus, the screens are largely confined to the sitting rooms of family houses. Shots of people watching television news are recurrent in *V for Vendetta*, and its 'BTN' news channel (a conflation of the BBC and ITN, Independent Television News) acts as a propaganda arm for the totalitarian government. The female protagonist, Evey Hammond (Natalie Portman), begins the film as a lowly cleric assistant at BTN, who later tells the revolutionary V (Hugo Weaving) that she can tell when a newscaster reads news which is untrue, as the newscaster blinks more often. The viewers often express outright scepticism at the news stories they are meant to believe, with good reason; here, the practices of media reception foreshadow the mass resistance which is the means of narrative resolution.

In Alan Moore and David Lloyd's *V for Vendetta*, a comic strip first published in *Warrior* magazine in 1982, there is no ubiquity of television; instead, in the 1980s, propaganda is delivered by the radio, the 'Voice of Fate', which approximates the BBC wartime broadcasts that Orwell himself was involved in scripting. Although surveillance cameras are everywhere in the graphic novel – the third panel of the entire book shows a camera, underneath which a sign reads 'For Your Protection' – the political urgency of a surveillance society is surprisingly downplayed in the 2006 film, where the British urban fabric is constantly monitored by CCTV. *V for Vendetta* was originally published in black and white, the artist Lloyd using a noir-influenced visual style to emphasize a bleak totalitarian future London, making a virtue of the economics of comics publishing at the time in Britain, in which comics were published on newsprint, with cover pages confined to the cover and the centre spread. Lloyd draws a *chiaroscuro* world, using strong inking and heavy use of shadow, and avoidance of the grey Lettratone process used for tonal purposes in other contemporary black-and-white comic art. In the graphic novel, the Labour Party wins the 1983 General Election (admitted by Moore as a prediction of crass political naïveté later in the decade), disarms unilaterally and thereby avoids being targeted in a nuclear conflict which follows in 1988, precipitated by superpower conflict over Poland, a not implausible scenario in 1981/82. In the film, this is changed to a situation whereby acts of terrorism, most notably the use of biological agents in a school, a London Underground station and in the water supply of a town that kills nearly 100,000 people. The Cold War scenario gives way to one which articulates the particular anxieties of the 'War on Terror'. The graphic novel of *V for Vendetta*'s future totalitarian Britain is a version of Thatcher's Britain of the 1980s; high unemployment, inner-city decay and riots in 1981 form the frayed cultural fabric from which the future world is woven. The screen version elevates the role of the dystopian Chancellor, Adam Sutler (John Hurt), to one that approximates that of Big Brother himself: Sutler is recurrently shown briefing his 'heads of department' by the means of a wall-sized viewscreen. This, and the casting of Hurt himself (who played Winston Smith in Michael Radford's *Nineteen Eighty-Four* (1984)), suggests that the intertextual markers are emphasized to re-locate the text from its time of original production, and also to attenuate direct connections between the Britain of *V for Vendetta* and the Britain of 2006.

Where the totalized dystopias of the 1950s and 1960s, which are strongly indebted to *Nineteen Eighty-Four*, structure their narratives through the trajectory of alienation of their *apparatchik* protagonists, *V for Vendetta* distributes the narrative function of the protagonist among several characters. The alienation of the Party official is represented through the experiences of Eric Finch, a detective who investigates the 'terrorist' activities of the anarchist rebel V, and through this investigation discovers his own self-deluding complicity with the oppressive system. Finch is appropriated from another form of narrative, the police television series which features the old-timer detective and his young sidekick, a familiar character pairing in British televisual culture. Finch's 'awakening' is mirrored in the development of Evey Hammond, who we first see as a 16-year-old orphan. The first pages of the narrative cross-cut between Evey and V, both of whom put on their make-up before venturing out into London's mean streets. This implicit parallelism foreshadows Evey's later training to replace the fatally wounded V (tracked and killed by his alter-ego and antagonist Finch), but this early episode ends with Evey propositioning some secret policemen on a stakeout. They are about to rape her when V intervenes, quoting from the first scene of *Macbeth* as he rescues her. V kills all but two of the policemen; as the narrative unfolds, he commits other acts of 'terrorist' violence (including the destruction of such symbolic buildings as the (now disused) Houses of Parliament, the Old Bailey, and finally Downing Street), in a systematic campaign of disruption intended to reduce the totalitarian state to chaos.

The film removes the sense that Evey is on the streets soliciting; instead, she is on the way to the home of Gordon Dietrich (Stephen Fry), a well-known television presenter, for an assignation. Late in the film, Dietrich is revealed as gay; he has his own 'Shadow Gallery', a secret room in which subversive art and a medieval Koran are kept, indices of his resistance to the state. The assignation was in fact a cover for his 'real' homosexuality. When Evey leaves V's sanctum in the first half of the film, she goes to Dietrich for help and stays with him until a satirical sketch on his TV show precipitates the security services to violently abduct and kill him, witnessed by a hiding Evey. This rewrites an episode in the graphic novel, where Gordon is a petty criminal in London who takes Evey in, after which they conduct a sexual relationship before Gordon's death (at the hands of other criminals). This insistent de-sexualization, particularly of Evey, is intended to de-problematize her relationship with V. In the graphic novel, Evey fantasizes that V is her father; upon V's death, she even imagines unmasking him to find her father's face, but declares 'No. No, I'm past that one. You weren't my Dad. I know that' (Moore and Lloyd 1990: 250). In the graphic novel, the relationship between V and Evey is not sexual, although it is loving, but neither is it strictly parental. In the film, a very curious scene, when Evey first awakes in the Shadow Gallery, has him finding V cooking breakfast, wearing uniform and mask and apron. This somewhat absurd image is a domestication of a problematic masculinity; V, a violent 'protector', must be rigorously differentiated from the violating masculinity of the Fingermen who were about to rape and kill her before V's rescue. This breakfast scene is repeated at Dietrich's house, to the extent that Evey comments within the film upon the parallel; the connection between V and the homosexual Dietrich is not only political, in terms of resistance or 'subversion', but also in terms of a non-threatening, non-sexual masculinity that is at once capable of revolutionary violence, but nurtures and protects Evey.

V's secure space, the 'Shadow Gallery', is a heterotopian and labyrinthine zone of escape and fantasy. When he first takes Evey there in the graphic novel, V soothes her by reading from Enid Blyton's *Magic Faraway Tree*, which involves a fantasy of the 'Land of Do-As-You-Please'. The narrative structure represents the contamination of the totalitarian order by the principles of the Shadow Gallery, the oppressive order replaced by 'Verwirrung' (chaos) and, then, perhaps, 'Ordnung' (anarchy). Anarchy is the ideological dynamic of *V for Vendetta*, and the rebel V's guiding principle. It is used as a revolutionary theory and practice, its tenets explicated in the course of the text. James Joll suggests that anarchism also has its roots in millenarian eschatology. He argues:

> On the one hand, [Anarchists] are the heirs of all the utopian, millenarian movements which have believed that the end of the world is at hand and have confidently expected that 'the trumpet shall sound and we shall be changed, in a moment, in the twinkling of an eye', On the other hand, they are also the children of the Age of Reason. (Joll 1979: x)

This ambiguity reflects that of Utopianism itself, which is the 'Shadow' of the state of V's Britain. The desire for change to the 'real world' in Utopian texts is manifested in visions of ordered societies, an order that *dystopian* writers perceive to be oppressive. Dystopias deploy the apocalyptic rhetoric of Utopia as a textual device, but exhibit a reaction from an over-application of order and rationality. Often, as in *Nineteen Eighty-Four*, this involves reliance upon an unexamined binarism of state and individual to critique the operations of state power. *V for Vendetta* inherits this structure, but it characterizes Anarchy as 'order without leaders', an explicitly organic and implicitly utopian social and political space. While many other twentieth-century dystopias end in suspension, the future of the protagonist and the society he was once a part of held in a precarious balance of forces, only Bradbury's *Fahrenheit 451* (1953) deploys explicitly apocalyptic or millenarian rhetoric to provide narrative closure. In Bradbury's dystopia, the society of Book-men walks towards the desolated city at the end of the narrative, returning to sow the seeds of 'civilization' and rebuild the city. Montag's texts are the books of Ecclesiastes and Revelation, signifying utopia's (and dystopia's) millenarian heritage.

The Utopian city, then, is the 'Land of Do-As-You-Please' (with an explicit nod to Aleister Crowley's 'Do What Thou Wilt Shall Be the Whole of the Law' on page 187), but one which is not achieved in *V for Vendetta*. V tells Evey: 'Anarchy wears two faces. Both *creator* and *destroyer*. Thus destroyers topple empires; make a canvas of clean rubble where creators can then build a better world' (Moore and Lloyd 1990: 222). In the final confrontation between the detective Finch and V, the anarchist allows himself to be fatally wounded, tainted as he is by murder and destruction. V is part of the old order, a reflection of its brutal imperatives, and so must be sacrificed for the creation of the new: an almost Jacobin conception. Here Evey understands her own future, and the parallelism of the opening pages is completed: she dons V's mask. Evey becomes a reborn V. In turn, she abducts/rescues Dominic, Finch's young sidekick, who V will again mentor to further the project of Anarchy.

V for Vendetta was begun by Alan Moore in 1981, and was first published in *Warrior* in 1982. However, after 3 years and 23 chapters of the narrative, *Warrior* magazine folded. The series was finally completed in 1989, when DC Comics issued a colour version of the original, which was then issued as a 'Graphic Novel' (or 'Trade Paperback') in the boom time for that form, 1990. Culturally, the beginning of the 1980s and the end are distinct periods, particularly with reference to non-official, youth culture. Most importantly, the end of the 1980s witnessed the rise of club culture, and the increasingly commonplace use of recreational drugs among clubgoers. Alan Moore's *Watchmen* series, issued in 1987, featured the Smiley badge as a recurrent visual motif, ubiquitous in the psychedelia-influenced 'second summer of love' of 1988. In *V for Vendetta*, unusually, it is the *apparatchik*, the detective Eric Finch, who uses LSD to produce visions. These visions complete his own trajectory of estrangement, and reveal his own delusive complicity. Finch's hallucinations are a kind of epiphany, in which he witnesses both the horrors of the former 'resettlement camp' where he takes LSD, and experiences once again the ethnic and cultural diversity this Fascist Britain has systematically erased. 'No Tamla, no Trojan. No Billie Holliday and no Black Uhuru' says V (Moore and Lloyd 1990: 18). Finch, who, in his visions literally becomes V, is locked in 'Room five' (signified by the Roman numeral), and then is freed, naked, reborn.

The final image of *V for Vendetta* is not V, nor Evey/E-V, but Finch, alone, walking out of the city along a deserted motorway. Ultimately, *V for Vendetta* can only offer the possibility of hope, the possibility of change, in its political and cultural moment. Like the mid-century dystopias, it ends in suspension, utopia waiting beyond the confines of the text. Unlike *Nineteen Eighty-Four*, however, it does not close off the possibility of political action, neither of (politically informed) individual action, nor of organized and communal action. Moore's 1988 introduction to the DC reprinted series professes an explicit political pessimism not unlike that of *Nineteen Eighty-Four* (with its lament, 'Goodnight England' echoing Orwell's sentiments). However, the images that follow move from the global bleakness of its intertext to an endorsement of radical, if not revolutionary, opposition. In a 'Behind the painted mask' article first published in *Warrior*, and reprinted in the collected edition, Moore reveals that, among the influences on *V for Vendetta* were Orwell, Huxley, Thomas M. Disch, Harlan Ellison and the British television series *The Prisoner*. That Britain's totalitarian systems are finally undone perhaps suggests the more open, less bleak politics of the 1960s' 'New Wave' of science fiction writers, rather than Orwell's vision of a 'boot stamping on a human face forever'.

The film of *V for Vendetta* emphasizes V's performativity. In a strange anticipation of the film *Prometheus* (2013), where the android David (Michael Fassbender) watches *Lawrence of Arabia* to imitate Peter O'Toole, V is seen by Evey enacting sword-play against a suit of armour, all the while watching the film of *The Count of Monte Cristo* (1934), starring Robert Donat. This almost childlike playfulness helps elaborate the signification of the mask, which is not something for V to hide behind, but the emblem of a constructed subjectivity that enables him to 'play' revolution: late in the film, when he asks Evey to dance, he suggests that he cannot conceive of a revolution without dancing. V's anarchism is spectacular (the blowing up of the Old Bailey and the Houses of Parliament) and it is also theatrical; the first words he speaks in the graphic novel are quotations from a speech in *Macbeth*, which provides a commentary on his rescue of Evey. This theatricality is both a strategy and constitutive of V's subjectivity in itself: he has been made (and in the film, Evey accuses him of being made monstrous) by the circumstances of political incarceration, torture and biological experimentation that accompanied the institution of the totalitarian British state. When he completes his role, he steps off the stage in a 'grand finale': his valedictory journey in a disused Underground tunnel, whereupon a train packed with explosives and carrying his corpse detonates beneath Downing Street.

This performativity works to different effect after his death, in novel and film. In the book, Evey becomes V, and appears to a crowd to exhort them to 'choose carefully' once the head (Downing Street) has been removed from the body politic. (The suggestion might be that V will continue, as the spectre of revolution, to haunt the political sphere, and would return if domination were to be re-established.) In the film, shots of the propagandizing televisions play to empty rooms as soldiers amass at Whitehall; the space is invaded by thousands wearing V masks and cloaks, who stand to watch the destruction of the Houses of Parliament (a much more striking symbol, and connected directly to Guy Fawkes's failed revolutionary act). Where, in the graphic novel, Evey becomes V, in the film V becomes the crowd, a sign of mass or democratic action. 'Beneath this mask is an idea,' V declares late in the film, and the multitude of V masks indicates the extent to which that idea has been transmitted. Rather than Evey forming a generational revolutionary cadre, who will carry on V's work, the film presents a popular revolution. While this gesture towards the mass indicates a progressive politics (one encoded in the narrative of resistance to the power of the state), it is also somewhat sentimental; Evey's change of mind and heart is won at considerable cost, just as V's had been, and although Evey rejects V's violent methods, the graphic novel is clear-eyed about the price to be paid for revolution. The one that occurs at the end of the *V for Vendetta* film is a soft revolution, a Utopian or fantastical one, inaugurated by fanfare and fireworks (and over the end titles, the Rolling Stones song 'Street Fighting Man'). The graphic novel suggests that it is much more likely to be won by revolutionary anarchism and gunfire.

Apocalypticism is at once foundational to dystopia – it is often the means by which the Utopian or dystopian world comes into being – and as we can see in *V for Vendetta*, it is also the means by which the totalitarian state comes to an end. The revolutionary subjectivity inhabited by V is necessarily millenarian: he wants to bring about a New World, a new political and cultural dispensation. From the ruins must come new beginnings, new life. Post-apocalyptic fictions and films such as Cormac McCarthy's *The Road* (2006, film 2009) negotiate a wasteland, but the means by which to effect change, whether that is concerted action of individual agency, have been lost. One of the comforts of dystopia is that, as in *The Hunger Games* (2012), the potentiality for agency and change is still open.

7

Alien Nations

Invasion narratives have long been associated with Empire, and in particular with anxieties provoked by the presumed over-extension and hubris that Imperial systems produce. The 'scientific romance', H. G. Wells's name for his particular mode of precursor of science fiction, drew upon the adventure narratives of the Imperial Romance (such as H. Rider Haggard's *King Solomon's Mines* (1885)) as well as developments in scientific theory and practice to create a mode of fiction that directly dramatized encounters between (Imperial) self and Other. In texts such as *The War of the Worlds* (1898), in which the late Victorian genre of the future war/invasion narrative is married to a narrative of encounter with the alien/Other, Wells inaugurated a mode of fiction that particularly articulates anxieties about the British Empire and its relation to indigenous peoples that it had subjugated. The culture that produced the future war story is described by I. F. Clarke thus:

> The new tales of future warfare had the marks of a new and frequently brutal epoch. At times they were violent and vindictive both in matter and in manner; they were often nationalistic to the point of hysteria; and they displayed an eagerness for novelty and sensation at the level of entertainment provided by the new journalism in publications like *Answers* and the *Daily Mail*. The cool tone, the objective approach to contemporary problems, the controlled emotion of Chesney now gave way on many occasions to excited language, crude emotionalism, and an often foolish idealisation of the nation as the sole source of justice and the supreme arbiter in human affairs. (Clarke 1992: 57)

The popularity of the future war story in late Victorian Imperial Britain is an index of a growing anxiety in Great Power relations caused by the unification of Germany and increasing Imperial competition on a global scale. The scientific romance becomes a means by which these anxieties can be explored and communicated by way of estrangement: reproducing the familiar in unfamiliar terms.

Wells's *The War of the Worlds* has been a signature text in critical thinking about the relation between Empire and SF/the scientific romance. Brian Aldiss suggested that the novel 'showed the Imperialist European powers of the day how it felt to be on the receiving end of an invasion armed with superior technology' (Aldiss 1973: 64); Adam Roberts writes that 'the deftness of Wells's conception is that he is able to simultaneously critique the European Imperial excesses, whilst also coding the "Eastern" threat against which European Imperialism specifically justified itself' (Roberts 2000: 64); and I. F. Clarke argued that 'Wells stood colonial expansion on its head, presented Britain as a backward area, and gave the Martians a degree of technical achievement that made the miserable defenders of imperial Britain look rather like the unhappy Tasmanians' (Clarke 1992: 84). John Rieder, in *Colonialism and the Emergence of Science Fiction* (2008), when discussing *War of the Worlds*, proposes a 'reversal of perspective' that Wells employs when asking his English readers to compare the Martian invasion of Earth with the Europeans 'genocidal invasion of the Tasmanians, thus demanding that the colonizers imagine themselves as the colonized, or the about-to-be-colonized' (Rieder 2008: 5). Rieder does not propose that such reversals overturn the ideological freight of Empire:

> The Wellsian strategy is a reversal of positions that stays entirely within the framework of the colonial gaze and the mechanism of anthropological difference, but also highlights its critical potential. . . . The science fiction novel, while staying within the ideological and epistemological framework of colonial discourse, exaggerates and exploits its internal divisions. (Rieder 2008: 10)

This tactic, Rieder suggests, leaves the structures of feeling of the British Empire intact, while attempting to disrupt them from within. One of the techniques of science fiction, however, is to bring these 'internal divisions' to light.

War of the Worlds

As we saw in Chapter 2, contemporary revisions of texts of Imperial provenance have an implicit tendency to recapitulate forms of masculinity that bear the traces of the formations and anxieties of Empire. Steven Spielberg's *War of the Worlds* (2005) dramatically alters Wells's text, particularly in the kind of masculinity inhabited by the protagonist, to articulate contemporary concerns about deficient masculinity, particularly in terms of fatherhood. Stella Bruzzi, in *Bringing Up Daddy: Fatherhood and Masculinity in Post-War Hollywood* (2005), suggests that the 'diversity and quantity of recent American father films in linked to the dominant idea connecting contemporary masculinity: that men are "in crisis"' (Bruzzi 2005: 153). In terms of Spielberg's career, masculinity and fatherhood have been a recurrent concern (mirroring his focus upon the viewpoint of the child), from *Close Encounters of the Third Kind* (1977) to *Hook* (1991) to *Minority Report* (2002).

War of the Worlds is the next Spielberg SF film after *Minority Report* (2002), and, of course, has the same star – Tom Cruise. These three films are significant revisions of the kind of visionary SF Spielberg essayed in *Close Encounters of the Third Kind* but continue that film's focus upon deficient fatherhood. Roy Neary (Richard Dreyfus), the boy-man who leaves his family behind and takes to the stars in *Close Encounters*, escapes censure for his seeming irresponsibility (the cosmological imperative outweighs the familial), but *Minority Report's* John Anderton (Cruise), a broken man suffering the loss of his young son and subsequently the love of his wife, is redeemed in the course of the narrative. (Precrime, as we see in Chapter 8, is explicitly characterized as pathological, predicated on the errant desire to forestall trauma and loss.) The final shots of *Minority Report* show husband and wife reconciled, with the wife pregnant again, the familial more important than the social.

War of the Worlds has at its centre Ray Ferrier (Cruise), a stevedore from New Jersey, who signally fails in his paternal duty when his daughter Rachel (Dakota Fanning) and son Robbie (Justin Chatwin) come to stay. His relationship with his teenage son has broken down, and his daughter seems to have more life skills than he does. When Bayonne, NJ, is attacked by electrical storms and then death-dealing tripods, Ray runs (like Anderton), but not back to his children, but to the scene of destruction. Ray, it seems, is not very quick-witted; he is seen at the edge of the crowd, watching while asphalt cracks wide open and then a huge mechanical tripod emerges from the suburban street. He forms no plan to escape other than returning the children to Boston, and their mother; his route there, in a stolen car, leads to near-disaster at the Hudson Ferry. While it is unusual to have a barely competent protagonist at the centre of the narrative, it is ultimately frustrating, particularly later in the film when he gapes at his son's attempts to join battle against the aliens, while his daughter is almost snatched away by another (albeit benign) adult couple.

The images of Ray with his back turned, or concentrating his somewhat feeble mental powers on something else while his children wander into, or hurl themselves into danger are recurrent in the film, and are an index of his incapacity as a father. As in *Minority Report*, however, the narrative is one of redemption for Ray in that he delivers his daughter safely to Boston and is reconciled with his son. In a sense, the film is a rites of passage for another boy-man, just as with Roy Neary, but here the resolution is Earth-bound. Ray finally matches up to the life skills of 'Tim', his ex-wife's husband, whose new SUV and prestigious house are shown to be in stark contrast to Ray's duplex and classic Ford Mustang. In a time of disaster, economic success is secondary to Ray's survival skills. 'Tim', the economically successful 'other man', is a recurrent figure in contemporary cinema; in Spielberg's own *Hook* (1991), the protagonist's yuppie 'other', who must be overcome to effect a reconciliation with his son, is actually himself (Peter Banning, who must become Peter Pan again).

In *War of the Worlds*, the central conflict between father and son is displaced by the closeness (often physical, when Ray carries Rachel) between father and daughter. Here we can see the vital influence of spectacle and spectatorship in Spielberg's cinema: the narrative switches between Ray's and Rachel's point of view (we never see Robbie's: both the stealing of Ray's car, and his joining battle with the tripods, take place off-screen). Robbie is active, leaping onto the gate of the Hudson Ferry to help those trying to clamber aboard: Rachel watches. The film privileges her point of view because, of course, this is the cinematic apparatus of which Spielberg's cinema is self-consciously a part. As in *Close Encounters*, the wonder on the faces of the intra-diegetic spectators is meant to be matched by that of the cinematic spectators.

In the course of *War of the Worlds*, Ray is taught to see: at the end, he points out to an army commander that the force-fields are no longer working on a tripod, rendering it vulnerable to attack. Several times in the film, the *mise-en-scène* shows a hole punched through glass – in a window of Ray's home, in a car windshield – through which Ray is seen. This 'tunnel vision', a visual enclosure, must be overcome. Rachel, by contrast, has her vision deliberately blocked on numerous occasions: on leaving Tim's house, destroyed by a falling 747; when she sees bodies floating down a river; when Ray kills the insane Harlan Ogilvy (Tim Robbins) to prevent them being discovered by the aliens.

Looking is even crucial to the active Robbie. When he attempts to run away from his father and join in the battle, he says, 'You've got to let me go. I need to see this.' Seeing, then, is vital to rites of passage, to becoming an adult: Ray protects his daughter's vision because she is too young to enter this process. When Rachel is snatched up by a tripod and placed in a cage with other humans,

Ray deliberately gets caught, to try to save her. When he reaches her, she is blank-faced, unseeing, traumatized: but Ray is soon able to recall her to herself. Considering how important it is to *Minority Report*, trauma plays a very small part for the main three characters: Rachel seems undamaged by her experiences, and Ray and Robbie 'grow' during the course of the film.

What remains is spectacle. A sense of wonder is, of course, the Spielbergian response to spectacle, but here I think it has a rather more political or philosophical dimension. When the people stand around on the streets of Bayonne and watch a huge mechanical monster emerge from below the asphalt, the principle of spectating overcomes basic human motivations to flee. In *War of the Worlds*, the mass of people, especially in crowds, are portrayed as stupid, and passive and affectless. For a film that draws on the invasion trope of human beings in conflict with alien others, it represents human activity as largely ineffective – and it is of course the Earth's biological environment which undoes the tripods in the end.

As we will see in Chapter 9, contact with the Other in contemporary science fiction cinema is not always predicated on invasion tropes, nor on the residue of Empire adventure texts and their masculine heroes at large in 'free' space (that is to say, the space formerly occupied by indigenous peoples). Overt critique of this mode of engagement with the alien Other is clearly central to James Cameron's *Avatar* (2009), in which a wounded and wheelchair-bound former Marine Jake Sully (Same Worthington) inhabits an artificial life form mixing human and alien DNA, called an 'avatar', in order to communicate with the alien species, the Na'vi, whose homeworld is the target of human exploitation. Sully's wounded masculinity, and ultimately his decision to side with the Na'vi against the invading human force, is contrasted with the brutal soldier masculinity inhabited by Colonel Quaritch (Stephen Lang), which corresponds to the armoured soldier-body that was investigated in Chapter 2 and Chapter 3. At an early point in the film, Quaritch and Sully enter a large hanger filled with military equipment, and Quaritch straps himself into a huge mechanical exo-suit, a combat armour which both amplifies his overt masculine physicality and reveals it to be the technological trace of an ideology of domination. By contrast, the avatar that Sully inhabits is biological, hybrid and effectively performs an 'alien' mode of subjectivity (one that understands Na'vi and nature to be part of a symbiotic system) that becomes Sully's own. In *Avatar*, the colonial intertexts are even more explicit than in Cameron's earlier *Aliens* (1986), where the exomorph predators of the title have overrun and destroyed the human colony on a far-distant planet. Here, as in *War of the Worlds*, we find a Wellsian reversal of perspective, where the humans are the invaders; the conflict is resolved through the agency of one of the colonial subjects who becomes alienated from the mission itself.

Star Trek Into Darkness

Star Trek Into Darkness (2013) was the second of the 'rebooted' *Star Trek* film series, which posited an alternative historical timeline to the original series (and films) and to the other television series that spun off those. While the first *Star Trek* 'reboot' film (2009) established an origin story for the Captain Kirk/Lieutenant Spock ensemble cast, the second was much more inflected by post-9/11 anxieties about the role of the Federation with regard to its mission and the rules by which it operates 'out there'. Scotty (Simon Pegg) says to Kirk (Chris Pine), when questioning the arrival of advanced missiles aboard the Enterprise, 'I thought we were meant to be explorers', making explicit what had largely been occluded in earlier entries in the series. The film asks: What kind of organization is the Federation? What are its aims, its ethics? The Federation is presumed to be a 'family' of planets and species, a democratic organization run on principles of mutual respect and benefit. Central to this is the Prime Directive, the 'non-interference' clause that Kirk violates repeatedly, most notably at the beginning of *Into Darkness* when indigenous peoples witness the Enterprise rising from where it is hidden on the seabed, and in turn mythicize the ship as a cargo-cult emblem. This action is necessary, in Kirk's consideration, in the name of a 'higher' ethics, whether that is to save a friend (here, Spock, where 'the needs of the one outweigh the needs of the many' in a reprise of *Star Trek II: The Wrath of Khan* (1982)) or in the service of a kind of liberation-theology, removing a developing people from an oppressive yoke. The 'Prime Directive' proposes the Federation as a liberal, post Imperial, non- or anti-hegemonic force, 'seeking out new worlds, new civilizations' to join the Federation 'family' (a word that is used repeatedly in *Into Darkness*), but refusing to expose themselves to the sight of developing species who might, as do indeed the denizens of the world at the beginning of *Into Darkness*, turn the technologically advanced 'alien' visitors into gods, thereby deforming their development. This is an ethical alibi, of course, allowing Kirk and crew to warp-drive around the galaxy doing all manners of things – including waging war against Klingons or Romulans – without the audience worrying unduly about the moral or material cost of their adventuring. The 'Prime Directive' is meant to keep Federation's hands clean; but it rarely does.

If the Federation, Gene Roddenberry's creation of the Space Age 1960s, is a projection of NASA, as it is often understood, then the ghosts that haunt the vaunted memory of the Apollo programme and its successors – Werner von Braun and the V-2 missiles that prefigured Apollo rocketry, the Space Shuttle's secret military missions – also haunt the Federation. The Enterprise embarks on a '5-year mission' to explore the galaxy, but its capabilities are offensive as well as defensive, and as the television series *Deep Space 9* (1993–99) in particular exposed, the Federation is also a military entity. *Into Darkness* brings this to the fore, although it really re-scripts the end-of-the-Cold-War narrative of *Star Trek VI: The Undiscovered Country* (1991), with Peter Weller's warmongering Fleet Admiral Marcus, the counterpart of Christopher Plummer's bellicose Klingon General Chang, as well as explicitly rewriting *Star Trek II: The Wrath of Khan*. One of the most revealing things about *Star Trek VI* is Kirk's, and the crew's, growing awareness that they themselves are Cold Warriors who have outlived their time, and in particular Kirk's unreconstructed belligerence towards all things Klingon has no place in the future coming-together of Klingon Empire and Federation that is key to the series *Star Trek: The Next Generation* (series 1987–94). This is modulated in *Star Trek Into Darkness* when Khan (Benedict Cumberbatch), himself a genetically modified human, reveals to the *Enterprise's* crew that he has been forced to build super-weapons for Admiral Marcus as a form of ransom for his own people, a plan which reveals that Marcus had intended the *Enterprise* itself to be destroyed by the Klingon Empire as a pretext for war. That it is Marcus who acts as the film's 'villain', and as its articulation of the warrior element of the Federation's foundational (and perhaps Imperial) structures, itself acts as a kind of ethical alibi. Audiences can rest easy with the heroics of Kirk, Spock (and Khan) knowing that Marcus is the real transgressor, and aggressor.

Star Trek has long been the site of critical discourse about the production of gendered subjectivities, largely though the work of Constance Penley. Penley, in the article 'Feminism, Psychoanalysis and the Study of Popular Culture' (1992) and in *NASA/TREK* (1997), brought the phenomenon of 'slash' fiction to wider critical attention. 'Slash', taken from the sign between K/S (Kirk/Spock), is a form of fan-produced fiction that appropriates characters from popular culture and imagines sexual desire between them; this fiction is predominantly written by women, and imagines homosexual desire between male characters. Penley, in 'Feminism, Psychoanalysis and the Study of Popular Culture', investigated the production and circulation (in *samizdat* fashion) of *Star Trek*–derived slash fiction from the early 1970s, and conceptualized this kind of reception/ production as a cultural phenomenon which resisted, through appropriation and re-inscription, models of consumption of popular culture. Penley articulated a resistant reading–writing practice in which female viewers took popular texts and revealed desire-scripts in them that had remained latent: in particular, the homosocial 'buddy' pairing at the centre of *Star Trek*. In this appropriative re-inscription, that 'continuum' between what Eve Kosofsky Sedgwick in *Between Men* (1985) called 'homosocial' male relationships ('male bonding' and other forms of friendship or emotional relationship that disavowed sexuality and desire) and homosexual relationships – a 'continuum' made invisible within patriarchal culture – is revealed, disrupting representations of masculinity.

The imagining of a *male* homosexual relationship re-scripted romance in utopian fashion, re-imagining desire *outside* of gender binaries and hierarchies. In a sense, the slash fan-fiction writers of the early period used SF as a means by which to re-write gender scripts in contemporary culture. Contemporary cinema, not least *Star Trek Into Darkness*, has often acknowledged the production of fan-written re-scripting of relations between characters along 'slash' lines, partly as a means by which to bind in fan reception into wider cultures of consumption. (The phenomenon of fan fiction, and its relation to circuits of production and consumption of major film franchises, is now incorporated into marketing and dissemination strategies by film production companies.) The importance of slash fiction to the *Star Trek* fan base means that a psychosexual hinterland has been created which allows for a high degree of ambiguity or allusiveness on the homosocial relations in the film, in particular, those between Kirk and Spock. Kirk's question in *Into Darkness* – 'why did I go back for you?' – receives Spock's stilted reply, 'because you are my friend', but this does not seem enough, and the viewer who is familiar with 'slash' fictions is easily able to intuit something more profound. That is not to say that *Into Darkness* embraces a polysexual utopianism; indeed, the film goes to great lengths to assert Kirk's heterosexuality. Kirk is discovered in bed with two be-tailed young women, and most notoriously, the reverse shot of Carol Marcus (Alice Eve) in her underwear – not point of view because it is shot from below so her whole body is on display – not only emphasizes Kirk's heterosexuality, but also places *Into Darkness* into traditional modes of gendered spectatorship and the presentation of the female body as spectacles that have been crucial elements of a feminist critique of Hollywood cinema since Laura Mulvey's 'Visual Pleasure and Narrative Cinema' (1973). Such explicitly gendered and heterosexually oriented shots occlude the central orientation of *Star Trek*'s emotional fabric, something that 'slash' fiction makes manifest: it is the homosocial – Kirk's relationship to Pike and to Spock, and even to Khan – that is the true centre of the film's relationships.

Khan is an ambiguous figure throughout the film. Pursued by Kirk as the assassin of Admiral Pike (Bruce Greenwood), he is then revealed as a leader of a captured people, who has been coerced into Admiral Marcus's plans. He joins forces with Kirk and Spock, only to betray them. After Spock has himself reneged on a bargain he makes, Khan directs his captured Federation ship – named the *Vengeance* – towards San Francisco and Starfleet headquarters. The scenes where the *Vengeance* plunges into the city, catastrophically damaging buildings, have inescapable echoes of 9/11 and the damage caused to New York. It is also, symbolically, a return of the Federation's own warlike violence (displaced as that of Admiral Marcus) to the Federal/Imperial centre, and one that binds the ethical, rational Spock into the necessity for violence to overcome the enemy Other. The passage of the Republic into Empire, as we saw in Chapter 3, is a recurrent concern for American cinema since 2000, as is the ethical blindness that this path requires; in *Star Trek Into Darkness*, its most critical edge is the suggestion that the Federation was always-already Imperial.

Monsters

Where *Star Trek Into Darkness* displaces the problematics of American military involvement overseas into a recognizably science-fictional future (the '*Star Trek* universe') as well as the machinations of a rogue Admiral, Gareth Edwards' *Monsters* (2011) is set in a recognizable present day, and revisits the discourses of militarization and the rupturing of borders in ways which invoke the United States' troubled relationships with its neighbours 'south of the border', and in particular the phenomenon of illegal migration across the Rio Grande. A NASA probe, carrying alien genetic material, has crash-landed in northern Mexico, which then becomes inhabited by the 'monsters' of the title, alien cuttlefish-pachyderm hybrids that lay waste to human settlements and which are the subject of US military airstrikes. As the film reveals towards the end, however, these are not 'invaders from outer space', but rather entities who form their own relationships with Earth's flora and fauna and whose seeming hostility to humans is simply the lack of knowledge or understanding of their impact upon human-oriented ecosystems, the very construction of which has often been predicated on lack of understanding of (or concern for) the destructive impact of human activities on a bio-diverse (non-human) Earth ecology. Two crucial scenes at night reveal that this alien 'infection' is not a simple invasion narrative that re-imposes ideological/species boundaries between human and alien Other, but something rather more sophisticated. Close to the huge concrete Wall that now separates Mexico from the United States, the American travellers Sam (Whitney Able) and Kaulder (Scoot McNairy) are escorted by a small group of armed Mexican men. Struggling with his efforts to understand Spanish (Sam is fluent), Kaulder questions the men for information, and then paraphrases them: 'There's no stopping nature.' The aliens, the men reveal, have been attacked by US planes carrying chemical weapons, and it is only when attacked that the creatures respond violently. Just as Kaulder struggles to communicate throughout the film, it is a failure of understanding or, more properly, *communication*, that ideologically imposes a discursive frame of 'monstrosity' upon the alien creatures. When the convoy chances into the path of a creature, a firefight ensues, during which the men are killed: Sam and Kaulder are left alone when he switches off the interior light in the car they shelter in. The aliens, it is revealed, are attracted to artificial light.

The reason for this is shown during a climactic scene at a deserted gas station after Sam and Kaulder have crossed the border back into the United States. The Wall is ineffective: they find empty towns and a dead alien in what has become a combat zone. Kaulder phones his 6-year-old son, breaking down as he speaks, and it is here that he is truly able to communicate, to reveal himself (as a father), ironically through a communications device; Sam, calling her fiancée and facing the prospect of an unhappy marriage, retains a closed facial expression and withdrawn manner in parallel, intercut conversations. After the calls have ended, two 'monsters' approach the station. The first examines the inside of the station with its tentacles, and as Sam witnesses it touch a television screen, light pulses passes cuttlefish-like up its mobile limb. Television screens had been ubiquitous in the *mise-en-scéne* in the first part of the film, but here, it seems as though the creatures are drawn to the light of the cathode ray screen, and try to achieve communication *with* it. As Sam and Kaulder walk outside, they witness two creatures come together in a kind of tentacular embrace, accompanied by emanations of light on their bodies. The purpose of this tactile communication is unclear, but it signifies that these creatures have a kind of life hitherto unknown to the human beings, and that their attraction to artificial light (of cars, televisions, towns) is a product of their desire to communicate. Where human interaction with the world is distorted by the lenses of global media (Kaulder notably develops a more urgent ethical sense towards his professional photography during the film), the importance of communication and connection with the Other is asserted here. It is deeply ironic, therefore, that the alien beings attempt to communicate with television screens, a technology itself other to human subjectivity. Direct human communication with the aliens remains, at the end of the film, frustratingly out of reach for the protagonists, even if they begin to understand the creatures more clearly.

Monsters begins with a point-of-view shot, through the night-vision scope of an American soldier; another sings 'Ride of the Valkyries', a clear reference to *Apocalypse Now* (1979). When they too become involved in a firefight with a creature, their vehicle is smashed, and we see two civilians injured on the road: these will be Sam and Kaulder, the film beginning where it ends. Immediately prior to the transition back to the beginning of the *histoire*, signified by a black screen, another point-of-view shot follows a 'smart' missile as it speeds towards its target, the creature. These images have inescapable visual connotations of the footage distributed by the US military during the first and second Gulf Wars that proved the 'precision' command-and-control structures now at work in contemporary warfare. As has become all too evident, however, and as *Monsters* itself demonstrates, it is this very mediation which distorts vision. The fate of Sam and Kaulder, offered at the opening of the film, returns us to a world where the aliens are known only through night-vision displays, gunsights and the visual feeds of smartbombs. That the 'ending' is transposed to the beginning of the film does attempt to ameliorate this closure, however.

Clearly, *Monsters* not only engages with the politics of the 'War on Terror' and projections of US military power overseas, but also works as a metaphor for Mexican immigration into the United States and efforts to patrol that porous boundary. The huge Wall built to keep out the 'monsters' has explicit real-world analogues in the border policing that stretches across the US Southwest, as analysed by Wendy Brown in *Walled States, Waning Sovereignty* (2010), but as Sam and Kaulder realize when they see the Wall from atop a Mayan pyramid, 'we are only imprisoning ourselves'. At the end of the film, in which the travelogue also serves as an off-beat romance, the symbolic emotional connection between the 'monsters' at the gas station is mirrored by the kiss shared by the two human protagonists. As they wait for the arrival of a US military patrol to 'rescue' them,

Sam responds to Kaulder's restrained, 'This is it' by saying 'I don't want to go home', and they then kiss. Still embracing in the foreground of the shot, the soldiers arrive, and physically pull the couple away from each other, exiting the shot on opposite sides of the screen. The separation of the lovers stands in for the disconnection between humans and 'monsters', between global North and global South, privileged and disenfranchised, the rich and the poor. In *Monsters*, re-crossing the border provides no security: there is no way 'home'.

Alien Nations

This return of the alien Other (and problematics of 'contact') from the spatial margins to the centre, a recurrent motif in contemporary science fiction cinema, is foreshadowed by the 1988 film *Alien Nation*. The film is, in essence, a 1980s' buddy–cop movie, but which shifts the racial dynamic of *Lethal Weapon* (1986) or, much earlier, *Dirty Harry* (1971) into a science fiction scenario wherein one of the two male cops investigating a crime is of alien origin: a 'Newcomer'. This begins with a provocative interest in media representations that the film does not follow-up; as in *Monsters*, television footage is inserted directly into the fabric of film. Grainy images of a large disc-shaped ship floating over the Mojave desert are taken from a purported news report, which explains that in 1991, 'a slave ship washed ashore on Earth'; footage of Ronald Reagan (who had, by 1991, been out of office for 3 years, but who would still have been president at the time of the film's production) is repurposed to make it seem as though he is proactive in accepting the Newcomers into American society. The film sets up the United States as a space wherein immigrants are welcomed and are allowed to make their own lives; but as the Newcomer Detective Francisco (Mandy Patinkin) says later in the film, Americans rarely live up to the ideals enshrined in its own Constitution.

The first sequence begins with Detective Matt Sykes (James Caan) and his African-American partner Tuggle (Roger Aaron Brown) cruising the part of Los Angeles, 'New Downtown', which has become a centre for the Newcomer community. Caan's expressed dislike for the Newcomers is played off the affection he has for his black colleague; the scene is an almost direct reprise of a scene in *Dirty Harry*, where Inspector Callahan (Clint Eastwood) drives around Haight-Ashbury with his new colleague Chico Gonzalez (Reni Santoni) expressing his disgust for the permissive attitudes of the young and wishing to 'throw a net over the whole bunch of them', to which Gonzalez replies, 'I know what you mean'. Just as in *Dirty Harry*, in *Alien Nation*, the racial attitudes inhabited by the aggressive, white, middle-aged cop protagonist are deliberately softened by a homosocial relationship with a partner coded as ethnically non-white (African-American or Chicano); in *Alien Nation*, when Tuggle is shot and killed during a robbery of a Mom-and-Pop grocery store in the Newcomer district, Sykes agrees to accept Detective Francisco (recently promoted from the uniformed division) in order to track down the perpetrators. The learning experience that is central to the buddy-movie dynamic here gains traction through the absolute centrality of coming to understand the Other in *Alien Nation*'s science fiction scenario. The fact that the Newcomers bear the burden of a history of slavery makes the racial analogy explicit, but the film is much less directly interested in exploring these issues than *Blade Runner* (1982) or, more overtly still, Philip K. Dick's novel from which *Blade Runner* was developed, *Do Androids Dream of Electric Sheep?* (1968). The buddy–cop dynamic in fact tends to repress some of the more interesting possibilities that the film opens up, but does not develop.

One of these concerns a night-club, run by a Newcomer, who was then murdered, where Sykes and Francisco watch as a female newcomer performs a mildly erotic dance routine. Attempting to question her in her dressing room, Sykes in particular uses a mirror to voyeuristically continue watching Cassandra (Leslie Bevis) while asking her questions. After Francisco leaves the scene at Sykes's behest, Cassandra reverses the polarity of the gaze and aggressively comes on to Sykes, despite his protestations: 'your voice says no, your body says yes', she says, unzipping his fly. Caan, in the light-hearted manner of the film overall, plays the character's discomfort broadly, but this is a scene that could have been used to add a great deal of complexity both to Sykes' character and to the film's analysis of relations between human and Newcomer. In an earlier scene in a bar, human women are seen with Newcomer partners, and so the element of inter-racial/inter-species sex is woven into the fabric of the film; the failure to develop Cassandra, even as a *femme fatale*, indicates the extent to which the Newcomer female is at once offered as a spectacle of desire and disavowed by both Sykes and the film itself. In a very short running time, Sykes's discomfort also allows the homosocial relationship to Francisco to play out without complication.

Although the film, particularly in the first half, makes interesting play with Francisco's knowledge of Newcomer language, allowing him to discover things that remain hidden to Sykes, and suggesting a city-within-the-city, a cultural enclave that resists assimilation, the buddy dynamic eventually renders Sykes and Francisco as a bonded partnership and close to an interchangeable pair. Where, at the beginning of the film, Sykes inhabits an aggressive machismo that largely prevents progress being made on the case, and Francisco seems to be an over-promoted functionary, too keen to do things 'by the book', the film reverses their positions. By the end of the film, it is Sykes who asks Francisco to restrain himself in their pursuit of the drug baron Newcomer, Harcourt (Terence Stamp) – whose assimilation as a businessman is shown when he is presented at a dinner by the mayor of Los Angeles, marking him as a typical businessman/criminal recognizable from the noir novels of Raymond Chandler – to which Francisco replies: 'Fuck procedure'. The Newcomer's abandonment of the rulebook indicates a reversal in the homosocial relationship and, in the codes of the buddy–cop action movie, his accession as a 'real' cop.

The film ends with a wedding, that of Sykes' daughter, which he has been threatening not to attend. With a bandaged hand, the result of saving Sykes from salty water (toxic to Newcomers), Francisco fixes his partner's bow tie and dress shirt outside the door of the church. Accepted by Sykes and his family – as Sykes takes his daughter down the aisle, Francisco and his wife watch from the doorway – this scene is less a paean to assimilation of the Newcomers than it is a celebration of Sykes' acceptance of responsibility as a father (as well as partner and friend to Francisco). The presentation of Sykes as a father seals the softening of the aggressive cop masculinity he had inhabited before, one that is revealed in the course of the film to be economically and socially disenfranchising (Sykes has unpaid bills and his small, grubby apartment is so dishevelled that Francisco 'thought it had been burglarised'). The ending not only heals the social and racial alienation of Francisco and his family from the (white) human denizens of Los Angeles, but more pertinently also overcomes Sykes's own alienation from home, from family and from happy productivity.

Alien Nation, partly through its Los Angeles setting, also inherits the spatialization of ethnic or racial difference that can be found in Roman Polanski's *Chinatown* (1974), and as in the earlier film, *Alien Nation* attempts to use its generic scenario to stand for wider matrices of exploitation and urban 'development'. Where *Chinatown* focuses on Los Angeles' history of disputes over water rights and use, and conflicts over land ownership and development, *Alien Nation* overtly connects the condition of the Newcomers to their employment in the oil and gas industries, where their tolerance for methane allows them to work in conditions that human beings cannot. In a scenario that seems directly lifted from *Outland* (1981), where off-world male miners are maintained in near-intolerable conditions through the importation of narcotics, the drug baron Harcourt uses the refining technology to synthesize a drug – harmless to humans – which is genetically keyed to the Newcomers' biology, not just to make them work harder but also to crave more of the narcotic, one necessitating the other in a closed economic cycle. *Alien Nation* does not have the resources to develop this narrative further, but it does suggest an embryonic critique of the exploitative conditions of capital into which the former slaves are assimilated. Unlike *Blade Runner*, in which the condition of slavery is ultimately revealed to be near-universal (the condition of both replicant *and* human in that film's Los Angeles), *Alien Nation* suggests the possibility of a class-based analysis of the Newcomers' conditions, but does not develop them. When Sykes watches Francisco with his family in a suburban villa enclosed by a white picket fence and murmurs 'Ozzie and Harriet' (a radio and then TV sitcom that ran from 1944 to 1966), a critique of Francisco's assimilationist imperatives is suggested by this reference to the All-American nuclear family (and, by implication, Francisco's failure to embody it), but the absence of Francisco's wife and son from the rest of the film closes this possibility, and enforces the focus upon the homosocial pair.

Alien Nation was developed into a television series that only ran for one season (1989–90), but its scenario is clearly influential on a contemporary science fiction film, not least in the images of a large disc-shaped alien craft drifting over dusty landscapes, made in South Africa: Neil Blomkamp's *District 9* (2009). A large 'mothership' drifts to a standstill above Johannesburg, and on board are discovered a small population of alien creatures in states of disease and distress. This alien population is then housed in a securitized shanty-town on the borders of the city, with overt connections both to the historical black townships of apartheid-era South Africa and to the scenario offered by *Alien Nation*. In *District 9*, security is handled not by the government of South Africa but by a corporate arms manufacturer, MNU (Multi-National United), who wish to develop alien technologies into usable weapon systems. Notably, both the bureaucratic structure of MNU and the military security forces they employ (explicitly 'mercenaries') are almost entirely white, and many are Afrikaners. The soldiers in particular seem transplants from the apartheid era, using racist language and violent suppression of the alien population. (The main black African employee of MNU is later revealed to be a whistleblower in the *verité*/ news media sections of the film). The camp that holds the alien population (themselves subject to the derogatory name 'prawns') is District 9 itself, but the film narrates the proposed clearances of these shanty towns and forced relocation into camps. While this has a particular resonance in the history of South Africa, when the protagonist Wikus van der Merwe (Sharlto Copley) confesses that these places are 'concentration camps', the metaphorical connection between species and ethnicity is made all too clear.

Van der Merwe, an Afrikaans bureaucrat elevated to the position of project leader for the clearances (played by Copley as a kind of naïf preferred to the position by his father-in-law), becomes infected with alien DNA while in *District 9* and his (literal) alienation from MNU and the racist imperatives of exclusion and repression is played out as a form of body-horror. Van der Merwe physically becomes an alien during the course of the film, his body hybridized. Here, then, the discourse of infection is used in the service of political estrangement (and understanding of the true nature of the camps). When an alien child sees his hybridized left arm and says, 'You're like me', van der Merwe reacts violently against this recognition of similarity and attempts to re-impose his self-constituting and blinkered idea of difference, but the film proceeds to unravel this difference biologically and bodily. The final shots of the films show an alien making metal flowers on the detritus of District 9 (or perhaps 10), but the film suggests that this is the 'disappeared' van der Merwe, now unrecognizable in his altered body. Whether this physical or biological transformation results in a translated subjectivity is unclear, however, and the film bypasses the possibility of a hybridized physical form in completing van der Merwe's trajectory from human to alien. Even though *District 9* offers a critique of the discourses of militarized security and emphasizes the racial or ethnic coding of exclusion, the final shot suggests a reconstituted binary (human/alien) rather than the hybrid and struggling form van der Merwe inhabits for the majority of the film.

Blomkamp's follow-up to this film was *Elysium* (2013), which re-drew the spatial boundaries between favelas (the 'outside', the place of Agamben's 'bare life') and the city, so that the entire Earth is a dusty, impoverished shanty, and a wealthy and privileged elite live in an orbital habitat that can be seen clearly in Earth's sky. Though less coherent than *District 9*, its narrative is overtly politicized, and the struggles of the protagonist Max (Matt Damon), a former car thief who is fatally irradiated in a workplace accident caused by negligent practices, to heal himself through entering the habitat and using one of its Med-Bays are mapped onto the struggles of the excluded to gain access to the privileges taken for granted by the elite. With 5 days to live, Max is surgically fixed into a mechanical exo-skeleton that will keep him mobile until he is able to enter Elysium. As the narrative unfolds, Max has a computer programme downloaded into his cortex that, when uploaded into Elysium's central core, will free all of Earth's citizens, but at the cost of Max's own life. *Elysium* thereby represents almost a compendium of key tropes and motifs that we have seen in this book: a traumatized and damaged masculine subject; the armoured male body; spatial borders and exclusions along economic, social and ethnic lines, between 'life' and 'bare life'; and motifs of sacrifice of the masculine subject for a 'higher' purpose. Max's violent heroics achieve a narrative rationalization upon the film's ending: with Elysium's medical craft on their way to give succour to Earth's starving billions, the means are justified by the revolutionary ends. The irony – that the narrative resolution is made possible by the technologies which have perpetuated social and economic division and exclusion – is perhaps unwittingly revealed in the film's title: this revolution is itself only achievable outside the boundaries of life itself, as a kind of a spectacular dream.

8

Everybody Runs

In this chapter we will analyse in detail two texts, Audrey Niffenegger's *The Time Traveler's Wife* (2005) and Steven Spielberg's film *Minority Report* (2002), itself freely adapted from a short story by Philip K. Dick called 'The Minority Report', first published in the 1950s. Both texts are concerned with mobility: in *The Time Traveler's Wife*, the dislocations in time suffered by the protagonist Henry deTamble, caused by a particular genetic mutation; and in *Minority Report*, the spectacular mobility afforded the 'Pre-Crime' policeman John Anderton (Tom Cruise) and its extension into unlicensed mobility when he attempts to escape the system of which he was a part. Both films are also concerned with temporality: time-travel, and also the precognitive ability of three young people in *Minority Report* which allows a police unit to intervene in a potential criminal situation before any offence has been committed. In both, anxieties about agency are particularly strong, as both texts presume a temporal structure in which the past and future are in some sense determined (although, paradoxically, in *Minority Report*, that very future can be voided by prophylactic action by the 'Pre-Crime' police). In both, debates take place in which the idea of individual agency or 'free will' is presented in a manner which complicates, rather than compromises, the global deterministic structure. The agency of the masculine subject at the centre of these highly mobile narratives is then under question, despite the science-fictional premises of the narrative themselves. In both, the male subject suffers from the effects of trauma; in both, fatherhood has a problematic relation to that trauma. Both *The Time Traveler's Wife* and *Minority Report* are indexical narratives with regard to the intersection of masculinity and mobility in the early years of the twenty-first century.

Before we analyse the texts themselves, it should be noted that mobility and trauma are indissolubly connected concepts. As Lynne Kirby notes in *Parallel Tracks: The Railroad and Silent Cinema* (1997), the anxiety surrounding train travel in the latter decades of the nineteenth century was partly produced by the suspicion that the 'passenger-spectator is vulnerable to unexpected events, or to "shock", as trauma was referred to before about 1880' (Kirby 1997: 57). Kirby goes on to suggest that 'the experience of shock was emblematized by the accident, both real and anticipated, which actually gave rise to a condition known as "railway spine", later called "traumatic neurosis"' (Kirby 1997: 57–8). Indeed, in *Beyond the Pleasure Principle*, Sigmund Freud notes that 'a condition consequent upon mechanical shock, train crashes, and other life-threatening accidents has long been described – a condition that has come to be known as "traumatic neurosis"' (Freud 2006: 137–8), a condition that Freud connects to an experience of sudden and unexpected 'fright'. In *Beyond the Pleasure Principle*, as we saw in Chapter 2, Freud outlines his theory of the 'stimulus shield' that protects the psyche from being overwhelmed by the shocks of modernity (which Kirby deftly connects to Walter Benjamin's conception of modernity as characterized by perceptual shocks). Kirby explores the work of Charcot on male hysteria to propose that extended mobility in the nineteenth century provided the conditions, particularly 'among vagabonds, tramps, society's peripatetic disenfranchised', for a kind of mental dislocation: 'mobility of social place is the male hysterical equivalent [of the female mobility of mind' (Kirby 1997: 67). The conditions of extended mobility produce the conditions of hysteria:

> In a kind of mirror image of otherness, one can see that cultural displacement as massive as nineteenth-century mechanization and urbanization – railway assisted – traumatized its victims into a condition akin to female hysteria. In other words, it 'emasculated' men. . . . The 'emasculated' male, the male hysteric, might then be seen as the boomerang of white, male, technological culture itself, a vision of the railroad neurotic as a man reduced to a female, or non-male state. (Kirby 1997: 67)

Heightened mobility has, from the nineteenth century, been fundamentally connected to anxieties concerning masculinity, trauma and dislocation. In the discussion that follows, these three elements will be brought together to analyse how science fiction texts have extrapolated from the mobile conditions of modernity to present a traumatized masculine subject, himself a product of the cultural conditions of the present day.

The Time Traveler's Wife

Audrey Niffenegger's *The Time Traveler's Wife* (2005) is an unusual text, a science fiction/romance crossover, written by an author outside genre science fiction (whose previous books were graphic novels or artist's books), which reached a very wide audience, with a degree of mainstream exposure that far exceeded other science fiction texts published in the same year. (It was shortlisted for the Arthur C. Clarke Award for science fiction, losing out to China Miéville's *The Iron Council* in 2005, as well as the Locus award, and the John W. Campbell Memorial award, where it was placed third.) It is a time-travel fiction, its very title advertising its generic connection to the Wellsian tradition, and yet it focuses not on the physics of time travel nor on the 'adventures' of the Time Traveler, but rather on the relationship between Henry deTamble, who is involuntarily dislocated in time through a hereditary and genetic 'Chrono-Displacement Syndrome', and his wife Clare Abshire, who is often forced to wait for Henry while he is absent. The novel is written from the point of view of both characters, with interleaving first-person sections; there is a rough chronology at work, but the narrative jumps backwards and forwards in time in a non-linear manner; and the relationship between Henry and Clare seems to form a kind of double loop, wherein Clare first meets Henry when she is 6 and Henry is 35, travelling from the future; but Henry first meets Clare (in 'normal' chronology) when he is 28 and she is 20. This results in a rather strange scene where Clare has known Henry for most of her life, but because Henry only time-travels back to see her after they have met at his age 28 he does not know who she is. In terms of the reader's experience of the narrative, this seems estranging, odd: but Niffenegger's narrative mechanics remain rigorous throughout the text. Discussion about the novel often focuses upon the ethical problematic with regard to Henry's relation to Clare: Does he 'groom' her in childhood to become his wife? This is only partly offset by the scene described above, where Henry meets Clare 'for the first time' aged 28, and Clare's responses to him as they enter an adult relationship. In some sense, it is clear Clare 'constructs' Henry, the Henry aged 35 who travels back in time to see her as a child (and the novel suggests that it is meeting Clare as an adult that provides the psychological and emotional 'anchor' for Henry to travel back to these particular points in time and space); the Henry of the early 20s that we see is a very troubled young man, whose actions are at least ethically problematic. When he meets Gomez for the first time, having physically beaten another man ('stomping the living shit out of a large drunk suburban guy who had the effrontery to call me a faggot and then tried to beat me up to prove his point' (Niffenegger 2005: 134)), Gomez marvels at Henry's physical prowess:

> 'You don't smoke? Anything?' [asks Gomez]
>
> 'I run.'
>
> 'Oh, shit, you're in great shape. I thought you had about killed Nick, and you weren't even winded.' (Niffenegger 2005: 138)

Gomez's suspicion of Henry's past and character are well founded; there seem to be, in a physical and psychological sense, 'two Henrys'. The physical doubling or splitting that occurs when Henrys from two ages are co-present is mirrored in the psychological fragmentation that seems to haunt him as he becomes an adult. Very often we see two different Henrys in the same scene, as in their first meeting at the Field Museum in Chicago, where the older Henry not only gives his 6-year-old self a tour around the museum and a loving inspection of Audobon's *Birds of America*, he begins the process of allowing him to survive the experience of chrono-displacement by showing the young boy how to steal, beginning with a t-shirt from the museum shop to cover his naked body. Henry engages in a curious auto-didacticism, but one which is oriented around practical skills that he has himself been taught (in the time-travel narrative's looping paradox) by his older self some years before. The first tour around the museum is the point where 'Everything changed. Starting now' (Niffenegger 2005: 31), but this is another displacement; the change has yet to come, and this is to do with the fatal automobile crash suffered by his mother, at which Henry is present (though he chrono-displaces out of danger), and to which he returns recurrently throughout his life, to the extent that one suspects that a good fraction of the people who witness it are Henry himself.

Time-travelling is connected explicitly to trauma; in particular, Henry's obsessive revisiting of the site of his mother's death in an automobile accident. Time-travelling becomes a kind of repetition-compulsion, as outlined by Freud in *Beyond the Pleasure Principle* (see Chapter 2). Henry returns again and again to the accident scene, acting as bystander, helper and witness.

My mother dying . . . it's the pivotal thing . . . everything else goes around and around it. . . . I dream about it, and I also – time travel to it. Over and over. If you could be there, and hover over the scene of the accident, and you could see every detail of it, all the people, cars, trees, snowdrifts – if you had time to really look at everything, you would see me. I am in cars, behind bushes, on the bridge, in a tree. I have seen it from every angle, I am even a participant in the aftermath: I called the airport from a nearby gas station to page my father with the message to come immediately to the hospital. I sat in the hospital waiting room and watched my father walk through on his way to find me. He looks grey and ravaged. I walked along the shoulder of the road, waiting for my young self to appear, and I put a blanket around my thin child's shoulders. I looked into my small uncomprehending face, and I thought. . . . I thought. . . . I thought, '*I should have died too*'. (Niffenegger 2005: 113)

Henry clearly suffers from survivor guilt, and his time-travelling must be read, symbolically, as a response to the catastrophic trauma of witnessing his mother's death, and his escape from the same fate. He is trapped, not only by his own sense of time, which is deterministic – 'it's like if you started the tape and played it for a while but then you said, "Oh I want to hear that song again, so you played that song and then you went back to where you left off but you wound the tape too far ahead so you rewound it again but you still got it to far ahead"' (Niffenegger 2005: 47); 'things happen the way they happened, once and only once' (Niffenegger 2005: 48) – but also by the Freudian, trauma-oriented structure of subjectivity that Niffenegger encodes in the novel. In none of his visits can he *alter* time, alter history: the past is material, fixed, and trauma may not be undone.

In some sense, Henry's time-travelling can be seen as an analogue of the return of memory that Freud diagnoses as being central to traumatic experience and to hysteria in *Studies on Hysteria* (1956), the volume he co-authored with Joseph Breuer. 'It is of course obvious that in the cases of "traumatic" hysteria', they write, 'what provokes the symptoms is the accident. The causal connection is equally evident in hysterical attacks when it is possible to gather from the patient's utterances that in each attack he is hallucinating the same event which provoked the first one' (Freud and Breuer 1956: 4). Henry's symptoms, his chrono-displacement, seem to be perfectly fitted to such a reading. Freud and Breuer continue: 'The disproportion between the many years' duration of the hysterical symptom and the single occurrence which provoked it is what we are accustomed invariably to find in traumatic neuroses. Quite frequently it is some event in childhood that sets up a more or less severe symptom which persists during the years that follow' (Freud and Breuer 1956: 4). Although Henry actually begins to chrono-displace (to the Field Museum) *before* his mother's death, his recurrent return to the site of the trauma seems to indicate its centrality to Henry's wounded psychology, as he himself confessed above. Time-travelling can, in *The Time Traveler's Wife*, be read as a science-fictional metaphor for the processes of memory, of trauma and neurosis, which find a material analogue in Henry's travelling. In the most famous quotation from *Studies on Hysteria*, Freud and Breuer declare: '*Hysterics suffer mainly from reminiscences*' (Freud and Breuer 1956: 7 [italics in original]). However, if Henry is a hysteric, then the procedures of psychoanalysis seemingly do not pertain. When they declare that '*each individual hysterical symptom immediately and permanently disappeared when we had succeeded in bringing clearly to light the memory of the event by which it was provoked and in arousing its accompanying affect, and when the patient had described that event in the greatest possible detail and had put the affect into words'* (Freud and Breuer 1956: 6 [italics in original]), this revelation of the traumatic event, to speak it in words, is no release for Henry. He is all too aware of the source of his own trauma, but cannot undo it. Indeed, because the chrono-displacement is genetic rather than psychological, Henry seeks a physiological 'cure' rather than analysis.

This aligns *The Time Traveler's Wife* with texts such as *Gattaca, Never Let Me Go* or *Code 46* that were considered in Chapter 5, and which form the core of Jackie Stacey's analysis in *The Cinematic Life of the Gene* (2010). Henry's 'real' trauma, which may not be undone through articulation, is at the level of DNA, the transmission of a 'faulty' gene which precipitates his time-travelling. In *The Time Traveller's Wife*, Henry's time machine is his own body. He suffers from a genetic mutation which determines that he 'chrono-displaces' to other historical moments. Throughout the novel, Henry desires to be 'normal', to seek a 'cure' for his problematic ability to move in time (and space). He explains thus:

> First of all, I think it's a brain thing. I think it's a bit like epilepsy, because it tends to happen when I'm stressed, and there are physical cues, like flashing light, that can prompt it. And because things like running, and sex, and meditation tend to help me stay in the present. Secondly, I have absolutely no conscious control over when or where I go, how long I stay, or when I come back. So time travel tours of the Riviera are very unlikely. Having said that, my subconscious seems to exert tremendous control, because I spend a lot of time in my own past, visiting events that are interesting or important, and evidently I will be spending enormous amounts of time visiting you, which I am looking forward to immensely. I tend to go to places I've already been in real time, although I do find myself in other, more random times and places. I tend to go to the past, rather than to the future. . . . So far, my range is about fifty years in each direction. But I rarely go to the future, and I don't think I've ever seen much of anything there I found useful. It's always quite brief. And maybe I just don't know what I'm looking at. It's the past that exerts a lot of pull. In the past I feel much more solid. (Niffenegger 2005: 162–3)

Notably, Henry understands his own 'syndrome' as at once pathological (connected to a condition such as epilepsy), psychological (triggered by stress) and driven by unconscious motives or drives. However, Henry is, foundationally, the subject of his own genetic code, his own predisposition to time-travelling, which is only partially one of the three categories outlined above. In a sense, Henry is 'hardwired' to travel; he literally becomes a 'time machine'.

The Time Traveler's Wife, in its narrative fabric, offers the potential for a radical critique of unitary subjectivity, despite its indebtedness to Freudian-inflected models of trauma and neurosis, and its biological/genetic determinism (one that reflects the determinism of its conception of time). At some points, this even cuts across the imperatives of the heterosexual romance narrative. Early in the novel, two 15-year-old Henrys are together 'doing what we often do when we have a little privacy, when it's cold out, when both of us are past puberty and haven't quite got around to actual girls yet. I think most people would do this, if they had the sort of opportunities I have. I mean, I'm not gay or anything' (Niffenegger 2005: 56). This final disavowal bespeaks a kind of anxiety, but opens the door to a rather polymorphous range of sexual desires that the novel tends to repress, even in scenes where Clare makes love (and conceives) with an 'other' Henry, while the Henry native to her time is asleep in the same room. It is a case of Nifenegger literalizing a phrase; masturbation becomes 'sex with oneself' in a direct, but different sense. The splitting or doubling of Henry in these scenes tends to suggest that there is no 'original' Henry; if two Henrys are present in a scene, they both are 'original', or neither are. This again tends to compromise the sense of the human subject as a unitary, unique identity; but in Henry's case, it leads to a further psychological dislocation. Henry is radically dis-located by his chrono-displacing 'abilities', alienated from other people, and even from his own father. Henry's temporal mobility leads to an evacuation of rootedness, a sense of anxiety and loss and emotional displacement, until he meets Clare. Until then, he is never at home, always elsewhere. In this sense, the narrative of chrono-displacement is an extended metaphor for the dislocating properties of contemporary life.

The genetic or biological imperative at work suggests, ultimately, an evolutionary frame to Henry's mutated genes, ones which are passed on to their daughter Alba, who has more control over when and where she travels to. Towards the end of the book, when Henry arrives to visit his daughter post-mortem, it is revealed that 'chrono-displacement' is now a publically recognized condition, and Henry's Lazarus-like re-appearance a matter for sympathy rather than horror. Several times in the narrative, Henry's sense of himself shifts from a register of identity to that of species categorization: 'I walk out if his office, down stairs, into the street, where the sun has been waiting for me. Whatever I am.

What am I? *What am I?*' (Niffenegger 2005: 312). Shortly after, Clare, again using the language of DNA coding, confesses:

> I look over at Henry, and I wonder that on a cellular level he is so different, so *other*, when he's just a man in a white button-down shirt and a pea jacket whose hand feels like skin and bone in mine, a man who smiles just like a human. *I always knew he was different*, but what does it matter? a few letters of code? but somehow it does matter, and somehow we must change it. (Niffenegger 2005: 322)

Henry is the Other-who-is-the-same, a double, uncanny. His own sense of normalcy is itself a burden; and as he cannot find the 'cure', cannot avoid his own fate or death, that is a burden that can only be resolved in the figure of his daughter, Alba.

Henry's time-travelling is exciting, but dangerous, and proves fatal in the end (when Henry's spatial mobility is curtailed by the amputation of frostbitten feet; temporal mobility is actually dependent upon the capability for bodily spatial mobility, running). It understandably proves a problem with regard to employment, and also in terms of the mobilities inherent in late modernity: vacations taken by air travel, and the ubiquity of the automobile in contemporary American social organization, for instance, are problems for Henry. For Henry, *immobility* is the great anxiety that haunts him, an immobility that ultimately comes to pass when he awakes, chrono-displaced, in a snowy park and suffers frostbite to his feet. When they are amputated, Henry's time-travelling becomes increasingly traumatic, and increasingly displaced from the narrative itself: from his wife Claire's point of view, we see Henry return bloodied or otherwise traumatized from his time-travelling, but we do not see Henry's own experiences themselves. Throughout *The Time Traveller's Wife*, Henry *runs*. He says: 'I am a beast of the hoof. If anything ever happens to my feet, you might as well shoot me' (Niffenegger 2005: 163). Running is survival, for Henry: physical mobility is crucial for him to be able to deal with his involuntary temporal mobility.

Minority Report

While often critically taken to task for his sentimentality, Steven Spielberg is in fact deeply invested in both the point of view of the child and the complementary figure of the father. In *E.T.* (1982) and in *A.I.* (2001), the experience and point of view of the child itself is central to the film (though in both of these, in *Jurassic Park*, and in the Spielberg 'produced' *Poltergeist* (1982), the child is put in danger); in *Close Encounters*, in the figure of Roy Neary (Richard Dreyfus), the child-man, is the focus of the sense of wonder; and in *Hook* (1991), anxieties surround the man who has forgotten what it is to be a child, Peter Banning (Robin Williams). Complementing this focus on the child is the recurrent motif of fatherhood, particularly anxious fatherhood: from Chief Brody's fears of water and fears for his children in *Jaws* (1975), to Banning's troubled relationship with his son in *Hook*, to Indy's desire to impress his father in *Indiana Jones and the Last Crusade* (1989). At the end of this line is John Anderton (Tom Cruise) in *Minority Report*, whose own son has been abducted and his wife 'lost', and whose relationship with Lamar Burgess (Max von Sydow) is that of father and son, but which is not all that it might seem.

If we understand fatherhood to be a recurrent Spielbergian motif, this begins to make sense of the changes between Dick's 'The Minority Report' and Spielberg's *Minority Report*. In Dick's short story, Anderton is approaching retirement. He thinks to himself, when meeting his young antagonist Witwer, '*I'm getting bald. Bald and fat and old*' (Dick 1994: 99). Anderton is the head of Precrime, a division of the police who use three 'Precog' talents (human beings who can see the future, or possible futures) to intercede and prevent murders before they can be committed. The narrative of 'The Minority Report' is organized around a power-struggle between the police and the army, in which a plot to frame Anderton for murder (and therefore produce the ultimate irony for Precrime) would bring the whole operation into question. The narrative proceeds to a crucial point in which Anderton must make a moral decision: to *not* commit murder, and bring the system of Precrime crashing down; or to fulfil the predicted future murder, and uphold the system. After first considering the former, Anderton decides upon the latter. I will return to the changes made in this scenario in Spielberg's *Minority Report* later in this chapter.

The crucial relationships in the short story by Dick are between Anderton and his wife (who Anderton sees as a threat, rather than as a source of support), and Anderton and Witwer (who Anderton distrusts as a younger man who appears to be planning to supplant him). There is no 'Lamar Burgess' character, just as there is no 'lost son'. Spielberg introduces both to make *his* John Anderton, played with boyish energy by Tom Cruise, both father *and* son. As in *Hook* and *Jaws*, fatherhood in *Minority Report* is suffused with irony and anxiety. Through little fault of his own, though he blames himself to such an extent that we see him reliant upon the illegal drug 'Clarity', Anderton is traumatized, and fatherhood is synonymous with loss and intolerable grief. The film suggests, as motivation, that Anderton's involvement with Precrime is a direct consequence of, and thereby symptom of this originary trauma, and his intercessions to prevent murders are a fantasy replaying of his own scenario of loss. He attempts to undo the past through 'undoing' or forestalling a traumatic future. Anderton's interactions with holographic video images of his son at play, treating photographic images as real, torture him while seeming to sustain. Spielberg's Anderton is a broken man, 'split' even, between Precrime cop and tortured father/drug user, between intolerable past and unacceptable future. In fact, Spielberg splits Dick's Anderton into *two* separate fathers: a younger head of Precrime, and an older father figure (Burgess) who constructs and oversees the system. The reason for this, I would argue, is to make Anderton a much more physically mobile figure, utilizing Cruise's 'action star' persona to the full. The translation from short story to film is also a generic transformation, here: from science fiction, to science fiction 'spectacle film'.

As Garrett Stewart and Christine Cornea note, the tension between representation of a 'real' world and the expressive possibilities of CGI imaging is often thematized in SF cinema through a narrative focus on the photographic image itself. Garrett Stewart also notes the connections between SF cinema and a self-consciousness about photographic and other representational or 'imaging' technologies. He writes:

> How might recent cinema contrive to figure its strategic capitulation, through so-called special effects, to a generalized computer technology that threatens to swamp wholesale, even while locally enhancing in the meantime, the motion picture's representational privilege?
>
> Closing in on an answer serves to rehearse an abiding tendency of the genre. Science-fiction cinema, it can be shown, has always taken media as its subject. In particular, the genre often takes such mediation to task for its violations of the real. This directs us to an equally long-standing tradition within film science fiction, exacerbated lately under the reign of the electron: the tendency to take cinema itself back to its roots in the science of photography. Within broad parameters, we can delimit further the photographic object as subject. (Stewart 1999: 226)

Cornea concurs, specifically citing *Minority Report* as a science fiction film that foregrounds photographic or 'imaging' technology as part of the film diegesis. She writes:

> Like *Blade Runner* (dir. Ridley Scott 1982), *Minority Report* was also based upon a
> Philip K. Dick story, and like its predecessor the truth of the photographic image
> is also placed in question in this later film. But here our detective is dealing with
> moving images created by the Precogs, rather than the still frame photographs
> of the replicants. The images are transmitted onto a flat transparent screen and
> Anderton is seen to carry out a kind [of] editing process in order to highlight
> the relevant information. . . . The supposedly real world that Anderton inhabits
> is actually juxtaposed with the literally flat and fluctuating photographic images
> that he handles throughout the course of the film. . . . [I]t is the photographic
> which is 'bracketed off' in *Minority Report*. (Cornea 2007: 261, 262)

This 'bracketing off' is, Cornea suggests, a term used by Melanie Pierson to suggest
the way in which CGI becomes 'a distinguished element within the narrative of the
film', foregrounded in the marketing and publicity of an effects-driven spectacle
film, 'obviously graphic and designed' (Cornea 2007: 258). Cornea suggests that,
in *Minority Report*, it is the photographic image itself which becomes a kind
of special effect, a spectacle placed in contradistinction to the 'real'. Of course,
in the film, the photographs are not indices of the 'real', but of the possible
future murders that Precrime is instituted to prevent. Even the photographs of
young children that John Anderton (Tom Cruise) discovers in the hotel room
at the crucial narrative juncture (which we will return to later in this chapter),
seemingly 'evidence' of wrongdoing, are fake. As we find out at the end of the
film, the 'foresight' of the precogs can itself be fabricated, and falsified. Where,
in *Blade Runner*, the replicants (and Deckard himself) cleave to photographic
images because they represent a concrete 'real' past that compensates for their
radical lack of memory (constitutive of subjectivity in the terms of the film),
in *Minority Report* the photographs are fluid, manipulated, unstable.

Cornea notes that the photographic images aligned with the visions of the
precogs are themselves subject to a particular kind of cinematic technology: the
'squishy lens' (filming through a soft plate which contains liquid) which *precedes*
digital imagining and manipulation. She writes: 'the flexibility of the lens allows
for the peculiar distortion of filmed images, which in the case of *Minority Report*
blurs and fans the outer edges of a central image or creates ripples of movement
across the frame' (Cornea 2007: 261). It is noteworthy that the distortions the
viewer sees in the 'precog' visions are *prior to* digital processing, and are instead
produced by optical or mechanical effects. It is then Anderton (Tom Cruise),
in the remarkable opening sequence of the film, who manipulates the images
digitally. The film begins with a 'report', a report of 'murder', in a minute-long

sequence of dislocated 'squishy lens' shots of a man returning home unexpectedly to find his wife with an adulterous lover, killing them both with scissors. After this sequence of shots, the camera holds on Samantha Morton's blue eye, and then zooms out. When the scene changes to the washed-out, glass-and-chrome office of Precrime, our attention is focused upon the kinetic form of Tom Cruise as he hurries into what seems to be some kind of AV suite. Here, the manipulation of the precogs' images begins. Lester Friedman describes the sequence thus:

> Only after slowing down the rapid images, and then re-arranging them into a seemingly logical narrative configuration of cause and effect, does the government take action. But the apparently precise montages sutured together by Anderton prove inherently ambiguous, a series of actions open to competing interpretations despite their ostensible clarity. (Friedman 2003)

The images that we see at the beginning of the film do not correspond to the structured time–space of Hollywood continuity cinema, and in fact what Anderton does is to reassemble these pieces into something which makes meaning as narrative. His digital manipulations, 'scrubbing the image', effected by the interaction of his data-gloves and a transparent screen upon which (or in which) the images are displayed, are themselves a dense layering of images. The classical music, Schubert's *Unfinished Symphony*, that plays (one presumes) to aid the process of image recombination suggests that not only is Anderton a kind of 'director' or editor of a narrative, but he also resembles the conductor of an orchestra. The interweaving and combination of image-tracks perhaps corresponds to the symphonic organization of orchestral instruments, which without direction and notation would produce *noise*, rather than *music*: sound as informational nullity, resisting decoding, ultimately meaningless. Ironically, Anderton's reassembling of disparate images into causal narrative not only reinstitutes the narrative–time organization of continuity cinema (visually, in the chase sequence which follows and supersedes the montage) but also locates it in *space*: Anderton's 'direction' of the images is oriented towards finding out *where* the murder would take place, rather than when, so it may be prevented.

Minority Report is everywhere suffused with images of seeing. As in *Blade Runner*, the insistent visual rhetoric of the film is introduced by an extreme close-up of an eye. In *Blade Runner*, the explosive bursts of flame from the cityscape are reflected in an unblinking (and unidentified) iris; in *Minority Report*, the camera swiftly zooms out from the eye of the precog Agatha (Samantha Morton). In both, the image suggests that there is a presence watching over the city and the protagonists of the film. In both films, recurrent motifs suggest that these are surveillance societies. While Deckard uses the ESPER machine in *Blade Runner* to 'penetrate' one of the replicants' photographs and reveal their identity, in *Minority Report* retinal scans flash as the fleeing Anderton enters a Gap store or subway train or the Precrime facility, and are used by the mechanical 'spiders' that skitter through an apartment building in the search for Anderton, stopping even love-making couples to check their retinal patterns. The film therefore makes an interesting connection between the kind of surveillance technologies used by the state (in typical dystopian fashion) and those used by the instruments of commodity capitalism. The blurring of the two is also signified by the televisual advertisement for Precrime (all too convincing, it must be admitted) which is interpolated near the beginning of the film. Running through a run-down part of the city, on his way to meet his drug connection, Anderton jogs past a wall-size screen that displays the emotive testimonies of the victims of crime, whose traumatic experiences would have been prevented by Precrime. Spielberg inserts this advert not only into the world of *Minority Report*, but it is also addressed directly to the viewer as part of the diegesis, attesting to its demagogical power.

The 'pusher' that Anderton visits to purchase the drug Clarity (presumably in order to see more clearly) is himself blind, two empty eye sockets revealed beneath his hooded, shadowed face. The film drives home the resonance of this image when the dealer intones, 'In the land of the blind, the one eyed man is king': is partial sight better than no sight at all? Considering that the titles of both short story and text refer to the 'minority report', the dissenting view offered in judicial review and by one of the precogs, partiality or incompleteness of vision is extremely troubling. Throughout the film, sight is distorted, and not just by the 'squishy lens' technology noted earlier. Vision blurred by water is a recurrent visual motif in the film. The precogs float in a quasi-amniotic pool; Anderton loses his son when playing a 'holding-your-breath' game underwater at the crowded public swimming pool; Anderton attempts to hide from the surveillance spiders by immersing himself in a bathtub; and the originary murder that Lamar Burgess commits to provide the impetus towards instituting Precrime, recurrently visioned by the precogs, takes place in water. All of these images indicate distorted vision, blurred vision, the *inability* to see clearly. If, as Lester Friedman notes, Anderton's experience in the swimming pool is an inverted baptism, from which he arises a changed man (seeing differently), then the way that he sees, through grief and loss, is itself distorting. It prevents him from appreciating the ethical problems at work in the Precrime system, that 'innocent' people are 'haloed' and placed in prison; he understands it as an intellectual argument, but it requires further traumatic experiences to change the way he sees the system.

If Anderton, at the beginning of the film, lacks ethical insight and requires the typical dystopian protagonist's trajectory of estrangement (displacement from his place in the system) to be able to see clearly, the idea of *foresight*, the subject as seer (able to predict the future), is also compromised in the film. The future, it is assumed by Precrime operatives, is seen *clearly* by the precogs; however, the existence of minority reports suggests that the future is undetermined, that choice is still a possibility. As Cynthia Weber states, 'previsions are not the same thing as predestination' (Weber 2005: 492). In fact, the very idea of Precrime intervention itself, to forestall a possible future, paradoxically signifies that future time is malleable and undetermined. If it were not, Precrime would be redundant: no matter what they did, the murder would occur. The precogs therefore 'see' a future that never comes into being. What, then, is the status of their 'visions'? Are they completely unreal? The film's narrative works to undo the certainties about Precrime offered in the emotive 'advertisement' for it that I referred to above; the film sets us up to partake of the Precrime ideology before undermining the status of that mode of thinking.

Anderton undergoes a second or even third 'rebirth' or baptism during the film. He arises from the bathtub with different eyes (literally a 'changed man'), having undergone an eye transplant to alter his identity; and he is also captured by Precrime and 'haloed', only to be rescued by his wife in a narrative *non sequitur* in the final section of the film. It is this final transformation, perhaps more a resurrection than a rebirth, that completes his trajectory towards alienation from the system. The change from the Anderton who believes in Precrime, that the future can be and should be forestalled because otherwise murder *will* occur, to the Anderton who believes that human free will or 'choice' renders the future indeterminate, is marked by two phrases repeatedly spoken by the precog Agatha to Anderton: 'Can you see?' and 'You have a choice.' At the beginning of the film, and all the way through until he is 'haloed', Anderton cannot *see*; he believes he is being plotted against, that he is being 'set up', but he cannot penetrate beyond his own assumptions about Precrime and his relationship with Lamar Burgess. Anderton is like the 'murderer' chased at the beginning of the film, who repeats his wife's phrase when confessing, 'I forgot my glasses. . . . You know how blind I am without them.' Anderton is ethically blind, blind to himself and his own motivations, blind to those around him (including his 'lost' wife, one assumes): he needs a change of eyes. He also believes, one assumes, that he does *not* have a choice; once the 'red ball' with his name on it comes down the chute at Precrime, he cannot decide *not* to murder the supposed victim. Agatha's repeated 'You have a choice' signifies, of course, that he does.

It is this moment of choice that is crucial to Philip K. Dick's 'The Minority Report'. There, Anderton has to choose whether to kill General Kaplan, his intended victim, thereby condemning himself while sustaining Precrime; or not to kill Kaplan, remaining 'innocent' of the crime but demolishing Precrime in the process. Anderton arranges to be present at a rally conducted by Kaplan, at which Precrime is to be 'exposed'. 'But there can be no valid knowledge about the future,' says Kaplan. 'As soon as the precognitive information is obtained, *it cancels itself out*. The very act of possessing this data is paradoxical' (Dick 1994: 136). Kaplan has planned for Anderton's presence as a demonstration of the failure of Precrime's principles, as the head of Precrime himself invalidates the report by refusing to murder Kaplan and fulfil the prediction of the crime. However, what Kaplan does not understand is that there is *no* 'minority report' in this narrative (in which one precog delivers a dissenting report: so two precogs 'see' Anderton murdering Kaplan, while one does not). The reports are sequential, out of phase: the first report indicates that Anderton *does* kill Kaplan; in the second, 'seeing' a future where Anderton has seen the first report, there is no murder; the third, the 'true' and final report, is where Anderton does kill Kaplan in order to preserve Precrime. In the film, the moment of moral decision comes in the scene at the hotel room.

This is where the 'plot' against Anderton leads him. He discovers a room in which the photographic evidence of child abduction and probable murder has been arranged, and in which he finds a photograph of his son. This is designed to provoke him to kill the purported kidnapper, and thereby seal a constitutional change to institute Precrime nationally and in perpetuity: even the head of Precrime is subject to its inviolable laws. When Anderton arrives at the hotel room, this, it seems, is the moment of moral choice relocated from the short story by Dick: he must decide whether to kill, sacrificing himself, or not to kill, bringing Precrime down. However, the film fudges and defers this decision. Anderton does not have to choose. He comes to realize that this moment has been set up, but in attempting to arrest the purported 'killer', the man commits suicide, making it seem as though the precogs' vision has been fulfilled. How the film resolves this narrative dilemma, instead of turning on a moral choice, is related to the 'splitting' of Dicks' Anderton into Cruise's Anderton and von Sydow's Burgess. In *Minority Report*, it is Burgess (much closer in age to Dick's character) who is determined to keep Precrime intact, and has in fact murdered Agatha's mother in the past to ensure her continuing functioning as a precog. In a sense, Burgess is Precrime's 'father'. Rather than sacrificing himself, though, he would sacrifice his 'son', John Anderton. The film defers the moment of choice, then disposes of it altogether, by turning to a father–son conflict between Anderton and Burgess, where the 'villain' is the betraying father.

In voiding the moment of choice, crucial to the narrative resolution of the Dick story, Spielberg betrays the generic transformation at work in the adaptation of 'The Minority Report' to the screen. Following the deferred/voided 'moment of choice' is a 30-minute coda, which seems like a different film entirely: Danny Witwer (Colin Farrell), the presumed architect of the plot, is revealed to be the 'good cop' and is then shot and killed by Burgess, who is revealed as the bad father. The film, in fact, itself splits into three distinct parts: the first is the Precrime dystopia, shown in the opening sequences; the second is a chase movie, making full use of Tom Cruise as action star, which can be summed up in the marketing tag line 'Everybody Runs'; the third, the coda, adheres to the conventions of the contemporary Hollywood thriller, where a deceiving father figure is finally confronted by the son. The narrative resolution of the film version of *Minority Report* turns the Dick story on its head: where Dick's Anderton sacrifices himself to maintain Precrime, the revelation of the primacy of 'choice' (free will) to Spielberg's Anderton means that he brings Precrime to an end. The final, sentimental shots of the precogs, themselves released from the prison of their amniotic pool and relocated to an idyllic cottage in the wilderness, are signature Spielberg images. As Cynthia Weber tellingly notes, Agatha 'resembles an infant' throughout the film, and the final shots (played against images of the restored Anderton couple, complete with unborn child) return the film to the typical Spielberg motifs of the child, and of childhood innocence restored (Weber 2005: 494). The change between source text and screen text irrevocably relocates the sensibility of the film: into Spielberg territory.

Minority Report was released in 2002. Cynthia Weber's article 'Securitising the Unconscious' notes the film's 'eerie allegory of the Bush Doctrine of Preemption', which holds that it is politically, legally and morally defensible for the United States to use force against a perceived foreign foe in order to prevent future harm against itself, even though that perceived foreign foe has not yet attacked the United States. (Weber 2005: 482, 483)

The film's release in the United States, in June 2002, followed just weeks after President George W. Bush announced this doctrine in the wake of 9/11. Of course, this is 'eerie' coincidence, as the film would have been in production for years before the 9/11 attacks, but Weber does suggest that the film keys into a debate about security that was current at the time. *Minority Report*, she argues, critiques the structures of thought (or 'moral geographies') that underpin the Bush Doctrine, in the shift from a judicial system or foreign policy which responds to *actions* to one which pre-emptively responds to presumed *intentions*. Although she does not mention it, the dystopian text that informs *Minority Report* here is Orwell's *Nineteen Eighty-Four*: Burgess, himself a splicing of Big Brother and O'Brien, oversees a system that punishes 'thoughtcrime' rather than criminal acts. The sentimentality that informs the final images of *Minority Report* are, as I wrote above, an index of 'Spielberg territory'; but it must also be noted that this territory, or 'moral geography' in Weber's terms, is unmistakeably a liberal one. The film bespeaks an anxiety about the erosion of civil liberties, the encroaching domination of surveillance technologies and fears of a 'police state' that have informed the left-liberal politics of dystopian fictions since the mid-twentieth century.

9

Annihilations

In this chapter, we will consider the relation between subjectivity and techno-logy, and in particular forms of masculinity inhabited by technical subjects in science fiction narratives (either the astronauts and scientists of space exploration films, or the 'androids' of the *Alien* films and *Blade Runner* (1982)). In particular, we will see how these films tend to stage a masculinity subject that, while encased within repressive technocratic structures (of ship-board routine, or the product of institutional training), seeks an ecstatic annihilation as a means by which to access some kind of transcendent experience, whether divine or represented by a radical alterity (or occasionally both). While the 'death drive' inhabited by these technocratic masculine subjects impels them towards annihilation (as we saw in Chapters 2 and 3), the very technicity of the artificial subjects of science fiction itself indicates a fundamental absence or lack which they seek to fill. Annihilation becomes a transcendent plentitude, symbolized by the knowledge (scientific and spiritual) that they come to at the point of dissolution.

Where, as we will see in Chapter 11, Orpheus has been the mythic figure whose journey for redemption has patterned several film texts which can be generally categorized as 'fantasy' or 'the fantastic', for many of the films we will encounter in this chapter, the key figure is Prometheus. We will investigate Bernard Stiegler's theoretical analysis of the Prometheus myth shortly, but here I wish to turn to the Freudian Marxist thinker Herbert Marcuse, whose *Eros and Civilization* (1987) posits Orpheus and Prometheus as two 'culture heroes' who embody polar opposite relations with regard to work, repression and what Freud called the 'reality principle' (the psychological work of repression of instinctual drives towards pleasure and satisfaction which is the motive force towards production, culture and 'civilization' itself). Marcuse writes:

> Orpheus is the archetype of the poet as *liberator* and *creator*: he establishes a
> higher order in the world – an order without repression. In his person, art,

freedom, and culture are eternally combined. He is the poet of redemption, the god who brings peace and salvation by pacifying man and nature, not through force but through song (Marcuse 1987: 170)

Prometheus, on the other hand, is 'the rebel who creates culture at the price of pain. He symbolizes productiveness, the unceasing effort to master life; but in his productivity, blessing and curse, progress and toil are inextricably intertwined' (Marcuse 1987: 161). Prometheus is associated with technology, having given fire to human beings (as we shall see, as a means by which to compensate them for their lack of other qualities), but he is also a figure who endures eternal pain, chained by the gods while vultures pick at his liver. Work, technology and suffering therefore combine in him to make, for Marcuse, an emblematic figure of the products and costs of repression.

That Ridley Scott titled his prequel to the *Alien* movies *Prometheus* (2013) is somewhat provocative in this light, particularly as that film proposes the development of the human being not as an evolutionary process, but as the consequence of intervention by an alien species of 'Engineers'. Just as in Stanley Kubrick's *2001: A Space Odyssey* (1968), *Prometheus* presents humans as themselves technical beings, products of work and science rather than 'natural' biological processes. The difference, therefore, between *2001*'s HAL 9000 computer and the astronauts who accompany him to Jupiter, or *Prometheus*'s David (Michael Fassbender), an android crew-member of the ship searching for the Engineers (and thereby the 'secret of life') and his human counterparts, is put into question. The androids, in particular, look human; the question of difference, in what these technical subjects might desire, is crucial to both film texts.

The sublime

In some senses, just like their human counterparts, as well as those viewers who are watching the films (especially on the cinematic screen), what these technical subjects desire is an experience of something transcendent, of the Sublime. As Mark Bould acknowledges, the history of technological 'seeing' and recording of the material world has been bound up with its supposed capacity to see *beyond* the material. 'This kind of logic', he writes, 'in which technological enhancement enables vision to extend so deeply into the world that it starts to perceive something beyond, something sublime towards which the subject is drawn and from which the subject also recoils . . . recurs in sf' (Bould 2012: 80). Scott Bukatman, in *Matters of Gravity* (2003), goes further to suggest that 'optical effects sequences generate revelation through kinetic exploration' (Bukatman 2003: 118) and that in the imaging technologies of contemporary spectacular science fiction, 'technology becomes a new source for exaggerated sensual and sensory pleasures' (Bukatman 2003: 130). The consequence of such a 'vertiginous sense of displacement and defamiliarization' (i.e., 'when it works, science fiction film's most significant accomplishment') is something more challenging for the subject (Bukatman 2003: 116). He argues that what connects the effects (and affect) of both experimental cinema and science fiction is

> a phenomenological excess that alludes to a reality beyond the ordinary – 'a world of endless, enchanting, metamorphosis'. This is very similar to Samuel Delany's conception of the paraspace in science fiction – a materially constituted other space, a field of heightened rhetorical performance where conflicts of the real world are played out, and in which the death of the subject (as we generally know and love it) is figured. Paraspaces redefine and extend the realms of human experience and definition, obliterating any vision of fixed space, subjectivity, or language as new, radically mutating, ontologies emerge. (Bukatman 2003: 119)

Brooks Landon, in his 1992 text *The Aesthetics of Ambivalence*, was among the first to rethink special effects as formal elements which define science fiction (SF) film as inherently spectacular, in that the 'technological wonder' of the effects sequences become an 'attraction' in itself. Therefore, rather than lamenting the way in which 'special effects have overshadowed or usurped narrative elements', as previous critics might have done, Landon suggests that SF film returns cinema to its oldest representational and formal strategies, the 'cinema of attractions' identified by the film historian and theorist Tom Gunning (Landon 1992: 72–4). Landon goes on to suggest that this emphasis on *spectacle*, on wonder, has been inherited by the SF film, and particularly in SF films' special effects sequences. Christine Cornea, in *Science Fiction Cinema* (2007), has complicated this critical manoeuvre in suggesting that while 'it seemed to many critics that the form and style of Gunning's "cinema of attractions" had re-emerged to dominate popular cinema in the post-classical era', it is necessary to differentiate the special effects in the SF films of the 1960s and 1970s (especially Kubrick's *2001: A Space Odyssey*), which demanded a meditative response, to the kind of blockbuster spectacle films that followed Lucas's *Star Wars* (1977) (Cornea 2007: 248–50). In this chapter, it is the mode of *2001: A Space Odyssey*, SF's potential for the representation of the sublime and transcendent, that will be crucial, particularly in considering narratives which offer the masculine subject the opportunity to transcend bodily limits and to become something else; as Bukatman argued, 'obliterating any vision of fixed space, subjectivity' (Bukatman 2003: 119).

My concern in this chapter is the desire for transcendence in the masculine subject circumscribed by technocratic institutions, which can be found in SF texts such as *Altered States* (1980), *2001: A Space Odyssey* (1968) and *Solaris* (1973/2002). The male scientists and astronauts I am concerned with in this chapter, the locus of a desire for transcendence of the technocratic institutions that are constitutive of their subjectivity, suffer from what Bernard Stigler has theorized as the 'defaut d'origine'. In *Technics and Time I: The Fault of Epimetheus* (1998), Stiegler takes Jacques Derrida's concept of the 'supplement' to analyse the relation between the human and the technical through a reading of the myth of Prometheus. In this myth, Prometheus and his brother Epimetheus are given the task of allotting different powers or attributes to mortal species by the Gods. Epimetheus persuades Prometheus to let him do the job; unfortunately so, Epimetheus distributes all the attributes among the animals and forgets to leave anything for human beings.

Prometheus is therefore forced to steal skill in the arts, and fire, to compensate human beings for this originary lack. For this, of course, he is punished. Stiegler reads this myth as a founding discourse of the relation between the natural and the technical, and more specifically between 'man' and his tools. It also points towards what Stiegler calls '*le défaut d'origine*' with regard to the human subject: an originary fault [*défaut*] or lack is compensated for by Prometheus's gift, but exposes the foundational state of human subjectivity as one of a radical lack, and, in fact, the defining characteristic of the human is a lack of characteristics: 'there will have been nothing at the origin but the fault, a fault that is nothing but the de-fault of origin or the origin as de-fault' (Stiegler 1998: 188). Stiegler goes on to posit the idea that instead of implying a hierarchy of precession or anteriority between the human and technics, that *technē* is a form of prosthesis to a 'natural' origin, the myth of Epimetheus signifies the 'originary technicity' of the human:

> Man invents, discovers, finds (*eurisko*), imagines (*mēkhanē*), and realizes what he imagines: prostheses, expedients. A pros-thesis is what is placed in front, that is, what is outside, outside what it is placed in front of. However, if what is outside constitutes the very being of what is lies outside of, then this being is *outside itself*. The being of humankind is to be outside itself. In order to make

up for the fault of Epimetheus, Prometheus gives humans the present of putting them outside themselves. (Stiegler 1998: 193)

Rather than being a compensatory addition to the human, the *defaut d'origine* suggests that technics are the necessary and constitutive supplement to the 'natural' and 'human' at their very point of origin. In the words of Arthur Bradley, 'technology is a supplement which exposes an originary *lack* within what should be the integrity or plenitude of the human being' (Bradley 2006: 78). Bowman and Poole in *2001: A Space Odyssey* in particular are characterized by a lack of characteristics. Why is it that the scientist, the astronaut, the technocrat, is the locus for the desire for transcendence in these texts? Bowman and Poole, Kris Kelvin in *Solaris*, Dr Weir in *Event Horizon* (1997), all inhabit a logical/rational worldview that dissolves, ultimately, into mysticism because of a transgressive desire for 'dangerous' knowledge. The rationality that is the foundation for their subjectivity is ruptured by their grasp on the radical incompleteness of this project: that the numinous, the Other, 'beckons' from the margins indicates the need to abandon the verities of scientific givens and 'risk' all in search of knowledge that will undo all rational paradigms – and complete the self that is constituted by an originary 'lack'.

This points towards a connection between the desire for transcendence and the desire for the dissolution of the subject that, according to Jonathan Dollimore, are intertwined in the long history of Western metaphysics. Dollimore, in *Death, Desire and Loss in Western Culture* (1998), suggests that, 'Time and again the representation of immortality [in Western metaphysics] is realized in the language of oblivion; transcendence and eternity promise the dissolution of identity, the cessation of desire, the still point of the turning world' (1998: 10). Dollimore sees Western metaphysics as being shot through with the following ideas: Individual identity is characterized as lack; Desire unbinds selfhood; there is a mutual implication of the Self and Other, Being and Nothingness; and that there is a prevalence of conceptions of a 'death drive' or 'nirvana principle', from Schopenhauer through Freud to Marcuse, which is a state of quiescence that is not just the end of desire, but also the end of lack. Desire's implication in lack also has a very long history; Dollimore references the Greek myth of human origin, that the original 'men' were made up of three sexes: hermaphrodite, male and female. The Gods, fearing these 'men' as rivals, split them in half. The principle of the immortality of the soul means that through human history, each split subject seeks its 'other' to reunify and complete the self. Even the 'whole' individual is then radically incomplete.

The 'death drive' is a recurrent motif in the group of texts I am analysing in this chapter. In both versions of *Solaris*, the psychiatrist Kelvin struggles to come to terms with the loss of his wife, who has committed suicide, and is himself no longer truly 'alive'; in *2001: A Space Odyssey*, Poole and Bowman are technocratic automatons, but even Bowman goes out in a pod to investigate the monolith; in *Event Horizon*, Weir's wife also commits suicide, and the doctor seeks the (ultimately evil) transcendent; in *Sunshine* (2008), the whole mission to save Earth is a kind of suicide mission (several of the crew come into willed too-close encounters with the sun's incandescence), and in the final delivery of the payload to restart the sun's nuclear fusion, the physicist smilingly embraces nirvana (literally, with arms outstretched); as we saw in Chapter 8, in *Minority Report*, John Anderson has lost a son (kidnapped) and wife (divorced), and now exhibits quasi-suicidal tendencies such as the consumption of the drug 'Clarity'; and as we will see in Chapter 12, in *Hannibal Rising*, to go back to the last of the Lecter texts (so far), the death of Lecter's little sister Mischa leads to a kind of death drive and Lecter only achieves a kind of peace at the end of *Hannibal* through the symbolic replacement of Mischa by Clarice Starling. In *Altered States* (1980), a film which narrates the transgressive experiments of Dr Jessup (William Hurt), which ultimately make him 'regress' into a primitive hominid form, Jessup clearly wants to find the pre-human (or pre-lapsarian, perhaps) state of transcendent insight patterned upon ecstatic religious visions. His 'regression' to apehood is a dissolution of human subjectivity (as biology) as much as it is a version of the degenerationist concepts that underpin Robert Louis Stevenson's Dr Jekyll and Mr Hyde, which otherwise are clearly very influential on Russell's film.

There are key structural similarities which connect these films. In each, first, a male protagonist is located in a technocratic institution: on board a spacecraft, in *2001: A Space Odyssey, Sunshine, Event Horizon* and *Solaris*; as part of a military/scientific experiment in *Stargate* (1994), as a researcher at a university in *Altered States*. (In *Contact* (1997), which will be examined in more detail in the next chapter, it is a female researcher in a scientific institution scanning for signs of extraterrestrial life; in *Gravity* (2013), a female astronaut is the survivor of a catastrophic orbital accident and must attempt to traverse space to find a way 'home' to Earth.) Secondly, this protagonist bears the traces of some kind of wounding or dysfunction: a wife who committed suicide in *Solaris* and *Event Horizon*, a 'nerdy' dislocation from family or society in *Altered States* and *Stargate*; this leads to a personal or private set of motivations and desires for which the institutional environment becomes but a vehicle or alibi. Thirdly, the 'scientific' project is implicitly (*2001: A Space Odyssey, Sunshine*) or explicitly (*Solaris, Event Horizon, Stargate, Altered States*) connected to the search for some kind of transcendent alterity. Here the 'alien' is often of such unknowable power that it assumes the lineaments of Godhead (*Solaris, 2001: A Space Odyssey*) or the diabolic (*Event Horizon, Stargate*). Fourthly, the male protagonist uses his willed proximity to radical alterity to dissolve, and thereby complete, the self. Either this project is successful and the protagonist enters some kind of altered state (*2001, Solaris, Mission to Mars, Sunshine*), returns having undergone a form of catharsis (*Altered States, Stargate*), or, if Enlightenment subjectivity is ruptured but transcendence is not achieved, what remains is insane (Weir in *Event Horizon*, Pinbacker in *Sunshine*).

It is often space travel that signifies the encasing rational discourses of Enlightenment, science and capital. These spacecraft, in terms of set design, tend to fall into two modes: *2001: A Space Odyssey* and *Gravity* are what I have called elsewhere 'NASA' fictions, the *mise-en-scène* of white interiors and environment suits recalling Apollo imagery in particular, or, following a related (but not entirely contiguous) film, *Alien* (1979), an industrial and ominous insistence on steel, iron and aluminium: *Solaris* (2002), *Sunshine* (2008), *Event Horizon* (1997). (*Altered States* (1980) could be typified as a 'real world' variant of this form of *mise-en-scène*, particularly in the initial shots of William Hurt suspended in a giant copper sensory-deprivation cylinder that looks like a domestic hot water tank.) Connecting both visual modes is a sense of physical constriction: the human being is encased not only within spaceship, environment suit and/ or tank, but also the composition of the *mise-en-scène* frames with human body within doorways, narrow corridors, communal spaces where the ceiling bears down upon the crew like a coffin lid. The human subject becomes an adjunct of the technology that is meant to serve them; the fate of *2001*'s HAL is only the most overt sign of the dominance of technology over these human subjects.

There are also repeated visual motifs in these films which indicate the connection between the willed dissolution of the subject and an explicitly Christian iconography. The crucial gesture appears in Soderbergh's *Solaris* (2002) when the space station Prometheus is about to enter the ionosphere of the planet Solaris. Kelvin has opted not to return to Earth, but to stay to uncover the mystery of the 'visitors' to the space station's crew, Solaris-engendered manifestations of human loss or desire: in Kelvin's case, his wife. As Kelvin (George Clooney) lies prostrated on the corridor floor, the light and noise of the station's disintegration overwhelming him, a young boy appears. It is another visitor, the 'son' of Kelvin's friend Gibarian who had committed suicide while on the station. ('It seemed like a good idea at the time', Gibarian tells Kelvin in a (possibly waking) dream earlier in the film.) The boy, standing above the prone man, reaches out his hand: Kelvin reaches up. The pose is held for a moment, whereupon the boy grasps Kelvin's hand, and the man 'enters' Solaris. In *2001: A Space Odyssey*, the gesture appears in the strange seeming-coda of the film, when Bowman (Keir Dullea) is translated to a room with an illuminated floor and Regency furnishings, having passed through the Stargate. He encounters rapidly ageing versions of himself, then is reduced (as a very ancient man) to laying in the double bed, a version of the monolith present at his feet. As 'Also Sprach Zarathustra' plays upon the soundtrack, he reaches out with his arm towards the monolith, one finger extended. Finally, in *Altered States*, in the climactic scene in the corridor where Jessup fights his transcendence/regression (while his wife, Blair Brown, is encased in some kind of sfx magma-suit), the two reach out for each other, and their salvation is dependent upon the touching of their hands.

The iconography at work here is obvious: it is Michaelangelo's fresco on the ceiling of the Sistine chapel, God's finger approaching that of the prostrated Adam in a moment of Creation. Here, the moment of transcendence is typed in cosmic SF terms (the alien planet Solaris, the monolith, the 'Absolute' approached by Jessup's experiments), but the insistence of the Christian tradition is clear. Why do we find these images at this point? Is it that the most powerful visual register available for SF filmmakers wanting to invoke a radically transcendent alterity is Christian iconography? In the case of Soderbergh's *Solaris*, this visual gesture is far more than throwaway or just a kind of shorthand: the film itself negotiates what we take as human subjectivity with that of the 'visitors', non-original beings engendered from the memories, emotions and desires of the humans aboard the space station. When Kelvin's visitor wife (the second such: Kelvin 'sent away' the first in an escape pod in a (self-)lacerating, callous and even quasi-murderous reflex of grief) meditates upon her relationship to her creator – Solaris – as one of radical unknowability, the film overtly opens up a space for us to read the analogy between her condition and Kelvin's. 'It created me, yet I can't communicate with it', Rheya says. Solaris is an analogue of God, but the final moments – when Kelvin is restored to his wife, categories of life and death don't matter any more, and all is forgiven – suggest that Kelvin has entered a transcendent realm so like Heaven that it is difficult to argue that Solaris is *not* an incarnation of the divine, and the state Kelvin enters is *not* the Hereafter.

The narrative of Soderbergh's *Solaris* is then one of redemption, the healing of the wounded subjectivity of the rational male protagonist through the acceptance of the 'reality' of the numinous Other, an alterity so radical that it exceeds the bounds of rational discourse and may only be approached through less material impulses as faith and love. The translation to the realm of the 'unknown' is, in *Solaris*, not a matter of spectacle effects (just as Kelvin's journey from Earth to the space station is almost entirely elided) but of an editing sleight of hand that simply reveals a state of being as 'concrete' as the one Kelvin left behind on Earth. (Indeed, it even looks like his apartment, but with minor differences – such as when he slices open his thumb while chopping a courgette, it heals immediately.) This is most unlike other films I have considered here. In *2001: A Space Odyssey* and *Altered States*, spectacle sequences are deployed to signify to the viewer access to otherness: 'Beyond the Infinite' or the realm of 'the Absolute'. In *2001: A Space Odyssey*, the translation is first effected by an extended SlitScan sequence (lights emerge in patterns towards the viewer to give the impression of a corridor or tunnel). These are followed by effects which seem like embryonic sacs spurting their contents across a dark universe/womb, clearly signifying the birth of galaxies/stars/individual beings. In *Altered States*, in the scene where Jessup's flotation-tank experiments result in the release of such energies that a kind of cosmic whirlpool is formed on the floor, a very similar embryonic imagery is used. The significance is clear. *2001: A Space Odyssey* deploys a quasi-evolutionary rhetoric which, at the end of the film, sees Bowman evolve into the 'Star Child' just as the hominids at the beginning of the film (the 'Dawn of Man') had evolved into *Homo sapiens*. (Revealingly, of course, this is effected by the hominid accession into technology – the animal bone is used as a tool. In *2001: A Space Odyssey*, there is an overt emphasis on the '*défaut d'origine*' and its correlative, what Stiegler calls 'originary technicity'.)

In *Altered States*, it is the inherited Gothic motif of degeneration (reverse evolution) which haunts the film. In Jessup's first 'regression', the hominid escapes from the tank, room and institution, to roam the streets and eventually end up killing an animal in Boston Zoo for its dinner. In the scene mentioned above, the hominid form is itself transcended as Jessup enters a primordial space where his body and consciousness are in a state of radical flux. This, unlike the end of *Solaris*, however, is no access to Heaven. More nearly, it is the reverse. Although Jessup's wife Emily ultimately 'births' him from the cosmic chaos that his experiments have induced, the experience of the transgressive experimenter is here catastrophic to a sense of integral subjectivity: in embracing the 'Absolute', Jessup discovers that 'the final truth of all things is that there is no final truth' and the Sublimity he endured is not the signature of the divine, but the knowledge that the conditions of the start of life (creation) is a terrifying 'Nothingness'. *Altered States* only finds the dissolution of the subject at the 'Absolute', the point of creation of life; anterior to it is, literally, nothing. For Jessup, then, the dissolution of the subject proves not to be pleasurable, but hellish, despite the wonderful image earlier in the film of Jessup and Emily, transformed into sand sculptures in Jessup's vision, carved by wind into nothingness, non-being.

The diabolic connotations of the dissolving of subjectivity are made most explicit in *Event Horizon* (1997). The banality of this film's conception shouldn't mask its indebtedness to the very same discursive structures I have outlined so far, nor the fact that its visions of the transcendent are hellish rather than divine. In this film, the ship *Event Horizon* is fitted with a 'gravity drive', a device created by one Dr Weir (Sam Neill) that 'folds space' and enables ftl-style interstellar travel. When operated, the ship disappears, only to return some years later without its crew. Weir is part of a salvage team sent to investigate: they find a ghost ship, haunted by the 'evil' embodied in a 'realm of pure chaos' that the ship has encountered. In effect, Weir is a transgressive experimenter in the classic mould, whose intended technology goes sinisterly awry and here, blows a hole in the fabric of the universe. As *Event Horizon* is an SF/horror hybrid, the salvage crew die in a series of gruesome tableaux (the medic played by Jason Isaacs is crucified in his ER). What most clearly reveals the banality of the imagination at work on the film is the footage decoded from the ship's voyage into chaos: the crew are shown in a sequence of flashed images in poses of torture, eye gouging cannibalism, vomiting blood in a kind of delirious or nauseous helter-skelter, the editing of this 'found' video denoting its 'evil' (as chaos). Neill himself enters the 'gravity drive', but returns a flayed man, the *Event Horizon*'s pilot/prophet. He doesn't last long. *Event Horizon* is interesting because of its reliance upon the most banal, stereotyped imagery in representing diabolic otherness. As the inverse of *Solaris* or *2001: A Space Odyssey*, this banality signifies the inescapability of religious iconography in the ways in which SF films have tried to (but fail to) imagine the divine, a state of alterity or transcendence. The price of entry, though, is still the dissolution of the self.

Sunshine is a contemporary film in the same mode. It marries the scientific, rational teamwork of the technocratic institution with the metaphysical speculations of transcendental SF; however, when the crew of the ship divert to investigate the hulk of the first mission to 'restart the Sun', in orbit around

Mercury, they inadvertently allow the insane Captain Pinbacker (Mark Strong) aboard, who sets about sabotaging the ship (as he had done the first ship). *Sunshine* then becomes a reprise of *Event Horizon* as Pinbacker sets about sabotaging the mission and killing the ship's crew. Narrative incoherency in *Sunshine* increases under the influence of this unlooked-for generic turn until the very end of the film, when the nuclear physicist Capa (Cillian Murphy) manages to deliver the payload. Here, on the surface of the sun, time and space become smeared together, and the film redeems itself in replacing *unintentional* incoherency with *intentional* incoherency. These final few minutes of the film are by far the most striking and return the film to the claustrophobic intensity of its opening act. As the payload moves towards the surface of the sun, space and time become fragmented. The experience of this fragmentation is achieved through *mise-en-scène* and particularly through editing. Some shots become smeared, the images made unclear through step-printing and other optical effects (not always in post-production, through CGI: Pinbacker's blurry, unstable image throughout the second half of the film was produced by special camera lenses rather than special effects work). Shots seem to end half way through, or are caught in freeze-frame; the horizontal plane becomes vertical and vice versa, the characters sliding down the surface they had been standing on; distance is elongated or collapsed, the actors appearing in long shot or close-up in consecutive shots. Continuity, in other words, is successfully abandoned at this point. This sequence is a kind of cinematic *tour-de-force*, a near-hallucinatory rush towards the end point (detonation), and then the cinematic otherness finally gives way to a kind of transcendent calm. As Capa detonates the device, the surface of the sun appears like a wall of plasmatic fire: Cillian Murphy stands, beatific, his hands open and arms held in embrace of the moment of transcendence/transfiguration/death. The (suicide/sacrifice) mission is successful, but the doubled figures at the end (diabolic Pinbacker/transcendent Capa), and the moment of transfiguration at the end (placing the film clearly in the metaphysical territory of *2001*'s Stargate sequence) ultimately move the narrative away back towards transcendence.

Technicity and the artificial subject

In *Alien* (1979), the android is Ash, played by Ian Holm as the 'science officer' (shades of Spock) who, as the film nears its climax, is revealed to be a totally amoral agent of the Company, pursuing the delivery of the alien species and mindful of the necessity that all 'other priorities' (the survival of the human crew, for instance) have been 'rescinded'. It is Ash who countermands Ripley (Sigourney Weaver) and allows the 'impregnated' Kane (John Hurt) back onto the ship, in direct contravention of protocol; it is Ash who researches the creature and declares it to be 'perfect' in its hostility. That Ash is an android is a shocking revelation in *Alien*: he is presumed by all to be human (even if a Company man). The scene where Ash's true otherness is revealed is when Ripley threatens to blow up the ship after the death of Captain Dallas: he attacks her physically, then attempts to choke her by inserting a rolled-up pornographic magazine down her throat, in an act which is at once a recapitulation of what the face-hugger does to Kane, and a symbolic oral rape. As the two struggle, Parker (Yaphet Kotto) tries to stop the violation, eventually smashing the back of Ash's head with a gas cylinder, decapitating him. Ash oozes white liquid, an echo of the white milk he drinks but also a sign of his otherness, his abjection: his internal structure is non-human, repellant. 'Ash is a God-damned robot', shouts Parker, though this is a word that (to me) signifies a mechanical entity, and a word that recurs in *Prometheus*; while Ash differs from the flesh-and-blood replicants of *Blade Runner*, he is clearly a fleshly rather than metallic being, even if that flesh is other and disgusting.

In 'The Virginity of Astronauts', Vivian Sobchack writes about the sexlessness of SF. This has a double dynamic. Women and sex are 'denied all but a ghostly presence in the genre . . . as if such a potent semiotic relation poses a threat to the cool reason and male camaraderie necessary to the conquest of space, the defeat of mutant monsters and alien invasions, and the corporate development and exploitation of science and technology' (Sobchack 1990: 103); at the same time, the 'male heroes who dominate almost all science fiction films are remarkably asexual . . . about as libidinally interesting as a Ken doll' (Sobchack 1990: 107). Sobchack reads *Alien* as a text that erases gender in the figure of Ripley, 'not marked as either woman or sexual' until the very end of the film, when in a 'disturbing and horrific' sequence Ripley believes herself to have escaped the alien threat when boarding the 'lifeboat' and undresses, down to skimpy pants and t-shirt, before realizing the alien is also on board. I have always found this scene deeply uncomfortable and seemingly out of keeping with the rest of the film in exposing Weaver's body to the camera's gaze, but the logic of presenting *the body of the mother* at this point in inescapable, particularly as a means by which to reassert normative human reproductive biology in the face of the monstrous reproduction (Kane's 'chest-burster', the 'rape' of Kane and Lambert) found elsewhere in the film. Sobchack argues that Ripley 'exchanges one kind of power for another, her sudden vulnerability at the narrative level belied by her sudden sexual potency as a visual representation on the screen' (Sobchack 1990: 106). In becoming a woman at this point, Sobchack states, Ripley becomes a victim; but she also becomes 'an irrational, potent, sexual object – a woman, the truly threatening alien generally repressed by the male-conceived and dominated genre' (Sobchack 1990: 107). In Sobchack's Freudian reading, the film here tips its hand: the symbolic relation between the abject otherness of the *body of the alien* and the abject otherness of the *body of the woman* is revealed. (Barbara Creed has persuasively investigated the film in Kristevan terms in a number of well-known articles.) I'd like to add to this reading; if Ripley is rendered sexless or genderless by costume choices, the way the character is written and the sexist and homosocial environment of the *Nostromo*, then there is also an uncoupling of gender/sexual biology and assumptions about power and victimhood: Kane's *male body* is the first victim of rape. The most significant markers of difference in *Alien* are not between male and female human bodies, but between that of the human and that of the android. *Alien*'s Ash and *Prometheus*'s David are both agents who abet the impregnation of human bodies by alien embryos; but they do not experiment upon themselves. Unlike the human body (male or female), the android body *is not a womb*.

The android, then, is the emblem of what Sobchack identifies as the sexless techno-body of the astronaut, the embodiment of the libidinal economy of the genre: 'science fiction denies human eroticism and libido a traditional narrative expression and representation' (Sobchack 1990: 103). It's interesting, therefore, that in her article, Sobchack analyses Ripley, but not Ash: the android's body is itself repressed, even in Barbara Creed's essays, where Ash is mentioned only in passing (for his eulogy for the alien's purity and perfection). Ash's body is a third term that disrupts gender binaries in terms of reading *Alien*, aligned neither with the terrifying potency of the alien nor with the reproductive vulnerability of the human, even if Ash acts to sacrifice the human crew to ensure the predator's survival. Ash seems to signify an in-human and obscene logic that takes no compass bearings from human ethics; indeed, the alien's very absence of 'conscience, remorse or delusions of morality' is something that Ash confesses he admires. When Ash, with the blackest irony, offers the remaining crew his 'sympathies' in their fight against the perfect killing machine, Parker demands that they 'pull the plug', and returns to incinerate Ash's decapitated head. This faked inhabitation of human emotion is, for Parker, even more obscene than the physical fact of Ash's bodily abjection, and he attempts to erase both with fire.

Like HAL in *2001: A Space Odyssey*, then, Ash seems to occupy a position of otherness-to-humanity that is threatening and destructive, because he operates according to the dictates of a logic that bears no signature of human emotion or sympathy. Like HAL, too, though, to see Ash as simply a version of *The Terminator*'s Skynet or *The Matrix*'s machines, implacably hostile non-human 'machine' entities bent on the destruction of the human race, denies the possibility of desire, libido, want, even subjectivity itself. For Ash, a (dangerous) libido is hinted at in the sexualized attack upon Ripley. It is impossible to ask the question 'what does he want?' of Sobchack's astronaut, as libido is repressed to an extent that evacuates desire: Is the same true of the android? What does Ash *want*?

One answer is, of course, that he only wants what the Company wants: the return of the alien to the Company's R&D division. Desire and agency are thereby external(ized), introjected into Ash as a set of commands. Ash would be no more than a marionette, operated from a distance. Little wonder, then, that Parker calls him a 'robot'. But we *might* wonder that the crew had no suspicion that Ash was not human before Parker decapitates him. Either his own masquerade as human is near-perfect, or the other crew members also occupy the same sexless condition of Sobchack's astronaut, and so cannot tell the difference. In terms of the dynamic between the characters in *Alien*, I don't think this is true: there is clearly some kind of relationship between Dallas and Ripley, and Lambert is the ongoing recipient of crude innuendo by Brett and Parker throughout the early part of the film. Ash might seem uptight and buttoned-up, but no more so than Ripley: they wear similar jump-suits at one point in the film. If Ripley is returned to the economy of libido at the end of the film, indexed by her nakedness, does Ash remain outside desire? One thing that Ash does not want *is to be human*; *Alien* does not trade on the Pinocchio trope (unlike *AI*, or *Star Trek: TNG*'s Data). This certainly marks a difference in conception between Ash and *Prometheus*'s David, and also a difference to *Blade Runner*'s replicants: Ash has no need to meet his maker, to demand 'more life, father' (or 'fucker', depending on which version of *Blade Runner* you're watching). Ash seems to accept his fate while also accepting the deaths of his crew-mates. His 'evil' is that of an absolute empathic blankness.

The excellent Lance Henriksen plays Bishop in James Cameron's noisy *Aliens* (1986), and was seen at the time as a revision of the android figure, almost an apology for Ash. Ripley is deeply suspicious of Bishop throughout *Aliens*, but he is ultimately revealed to be a redemptive and heroic figure. In the 'knife trick' scene, Henriksen puts his hand over that of the 'grunt' Hudson (Bill Paxton) and whirrs a combat knife between their fingers: 'trust me', he says to Hudson. During the course of the film, Ripley does indeed come to trust Bishop, though she is antagonistic for much of the film, and on first realizing Bishop is an 'artificial person' (his preferred term) had threatened him and told him to stay away from her. That Bishop insists upon self-definition, not as robot but as 'artificial person', indicates a subjectivity that is denied to *Alien*'s Ash, and this subjectivity is an index of the android's redemption in the figure of Bishop. At the climax of the film, Bishop is himself violated by a spear-like appendage of the alien 'mother' and then torn in half, but his dismembered, abjected body carries on heroically until it is itself saved by Ripley. Henriksen makes a small appearance in *Alien 3* (1992), which otherwise concentrates upon the dynamic of the female body within a strictly homosocial environment; in Jeunet's *Alien Resurrection* (1997), however, one of the cast members is again revealed to be an android, but again, in a revision of the malign role of Ash, one who is helpful to the human survivors, and female, played by Winona Ryder.

The long-awaited 'prequel' to *Alien*, *Prometheus*, was released in 2013. The opening minutes of *Prometheus* feature David (Michael Fassbender) roaming the ship *Prometheus* while his human colleagues remain in stasis. The shots of him cycling the spaces of the ship (and shooting hoops while he did so), or watching *Lawrence of Arabia* (1962), evoke the one- or two-hander scenarios of classic 'serious' space fiction: *2001: A Space Odyssey*, inevitably, with Bowman and Poole running around the circumference of their living quarters on the *Discovery*, or Sam Rockwell's tics and habits in *Moon* (2009), or the rather less calm demeanour of Bruce Dern as the ecologist (and murderer) Freeman Lowell in the geodesic domes of *Silent Running* (1971). David's imitation of Peter O'Toole as T. E. Lawrence is at once touching and disquieting, because it bespeaks a kind of yearning for subjectivity on David's part (a performance that, like Ash's, may be indistinguishable from human) and also a callow narcissism: the shot of David brushing his hair while watching O'Toole could be used to illustrate Laura Mulvey's Lacanian arguments about the cinematic apparatus and the spectator's mis-recognition of the ideal image of the subject. Fassbender's appearance not only imitates O'Toole; but he is also significantly named David, and resembles the ill-fated alien of Roeg's *The Man Who Fell To Earth* (1975), Thomas Jerome Newton (David Bowie). Bowie's portrayal of Newton, whose weakness is all-too-human (addiction an index of his true humanity, despite the fact that he comes from another world) and his slow-motion betrayal of himself, his family and his homeworld renders him a pathetic figure by the end of the narrative, clearly stands behind the rather uncannily stylish David. Newton's *alien*ation is expressed most deeply in his succumbing to the temptations of human vice (especially alcohol); this blurring of the divide between human and alien, the 'man who fell' offered as the focus of sympathetic identification and pathos, suggests a revision of the potentialities of the android as narrative focus. David is the emotional 'hero' of *Prometheus*, but one whose agency is consistently repressed in the narrative, and in fact the film consistently fudges the fact of David's centrality by reinstating a human/other binary. If Ash is a marionette operated by the Company, David is a costumier's mannequin, albeit one who understands his own condition to be deficient in comparison to human beings.

David taps into the dreams of the hyper-sleeping scientist Elizabeth Shaw (Noomi Rapace) as a kind of voyeur, but this somewhat sinister act signifies a curiosity and sense of wonder that is entirely absent from the rest of the human crew of the Prometheus. Indeed, the crew are a group of unattractive and barely credible yahoos who seem to have no reliable methods, practices or intellectual framework through which to grapple with what they are encountering. In *Alien*, the collective ignorance of the crew in the face of the alien creature is understandable and commensurate with the fact that the crew are all working stiffs, subject to 'the contract', and ultimately expendable. In *Prometheus*, there is no such rationale; no one seems to know what they should be doing. When David asks Shaw's partner Holloway (Logan Marshall-Green) why human beings made androids, the reply is 'because they could'. David's rather dismissive response, that human beings might be disappointed if they received the same reply from their Creator, reveals the shallowness of Holloway's appreciation and insight into the nature of being: Holloway simply assumes that David is significantly inferior to human beings, as a 'robot'. Considering David's self-possession, and the significant fact that he saves Shaw from some kind of pyroclastic storm-front soon after they have landed, such assumptions on Holloway's part are self-evidently unfounded.

Fassbender is the most impressive part of the film, his casting in this role, and the connections to O'Toole and Bowie, destabilizes any sense that David might be a mere 'butler'. David is, in fact, the protagonist of *Prometheus*. Where Ian Holm was physically small and slight, downplaying his significance, Fassbender is tall, imposing, aquiline, glamorous: a literal star/man. Not only that, but the film goes out of its way to mark David as the only true repository in the film of one of SF's oldest motifs: a sense of wonder. When he penetrates the fallen ship of the 'space jockey', recognizable from *Alien*, David is able to follow the holographic 'ghosts' of the Engineers (an unexplained and rather convenient phenomenon, one might add) to start up the ship's navigational array. The circular rostrum of the flight deck becomes an illuminated globe, a star-map, and here the film switches into the register of classic space fiction: David has made an awe-inspiring 'discovery'. Again, David is placed in the role of the masculine hero, and in many ways, he conforms to Vivian Sobchack's characterization of the 'superb physiques, wooden movements, hollow cheerfulness, and banal competence . . . cool, rational, competent, unimaginative, male, and sexless' (107). Not unimaginative, though; it is difficult to imagine any other character in *Prometheus* responding with such awe and delight to the universal star-map.

The question of virginity, however, is important to consider in relation to David; while there is no Ash-like symbolic oral rape, he does end up in a parodic *Reich der Zwei* with Shaw at the end of the film and, as I noted above, saved her from the storm earlier in the narrative. What does David want? Not sex, perhaps, but romance. David's spiking of Holloway's drink with alien DNA, thereby killing the scientist, seems to place him as just another android villain, as bad as Ash had been. However, if we remember that David has seen into Shaw's dreams, surely he must know that she is incapable of conception, that she is unable to 'create' (revealed in one of the most weakly scripted scenes in the film). By poisoning Holloway, David is able to romance Shaw at one remove, to give her what she wants, what Holloway cannot: a baby. That the foetus is alien and monstrous is, in a sense, irrelevant; the fact of pregnancy is enough. It is telling that the word that the film cannot use in the scene where Shaw uses the surgical pod to remove the alien embryo is 'abortion', for this is, essentially, what she conducts, a termination by caesarean section. Where *Alien* represented the *body of the woman* as the *body of the alien*, *Prometheus* represents the body of the mother as itself a techno-body, eventually stapled together and sprayed with antiseptic paint.

Ridley Scott himself staples together elements of *Blade Runner* (1982) with the *Alien* series in *Prometheus*'s emphasis on meeting with one's maker, but the aged Weyland is no Roy Baty, and cannot demand of the Engineer, 'I want more life, father [fucker]' (though this is clearly what he's after). In fact, he cannot even speak the Engineer's language; this is left to David, who receives a pat on the head, like a schoolboy, for his efforts, before he suffers the same fate as Ash and Bishop. The Frankenstein motifs that give *Blade Runner* such depth, and the meeting between Baty and Tyrell such awful resonance, are thrown away in *Prometheus*, largely because the meeting takes place between the Engineer and a character who has been largely absent (secreted away aboard the ship in hyper-sleep) in a language that remains untranslated. There is no grandeur, no horror, no climax, and the father visits fatal violence upon the sons (rather than vice versa). 'It's not an easy thing to meet your maker', says Baty, but David has already done so, every day. The question he asks Holloway is moot; perhaps he is already disappointed. For a human being to meet their maker is to undergo an extremity of terror and violence, in *Prometheus*; but not for David.

The connection between Creation and space fiction is a very long one, as indicated at the beginning of this chapter, and it is a signal feature of the 'transcendent' vein of SF that encountering the alien Other is represented through a register of Christian iconography: as we saw above, *2001: A Space Odyssey* and Soderbergh's *Solaris* repeat the gesture between God and Adam on the Sistine Chapel frescos. With its classical allusions, *Prometheus* seems to offer a variant on the Christian Creation, where the origin of human beings is founded on an external transgression (the theft of fire) rather than an internal one (the Fall). This would seem to suggest not that *Prometheus* re-situates human beings as part of a divine cosmology, but that it suggests human beings are a *technical* by-product of some kind of radically unknowable Engineering project.

Prometheus offers an imaginative rendering of a Stieglerian conception of human beings *as technological artefact*. It is not hubris or overreaching ambition that drives human beings to the stars: it is *lack*, begetting the questions, who, or what am I? Is this all there is? The greatest sense of 'lack' is felt by a triumvirate of characters, rather than one (as with Roy Baty), and this disperses, rather than intensifies or makes more complex, the need to 'meet one's Maker'. Baty, as played by Rutger Hauer, manages to combine both a childlike energy and capacity for wonder with a fundamental sense of his own mortality; in him, innocence and experience exist side by side, and this gives the concept of his character both power and pathos. Baty is not a fallen being, despite the (altered) quotation from Blake he offers to Chu: 'Fiery the angels fell; deep thunder rolled around their shores; burning with the fires of Orc.' His is not an Infernal subjectivity, a fallen angel in search of redemption from his God. Rather, Baty is outside sin itself: 'I've done . . . questionable things', he confesses to Tyrell (Joe Turkel), which is ambiguous at best. Baty commits acts of monstrous violence but remains a child: when he looks down, at the end of the film, at Deckard hanging on to the girder by two fingertips, and says, 'It's painful to live in fear, isn't it?', his face betrays curiosity rather than anger, lust for life rather than world-weariness. David's innocence is of a different kind, but similar order. As an explicitly technical being, defined by *lack* but not driven to compensate for it, David is not subject to the myth of lost plenitude that haunts the Fall, the desire to redeem lost Eden. He is not driven by Baty's rage against mortality, to demand 'more life': his agency (such as infecting Holloway) is without a defined purpose or end. He simply *does* and observes the results. David occupies a space of radical innocence, the innocence of the Alien other, unconcerned with 'conscience, remorse or delusions of morality'.

Part Three

Gothic/Horror/The Fantastic

10

Tape Spectra

The film *Contact* (1997) begins with a striking effects sequence. After the title, the film begins with a shot of the Earth from low orbit, in shadow. On the soundtrack, contemporary rock music plays. Both visual and aural signs mark this to be 'now', our present day. The camera (virtually) begins to recede, and as it does, the sound stage alters. A phrase 'obviously a major malfunction' is heard, taken from the reporting of the *Challenger* space shuttle disaster of 1986, and the music segues through 1980s pop into disco. A phrase from the theme music of the long-running TV series *Dallas* (1978–91) is heard, as the Earth and then Moon shrink, in silhouette, displaced by the brightness of the Sun. As the camera recedes from Earth and travels outwards in the Solar System, other phrases from twentieth-century America are heard: Richard Nixon saying 'I'm not a crook'; Neil Armstrong's 'one small step for man'; Martin Luther King's 'free at last'. As the camera swings past Jupiter, we hear of John F. Kennedy's assassination, then Dean Martin singing 'Volare', and a member of HUAC demanding, 'have you ever been a member of the Communist party?'; at Saturn, the Lone Ranger calling 'Hi-ho Silver', and an FDR 'fireside chat'. All the while, the volume decreases, descending towards silence as the intensity of broadcasts decrease, as the camera 'travels' further out, leaving the Solar System then the Milky Way itself behind, then moving ever faster away from tiny spiral galaxies disappearing into the distance. The screen is then overcome with whiteness, the edge of the universe; the screen then fades up from white, still 'zooming out', as the camera shows the reflection of a window in a young girl's pupil, who we see finally at a desk, transmitting on short-wave radio: 'This is CQ, W-9 GFO.' She picks up a contact, receiving in Pensacola, Florida, some thousand miles away, 'the furthest one yet', as her father watches benignly. She marks this on a map of the United States.

In this sequence, political history (of the United States) is mixed up with musical markers from popular culture and music, recognizable emblems of particular eras. Space is signified by time: the further out from the Sun we travel, the further back in time we seem to go. Earth is itself a 'planet of sound', a tiny mote of dust in the sky, soon lost to our vision, but human broadcasts penetrate the vast distances of space in a way that human beings themselves cannot. The earliest human broadcasts, travelling at the speed of sound, may (without degradation) have reached around 100 light years distant by the end of the first decade of the twenty-first century, though it would take alien intelligences to have developed receiving equipment far beyond the tolerances and sensitivity of even the most advanced arrays on Earth to be able to hear (and later, watch) them. *Contact* plays a strange double game in its opening minutes: while the opening effects sequence emphasizes physical *distance* (the time taken for signals, at the speed of sound, to travel across space), the images of the girl at her ham radio emphasizes *instantaneity* of 'contact', that distance *in space* is countermanded by broadcast technologies, where a form of telepresence makes it seem as though someone a thousand miles away is sitting right next to you. The physical realities of sound, distance and time are then subject, in *Contact*, to a wider fantasy of instantaneity of contact, one that will have increasingly metaphysical (as well as psychological/emotional) implications as the narrative progresses.

Haunted technologies

Despite its Anglophone and North American bias, *Contact*'s opening is of particular interest because it reads contemporary history through sound broadcast technologies: radio (wireless), in particular. The universe itself, of course, emanates radio-frequency signals as part of its fabric, not only from sources such as pulsars but also as part of background radiation, and the Search for Extra-Terrestrial Life programme (SETI) has used radio-telescope arrays to try to filter out possible extraterrestrial transmissions from the background 'noise' of the universe. By focusing on radio, *Contact* emphasizes the fundamental contiguity between human activity (sound broadcasts) and the universe itself, and marks human history through its audio footprint, almost as if human life began with radio, Marconi as Adam. Extraterrestrial scientists, perhaps, will gauge human 'intelligence' (or otherwise) through its capacity to produce audio transmissions. Paradoxically, Earth becomes *visible* as a 'planet of sound'.

Radio is one of the sound technologies which came into being in the second half of the nineteenth century, which also included telegraphy, the telephone and recording via phonograph cylinders (principles later developed into the gramophone/phonograph and audio tape). Jonathan Sterne, in *The Audible Past* (2003), has argued that sound recording is continuous with the nineteenth century's cultures of death, in that it seeks to *preserve* the voice of the dead subject and prevent decay. Sterne connects this to the development of canning technologies in the food industry and also to the arts of embalming. In a sense, preservation of the voice is then a way to efface or overcome time and its depredations (allowing that the recording technologies themselves do not degrade over time). Sterne argues that emblematic of the reifying imperatives of what he calls (derived from Matei Calinescu) 'bourgeois modernity', a way of 'managing time' itself: sound recordings offer 'repeatable time within a carefully bounded frame' (Sterne 2003: 310). However, Sterne goes on to suggest that 'the scheme of permanence . . . was essentially hyperbole, a Victorian fantasy. Repeatability from moment to moment was not the same thing as preservation for all time' (Sterne 2003: 332). Recorded sound offered the possibility of repetition, of *playback* of the voice after death; however, playback itself, on cylinders or gramophone records, relies on the same technologies of *material inscription* that constitute recording: the needle touches the vinyl groove, and in touching, marks it, degrades it. Repeated playback is another slow fade into white noise, undifferentiation, death. The term 'white noise' is drawn from the frequency spectrum. Within the audio range, we hear different tones or notes when a particular frequency length predominates. When all frequencies within the audible range are equally present, resulting in a 'flat' sound spectrum, then what the human ear hears is 'white noise'. White noise is undifferentiated sound, deemed 'white' through analogy with light, where the presence of all visible frequencies results in white light. The relation of transmission or signal to white noise is one that that has haunted analogue sound reproduction technologies from their inception.

Most notably, Jeffrey Sconce has investigated the history of this 'haunting' with regard to sound and vision technologies. In *Haunted Media* (2000), Sconce outlines three recurrent 'cultural fantasies' that have accompanied the development of telecommunications technologies: (1) 'these media enable an uncanny form of disembodiment'; (2) the imagination of a 'sovereign electronic world', an 'electronic elsewhere'; and (3) 'the anthropomorphization of media technology', most visible in a fascination with androids and cyborgs (Sconce 2000: 8–9). In his chapter on radio, Sconce suggests that 'enthusiastic celebration of the emerging medium [was accompanied and challenged by texts] suggesting an eerie and even sinister undercurrent to the new electronic worlds forged by wireless' (Sconce 2000: 62). In fact, we might suggest that sound broadcast technologies enabled an uncanny form of *embodiment* through telepresence, the belief that the other was somehow present in the room as you spoke to them via radio or telephone. In either sense, we can ascertain that telecommunication technologies disrupted the 'metaphysics of presence' diagnosed by Jacques Derrida and others as central to Western metaphysics, a privileging of speech over writing, of the voice-over text, that makes the *voice* the embodiment of truth and of authenticity. In this *phonocentrism*, as Derrida called it, writing is seen to be derived from a pre-existing orality, a 'natural' form of communication that is prior to 'the fateful violence of the political institution' (Derrida 1976: 36). Derrida, of course, sought to undo this binary which privileged voice-over writing, and argued that writing preceded, and was the condition and ground of speech. After the advent of telecommunications technologies, voice itself becomes disembodied, no longer physically connected to a subject who speaks. Telepresence is at one and the same time presence and *not*-presence, offering the fantasy of 'instantaneity of contact' but at the same time emphasizing that the *other speaker* is *not* there.

When talking with Bernard Stiegler about television in *Echographies of Television* (2002), Derrida asserts that technologies of the image are bound up with acts of 'magic' or 'faith', 'by our relation of essential incompetence to technical operation' (Derrida and Stiegler 2002: 117). 'For if we don't know how something works', Derrida continues,

> our knowledge is incommensurable to the immediate perception that attunes us to technical efficacy, to the fact that 'it works'; we see that 'it works', but even if we *know* this, we don't *see* how it 'works'; seeing and knowing are incommensurable here. . . . And this is what makes our experience so strange. We are spectralized by the shot, captured or possessed by spectrality in advance. . . . What has . . . constantly haunted me in this logic of the spectre is that it regularly exceeds all the oppositions between visible and invisible, sensible and insensible. A spectre is both visible and invisible, both phenomenal and nonphenomenal. (Derrida and Stiegler 2002: 117)

Although Derrida uses the discourse of visibility here, his addition of 'sensible and insensible' crucially extends the idea of the 'specter' to the frequency range of audio, in its disruption of presence. In his attempt to situate the problematic of how telecommunication technologies in relation to human knowledge, Derrida allows media to escape discourses of science, the rational (or of knowledge itself) and so it enters the numinous, the 'electronic elsewhere', where our relation to it *can only be* uncanny (and/or theological: we must *believe* that it works, even if we don't know *how* it works, a 'technical efficacy' that must always elude us). Telecommunications technologies, broadcast media, are then spectralized, 'haunted', by this strangeness.

In terms of the developing communication technologies of the late nineteenth and early twentieth centuries, both *transmission* and *reproduction* of sound are 'haunted' by ghosts. Recording the voice, according to Sterne, is part of a culture of preservation and memorialization of the dead; Joe Banks, in 'Rorschach Audio', reports that 'Edison and Marconi both believed that radio technology might enable contact with the afterlife' (Banks 2001: 83). In his short story 'Wireless' – analysed by Sconce and Warner – Rudyard Kipling imagines a young man who, entering into a kind of fugue state, becomes a kind of human 'receiver' (or we might say 'medium') for the transmission of one of Keats' poems, which he writes down as if transcribing a message: a poem the young man does not consciously know. The mystery of this act is maintained by the short story until the end: the act of transmission itself, a kind of aetheric emanation picked by a 'sensitive', remains unexplained. Here we might also return to the film *Contact*. The young girl, Ellie Alloway, asks her father, if she had powerful enough equipment, 'Could I talk to . . . the Moon?', going on to add 'Jupiter?', 'Saturn?', and then, 'Mom?'. When her father unexpectedly dies, the loss of her mother is compounded, and after the father's funeral, immediately prior to a cut across time to the older Ellie (played by Jodie Foster), we see the girl, once again transmitting on her short-wave radio, calling 'Dad, this is Ellie: come back? Dad, are you there? Come back.' Talking across space is twice encoded as talking to the 'electronic elsewhere', hoping to hear the voices of the dead. In *Contact*, the gender polarity of loss and restitution is inverted: here, it is the daughter who grieves for, and seeks out the father.

In the film *Frequency* (2000), John Sullivan (Jim Caviziel) plays a man who lost his own father Frank (Dennis Quaid) in a fire when he was young. It begins in a similar way to *Contact*: on the soundtrack, dislocated phrases from radio broadcasts are heard, while the visual track shows images taken from space, here the plumes of solar flares that will create unusual atmospheric conditions on Earth on 2 days 30 years apart, 10 October 1969 and 1999. Effects-shots of the aurora borealis behind the Queensborough Bridge in New York emphasize both material locatedness (this is a New York story: Frank was a fireman, while John is a detective in the NYPD) *and* strangeness, the presence of the uncanny, the sky 'haunted' by the lights. The bridge also symbolizes the connection between the two time periods, as the film intercuts between them, and largely focuses on the relationship between Frank and his young son. The technological 'bridge' between the time periods is short-wave radio, and the backyard mast is prominently displayed against the borealis several times. *Frequency* matches time through space: John still lives in the house he grew up in, while his widowed mother lives elsewhere, and the film regularly intercuts the older John pacing around the house, himself haunting its spaces, with images of the family life he lost upon the death of his father. The ham radio itself, discovered in the NYFD trunk of his father, becomes an uncanny object; its old valves fail, but the receiver seems to start into life of its own accord when Frank begins to broadcast on it, and John receives its messages across time. When John informs his father that he is to die in a warehouse fire on the 12th, he alters the timeline (we see direct evidence of this when contact with his father on the radio causes his father to burn the desk he is sitting at, the burn mark appearing under John's hand as he speaks): his father survives, but it is only at the end of the film (after a long diversion into a serial killer procedural narrative) that a kind of wish-fulfilment of emotional restitution is enacted. John's final 'new' timeline gifts him with the family life he lost once his father died: *Frequency*'s imagination of haunted radio directly undoes the trauma of loss.

Both *Contact* and *Frequency*, although science fiction films (one a 'first contact' narrative, the other a time-paradox story), can both be said to incorporate elements of what is known as 'EVP', or electronic voice phenomena. This is a focus of para-psychological research whereby it is understood that the 'voices' of the dead can be found imprinted upon the ambient sounds (or 'noise') produced when recording in an ordinary empty room. This began in the mid-1930s with the artist Attila von Szalay, who, in his darkroom, heard 'the voice of his deceased brother calling his name' (Sconce 2000: 84). After unsuccessful attempts to record these voices on a phonograph, he was finally successful when using a reel-to-reel tape recorder in the 1950s. This technological advance is important. Around the same time, Friedrich Jürgenson, a Swedish documentary film-maker, attempted to record birdsong (also on tape recorder) in his garden, but found, on playback, that he 'heard his dead father's voice and then the spirit of his deceased wife calling his name' (Sconce 2000: 84). Upon publishing his findings in 1959, his book *Radio Contact with the Dead* was read by the Jungian psychologist and philosopher, Dr Konstantin Raudive. Raudive's book *Breakthrough* (1971) was literally that in the popular imagination, and is a curious example of what might be termed 'spiritualism in the age of electronic reproduction'. The book's subtitle, 'An Amazing Experiment in Electronic Communication with the Dead' marks its significance as a 'scientific' text that purports to reveal the intersection of spectrality, life-after-death communication and analogue recording devices. In the book, Raudive 'hears' or decodes voices of the dead ('speaking' in English, German and Raudive's native Latvian) emanating from the background hiss and rumble of recorded ambient sound: he asks questions of an empty room and records the 'answers'.

Raudive's work is a common touchstone for critics considering haunted media. For Sconce, Raudive presents himself and the EVP project as radically antithetical to Freudian depth psychology:

> [t]he Raudive voices did speak of an immortal essence that transcends alienating models of Darwin, Freud, Sartre, and all other demystifying assaults on the transcendental dimension of the human psyche. The irony, of course, is that Raudive remystified the soul through the validating authority of an electronic technology. (Sconce 2000: 90)

However, Sconce asserts a fundamental homology between Freud's and Raudive's intentions: 'At their core, both of these "interpretative" sciences shared the hope that their practices overcome *the trauma of a profound loss*' (Sconce 2000: 90, 91). Joe Banks, in 'Rorschach Audio', takes an extremely sceptical view, suggesting that 'EVP experimenters are psychologists who have misunderstood their own work; . . . [they] are inadvertently reproducing acoustic projection experiments', making the analogy to Rorschach ink blots (Banks 2001: 80). Mike Kelley, in 'An Academic Cut-Up', also refers to Rorschach blots, but understands Rorschach's experiments both as technological Spiritualism and as a way station in the history of twentieth-century experiments in sound, particularly in the musical avant-garde: 'one is hyperconscious of the fact that the distortion of the recording process [in EVP] is the primary experience', he suggests (Kelley 2003: 38). My own reading of Raudive's work would emphasize three main elements:

1. the centrality of *naming* in EVP. Von Szalay hears his brother call his name; they call Raudive by name, over and over again: Konstantin, Koste, Kosti. Naming, interpellation, calling into being: a crucial way of making meaning in EVP seems to circulate around the name, the act of being identified by EVP event, call into *presence* by an act of hearing/decoding.
2. The centrality of trauma to the experience. Von Szalay and Jürgenson hear the voices of dead relatives; Raudive's recently departed mother looms

large in the catalogue of voices, and she is the first catalogued figure to be identified in *Breakthrough*; on reading transcriptions of the EVP events, Raudive 'hears' many dead friends. (Raudive 1971: 35)

3. Thirdly, the common technological device here is magnetic audio tape.

Where Kittler notes the gramophone as a storage device/externalizations of memory becomes a metaphor for a figure for human consciousness itself, *tape* has different qualities: 'tapes can execute any possible manipulation of data because they are equipped with recording, reading, and erasing heads, as well as with forward and reverse motion' (Kittler 1999: 108). (Kittler also notes, *pace* Paul Virilio, that it is war, here the experiments by BASF and AEG used by the Abwehr in World War II, that accelerates magnetic tape production, rather than steel tape, towards general or consuming usage in the post-war period (Kittler 1999: 106).) As N. Katherine Hayles has it, in *How We Became Posthuman* (1999), 'audio tape was a technology of inscription, but with the crucial difference that he admitted erasure and rewriting':

> Whereas the phonograph produced objects that could be consumed only in the manufactured form, magnetic tape allows the consumer to be a producer as well. The switches activating the powerful and paradoxical technoconceptual actors of repetition and mutation, presence and absence, were in the hands of the masses, at least the masses who could afford the equipment. (Hayles 1999: 209, 210)

Hayles writes of how 'audio tape may already be reaching old age, fading from the marketplace as it is replaced by compact discs, computer hypermedia, and the like' (Hayles 1999: 208). The compact cassette is now one of Bruce Sterling's 'dead media', and its successor, the CD, is also on the way to obsolescence (Sterling 2008: 73–82). However, it is the very imperfections of magnetic tape, the 'wow' and 'flutter' of the thin, flexible tape passing over the heads, which renders it perfect as a 'haunted' technology. Like the 'ghosting' of analogue television signals (soon also to be obsolete), the imperfection of the analogue media artefact is part of its quality, its form. It is, of course, its very imperfection as a recording media – its hiss, its rumble, its flutter – which is the very condition of possibility for EVP. As documentary features on the DVD of *White Noise* point out, without the hiss of tape – or in contemporary technology, used by EVP experts, the noise generated by the hardware of solid-state Dictaphones – they can be no coalescing of the EVP 'voice', no recording of the phenomenon. Without *noise*, there physically can be no *signal*.

The main association for popular research into EVP is now called the Association Transcommunication. From the ATransC website, it is clear that the crucial motivation for the EVP practitioner is *to contact a lost loved one*: to undo trauma. One of their projects is called 'Big Circle', which attempts to contact the lost loved ones who now reside in the 'etheric'. Its directors, Lisa and Tom Butler, encourage DIY: all you need is a tape deck (portable compact cassette recorder), microphone and, if possible, a computer with spectrum analysers and filters and other sound processors to enhance the listening experience, to hear the voices. As Raudive himself writes, 'the ear cannot hear the voices without technical aids' (Raudive 1971: 108). It is clear from the AA-EVP/ATransC work shown on the documentary that the voice phenomena are much simpler to decode than Raudive's: the voices of monoglot (English, in the United States) and seem much more immediately comprehensible. (Indeed, on page 19 of *Breakthrough*, it seems that the polyglot discourse is a condition of a claim to paranormal status for a voice event: polyglot + 'sensible meaning' = 'voice is paranormal'). It is the demo-cratization (and technologization) of mediumship that is so striking here – this is not a spectacular event, complete with female medium, ectoplasm, table rapping, or other visual spectacle: it is seemingly demystified, as simple as taping while asking questions of an empty room.

Where, then, do these voices come *from*? Kelley offers several means by which to explain the EVP phenomena. The first is that they are indeed some kind of extra-sensible emanations, 'the tortured voices of those in Hell, . . . the taunts of demons, or . . . the by-products of some numbing mental process that occurs after death'; the second, that they are psycho-acoustic patternings of geography: 'the haunted house, the poltergeist phenomenon, are explained as a result of the continuing presence of traumatized spirits or stored psychic energy, associated with a given place' (Kelley 2003: 25, 29). William Burroughs, in his own essay on Raudive, 'It Belongs to the Cucumbers', is highly sceptical, and suggests that the voices are more likely 'imprinted on the tape by electromagnetic energy generated by the unconscious minds of the researchers or people connected with them' (Burroughs 1985: 58). I find a third possibility more suggestive: that EVP phenomena are the coming to attention of the human ear to the 'planet of sound' around us. Kelley writes:

> We are programmed in such a way to screen out as much extraneous information as possible; otherwise we would not be able to deal with the amount of external stimuli that constantly bombards us. A tape recorder does much the same thing

that putting a seashell, or a simple tube, up to our ear does – it makes us aware of the amount of white noise that continually surrounds us. (Kelley 2003: 37)

Jonathan Crary, in *Suspensions of Perception* (2001) argued that the idea of attention became increasingly investigated in the fields of both psychology and optics in the nineteenth century. This is because of the perceived tendency in human beings (particularly workers, it should be noted) towards *distraction*, in what Crary calls 'an emergent economic system that demanded attentiveness of a subject in a wide range of new productive and spectacular tasks, but whose internal movement was continually eroding the basis of any disciplinary attentiveness' (Crary 2001: 29). The conditions of a 'modern', industrial, increasingly consumption as well as production-oriented economy pulled the human subject in two directions: first, the bombardment of what Walter Benjamin has called the 'shock' of modern existence (urban living, machinery, speed, advertising, etc.) creates an increasingly distracted subject in an increasingly kaleidoscopic world; and second, that the very economic conditions that produce this kind of world require a working subject who is able to maintain long periods of attentiveness to complex and repetitive tasks (over a 10- or 12-hour working day in a factory, for instance). The disciplining of *visual* attention that Crary diagnoses can be extended to the field of sound reproduction and transmission; *aural* attention is required to prevent a kind of distraction of the senses through sonic overload in a world where the skies are filled with 'aural garbage . . . aether talk [. . . and] dead city radio transmissions' (Toop 1995: 270). EVP, then, in Gothicized form, makes this disciplining of attention itself 'visible': it is what we do not, or cannot, hear. The image that is repeated continuously in *Contact*, of Ellie Alloway concentrating on the sounds transmitted through her headphones ('no-one listens any more', says her immediate superior) is emblematic of the necessity of aural attention in modernity: Ellie must shut out the very 'planet of sound' that the film begins with in order to contact the 'electronic elsewhere'.

Technology and trauma

Fictional or filmic EVP narratives are, like the phenomenon itself, organized around overcoming 'the trauma of a profound loss' (Sconce 2000: 91). *Contact*, which, despite being about the search for extraterrestrial intelligence, is a classical EVP narrative, expresses Ellie Alloway's search for transmissions explicitly as a recuperation from the loss of her mother and father, and when she does indeed achieve 'contact' with extraterrestrials, they appear in the very physical form of her Dad. *Frequency* also has at its centre the loss of a parent, where radio-transmitted EVP phenomena become stitched into a time-paradox narrative where the trauma of loss may not only be overcome, but also *undone*. Both of these films concentrate upon *audio* transmissions, but another, better-known film that incorporates 'spirit voices', Tobe Hooper's 1982 film *Poltergeist*, has at its centre the 'snow' of a television screen after transmission on a channel has ended (in the days of analogue signals and 'closedown'), the audio white noise accompanied by the unsettling light of a cathode ray tube broadcasting no signal. The poster for the film featured the young girl Carol Anne (Heather O'Rourke) sitting directly in front of this television, listening intently to 'voices' only she could hear. The tagline for the film, dialogue spoken by Carol Anne, is: 'They're here.'

Where *Contact* and *Frequency* concentrated upon the loss of the father-figure, the crucial triangulation in *Poltergeist* is female, and maternal. While the father Steven Freeling (Craig T. Nelson) has been morally compromised by his complicity on dubious land deals that have sited housing developments on old Native American burial grounds (a failure of paternal authority more common in the films of producer Steven Spielberg), it is the daughter Carol Anne who becomes the subject of the malign attentions of the poltergeists. When she is taken to the 'elsewhere' in this film, the family call upon the services of a team of parapsychological researchers from UC Irvine. When the 'scientists', with technological gear of high-end EVP experimenters (video and audio recording, motion sensors and so on) cannot solve the problem of poltergeist activity, they call in the medium, Tangina Barrons (Zelda Rubinstein). It is she who realizes that the phenomena are 'spirits' who have not gone into the 'light' of the Hereafter, and that a malign entity has captured both Carol Anne and the attention of spirits, preventing them from 'passing'; and it is she who sends Carol Anne's mother Diana (JoBeth Williams) into the 'portal' to retrieve her daughter. When they emerge back into the 'real' of the house, mother and daughter are covered in some kind of ectoplasm, a (re)birth-fluid that emphasizes feminine and maternal materiality. The core of *Poltergeist* is the recuperation of the mother–daughter bond through the ministrations of the female medium/midwife, preserver of arcane knowledge and practices that always-already escape the scientizing discourses of the UC Irvine team (who are led by a female scientist, but whose practices are resolutely coded as masculine: rational, technological and deeply flawed).

In *White Noise* (2005), communication devices abound: cell phones, answer phones, TV, video, computer screens all feature heavily in the *mise-en-scène*. These devices allow a bridge to be formed between quotidian and other- or under-worlds. The haunted nature of telephonic/telegraphic communication is figured directly as communication with ghosts, and particularly with the spirit of a lost wife. Michael Keaton plays Jonathan Rivers, an architect whose second wife tells him she is pregnant before she drives into the city for a meeting. She never returns. Her car is found by the river with a flat tyre, and her body is eventually discovered upriver, taken there by the tide. In the protagonist's name and this location we find reference to not only the Styx/Lethe imagery that is much more overt in *Frozen*, but also the birth imagery that Brian Jarvis notes as significant in the J-horror variant on haunted tape and the invasion-horror narrative, *Ringu* (Jarvis 2009). (In *Frozen* (2005), discussed in more detail below), Annie, the lost sister, has also recently had a child; we see the baby with the 'abandoned' father.) Ultimately, the narrative descends into both spirit-invasion horror (malignant spirit entities as in *Poltergeist*) and, in a curious genre-swerve, serial killer narrative, where the wife's death was murder, not accidental, and is one of a sequence that the serial killer offers up to the malign spirit entities. *Frozen* makes the same swerve when revealing, at the point of the female protagonist's death at his hands, that the abandoned father of his sister's child is in fact the murderer of both sisters.

At first, in *White Noise*, televisual imaging technology (home movies shown on TV) is not connected to EVP. As in the figure of John Anderton in *Minority Report* (2002), whose watching of holographic images of his lost son are meant to comfort but merely compound the trauma of loss, Rivers seeks out videotapes of his life with his lost wife as an index of unrecuperated trauma. The promise of all these haunted technologies is, ultimately, the restoration of a form of life to the dead: as Terry Castle notes in *The Female Thermometer*, the phantasmagoria entrepreneur/inventor Etienne-Gaspard Robertson, when introducing the show 'emerged, spectrelike, from the gloom, and addressing the audience, offered to conjure up the spirits of their dead loved ones' (Castle 1995: 147). The bridge formed by these tape technologies is not only to the spirit world, but also to the past, the time in which the loved one was not lost.

This literal nostalgia, this return home to a time before loss/trauma, is indicated in the *mise-en-scène* of *White Noise*. Rivers' home and office are photographed with a cool, grey-blue palette: chrome, brushed steel and glass predominate. After he moves to an apartment following his wife's death, this becomes still more emphasized, the blue light of cathode ray screens reflecting from glass-brick walls. When Rivers is approached by an EVP specialist, Raymond Price (Ian McNeice), who tells him Rivers' wife has contacted him, the initially sceptical Rivers visits Price's home. The *mise-en-scène* here is markedly different: the clapboard house contains rooms lit in shades of red and brown, the space cluttered, old rugs on the floor. Unlike Rivers apartment, this base is homely, *heimlich* perhaps, although part of the clutter is the EVP equipment itself: tapes, video recorders, computer and a DAT player. The room bespeaks the past, and the technology of the past; it is as though Price has heard voices through a crystal radio set in his front room (echoing the ham radio activities of Ellie Alloway in *Contact*). In a sense, this is exactly what he has been doing; EVP as do-it-yourself radiophonics.

If Price's house is homely, then Rivers deliberately dislocates himself from 'home'. He moves from a house shared with his lost wife to a cold, modern apartment building in the city. Perhaps the house is haunted by the memories of his wife, and indeed it is here that Rivers is seen watching home movies; and the move to the blank new apartment becomes an attempt to escape these ghosts. But it is here, through tape and EVP, that the ghost of his wife manifests itself. It is the very blankness of the modern apartment that calls forth the ghost.

This narrative, like others mentioned above, places a male questing protagonist at the centre of narrative agency. Von Szalay, Jurgenson, Raudive, and in *White Noise* Rivers and Price: EVP is figured as a male activity, the technology perhaps inverting the paradigm of female mediumship. The history of mediumship is, of course, a female one. As Sconce and Warner note, from the Fox sisters on, there is an interesting implication of gender in Spiritualism – a gender politics. Sconce writes, 'spiritualism empowered women to speak in public, often about very controversial issues facing the nation' (Sconce 2000: 49). In spirit photography, William Crookes or William Hope photograph female mediums; and in spiritualism, the female *does not speak*: she is a medium for others. The media (photography/tape) that will prove the scientific fact of the existence of post-mortem life (spirits, voices) is coded as male; the mediums that are the focus are female. In *White Noise*, Rivers visits a blind female seer, a medium, who cautions him against EVP, warning him not to 'meddle'. The conflict between the archetypal female medium, and the technophile male EVP experimenter, bespeaks a kind of gender problematic in these Orpheus narratives, and perhaps an attempt to wrest the figuring of the 'electronic elsewhere' into the realm of the masculine.

Frozen (2005), on the other hand, is certainly a text which uses EVP motifs – the imprinting of a strange image on to surveillance CCTV tape – but in the service of a narrative which focuses on female, and sisterly, loss. When Kath, the surviving sister (Shirley Henderson) of a disappeared woman, visits the alleyway where CCTV images of her sister were captured, she has a vision whereupon she stands upon tidal sands, while what she takes to be her sister walks upon a sandbank across and inlet or creek. As the film progresses, the number of these visions increases: a boat is seen, rowed by the blind ferryman Charon, and when she discusses her visions with a counsellor/priest (Roshan Seth), he explicitly decodes them as a Greco-Roman underworld.

The counsellor/priest's discourse runs directly counter to the scientific, demystifying impulses of Raudive and other EVP experimenters. The priest says to Kath: 'some things are beyond understanding and we just have to accept them as mysteries'. At the same time, when Kath shows him a printout of the uncanny image on the CCTV tape, in return he shows her a Rorschach ink blot, indicating that her meaning-making, of Annie as a dead and her visions as uncanny, is faulty. Later in the film, the image on the 'blot' becomes clearer, like a very slowly developing Polaroid photograph. It is revealed to be a close-up of a two-shot taken while Annie and Kath were on a roller-coaster, their happy faces pressed together. While Kath only finds herself, not Annie, wandering the underworld sands in her visions, this image does suggest (albeit sentimentally) that the two sisters are reunited in death. Through Kath's visions, which we see as a cinematic 'real', the afterlife is presented as a kind of truth or reality, just as in EVP.

Frozen returns to the figure of the female visionary, though Kath's medium-ship is overtly bound up with trauma and loss, and possible psychological disintegration. Kath ends up 'channelling' her own death, seeing her own face, when Jonathan Rivers in *White Noise* sees the deaths of others. He does not see his own death, even though his EVP visions become proleptic/prophetic/prophylactic in form. However, the last image of *White Noise* is Rivers, with his wife, amidst the visual snow of blank videotape playback, looking back out of the screen at us. Where Kath and Annie are bound up with each other, *White Noise*'s final visual gesture is to turn to the audience. *White Noise* is explicitly a cautionary tale, and on-screen titles warn that one in twelve EVP events is threatening in nature. It is also a warning against nostalgia, and becoming over-burdened by loss so that one can no longer see the world and the people that remain. What is striking about certain sequences in this film is not the use of EVP, nor the spirit-invasion narratives, but the images of the son, playing alone, on the father, in another room, watched blank tape in a search for his wife. In inhabiting nostalgia, in wanting to restore the past, in an inability to overcome the trauma of loss, Rivers neglects his son, and present time. The real locus of anxiety (and pathos) in *White Noise* is not the bereaved lover, but the neglectful/ forgetful father.

There is one film that uses EVP motifs I have deliberately refrained from mentioning so far: M. Knight Shyamalan's *The Sixth Sense* (1999). There is indeed a 'lost wife' in this film, but, of course, the 'twist' in this narrative is that Dr Malcolm Crowe (Bruce Willis), the psychologist who treats a traumatized child who 'sees dead people' (Cole Sear, played by Haley Joel Osment) is himself dead, only a ghost. Cole tells Crowe that the ghosts 'only see what they want to see', and while this bears upon Crowe's ongoing self-delusion as a ghost who believes himself to be alive, it also indicates the failure of rationality and scientific/medical discourse to deal with the real cause of Cole's trauma: he really does see dead people. As the narrative nears its end, Dr Crowe realizes that the causes of his own death lie in the roots of his rational worldview. His home invaded by a traumatized former patient, Crowe is shot, and the film seems to take place after his recovery, but in fact occurs after his death. Crowe 'fails' Vincent Grey (Mark Wahlberg) because he can only see Vincent's symptoms as internal and psychological terms, whereas the truth lies externally: he, too, contacts the dead. On playing back a tape of an interview with Grey, Crowe hears what he has blocked out all this time, the voices that haunt and torture Grey. The EVP manifestation finally makes clear to Crowe the limits of his own discourse; and this way is the path not only towards understanding his own condition (as ghost), but also a form of healing for himself and Cole, who stands in for and recuperates the damage that he could not undo with Vincent Grey. *The Sixth Sense* is then another recuperative narrative, and as he leaves the film (and Earth), Crowe is rewarded with the knowledge of his wife's ongoing love for him.

It is important to note that the films I have been considering here deal with analogue technologies: radio, audio tape, video, CCTV. As I have argued in the course of this chapter, it is the very properties of these media which are the ground and condition of their 'haunted' phenomena, the imperfections of aural and visual reproduction. Without noise, as I have stated, there can be no signal. Does the sonic 'cleanness' of digital reproduction mean that communication technologies will no longer be uncanny? The use of digital sound recorders by contemporary EVP experimenters suggests not: computers, hard disks or digital cameras have their own ambient footprints. There is a difference between analogue and digital reproduction; however, Bernard Stiegler suggests that both can create anxiety:

> Analogico-digital technology continues and amplifies a process of suspension [that interrupts one state of things and imposes another] that began a long time ago, in which the *analogy* photograph was itself only a singular epoch. And so the process in ancient, but the current phase of suspension – in the form of digital photography – engenders an anxiety and a doubt which are particularly interesting, but particularly threatening. (Stiegler 2002: 149)

It is, then, perhaps sound and visual reproduction itself which is haunted, rather than specific technologies. In digital artefacts and glitches, we may still see ghosts.

11

Orpheus Descending

Orpheus has, in the twentieth century, been a myth recurrently taken up by artists and writers who wish to explore artistic creation and transmission, and also the imperatives of loss and recuperation. In his Afterword to his translation of Rainer Maria Rilke's 'Orpheus' sequence of sonnets, the poet Don Paterson writes that Rilke produced the poems at such speed that it seemed to Rilke as though they were being broadcast from elsewhere (as in Kipling's 'Wireless', as we saw in the previous chapter), where poetic creation took the form of an 'enigmatic dictation'. This exterior conception of writing leads Paterson to propose the poet as being a kind of medium:

> Someone so sensitive that they become not only a lightning rod for all the crackling static of the culture, but also a satellite-dish, a 'receiver' (to use a Rilkean favourite) for things a less precisely attuned and calibrated sensibility would never be aware of. These individuals possess no supernatural powers, but do have abnormally strong sense of what's on the wind for us. (Paterson 2006: 63)

Orpheus is, of course, a mythic figure of the poet, one whose gift is bound up with loss. Orpheus, once a priest of Dionysus, is, at the time of his marriage, a priest of Apollo. The son of a river god (or perhaps Apollo) and Calliope (the Muse of epic poetry), Orpheus is gifted with a supernatural ability to play the lyre: his song charms the trees (who uproot to come nearer the singer), softens stones, alters nature itself. On his wedding day, his bride Eurydice, fleeing the bee-keeper Aristaeus, treads upon a snake, is bitten and dies. The grief-stricken Orpheus thereby descends into the Underworld, and through song, persuades Persephone and Hades to allow Eurydice to accompany him back to the upper world, on one condition: that he does not look back at his wife as they ascend. Unfortunately, as they near the upper world, Orpheus does look back, either in fear, or anxiety, or through love of his wife – and her shade retreats to the underworld. Despite his efforts, she may not be released a second time. In some versions of the myth, Orpheus then forswears the company of women and takes young male lovers. Precipitated by this rejection, women of a Dionysian cult, in an intoxicated frenzy, tear Orpheus to pieces; his head and lyre float down the river, still lamenting the loss of Eurydice, until they are washed ashore on Lesbos, while his shade is reunited with Eurydice in the underworld. The head of Orpheus becomes an oracle until Apollo, fearing competition with his own oracle at Delphi, silences the head and places Orpheus among the stars.

The figure of Orpheus has, from the Medieval period, through the Renaissance, Romanticism and to Modern and Contemporary literature, been re-imagined as (a) an emblematic narrative of loss of the loved one; (b) a figure of the transcendent power of art and poetry; and (c) the imagination of the boundary between the real or quotidian and the transcendent or divine. Contemporary science fiction, fantasy and gothic/horror fictions have used an Orphean narrative pattern, of a journey to an 'underworld', to construct narratives of anxiety, trauma and loss. These include films we analysed in Chapter 9, such as *Solaris* (2002), where a voyage to a sentient star, and thereby contact with a transcendent other, is patterned on the male protagonist's search for the restoration of his lost wife; or horror/SF crossover texts such as *Event Horizon* (1997), where the scientist Weir's interest in the demonic ship is predicated on undoing the trauma of his wife's suicide; and, in different ways, both *White Noise* (2005) and *Frozen* (2005), films considered in the previous chapter. In this chapter we will look in detail at two films that explicitly use the motif of the male journey to the underworld to recover the loss of a wife: Vincent Ward's *What Dreams May Come* (1999) and Christopher Nolan's *Inception* (2010). To begin with, however, we will consider Jean Cocteau's *Orphée* (1950), and the writings of Tom McCarthy, who we encountered in Chapter 2, and in particular his non-fiction texts that propose Orpheus as a key myth of the twentieth century.

In 'Transmission and the Individual Remix', a digital only essay published in 2012, McCarthy aligns Orpheus with a poetics of repetition. 'He comes to us already reconfigured and repeated', he argues, through the work of the Roman poet Ovid; and when he sings, 'not of himself but of Pygmalion, Hyacinthis, Myrrha and Cinyras' he is 'like some ancient jukebox, replaying stories on demand' (McCarthy 2012c: section iii). Orpheus, in McCarthy's imagination, is the poet of transmission: his 'hilltop concert' is followed by his dismemberment and scattering ('broadcast') among the Thracian hills. Orpheus is also the poet of loss and lament, the male figure who loses his wife *twice*: once when she steps upon the serpent and is taken to Hades, and once again when his mission to save her fails at the threshold of the upper world, when Orpheus looks back. Even loss and trauma is, for Orpheus, repeated. The connection between repetition and trauma is central to Freud's *Beyond the Pleasure Principle* (1920), in which Freud proposes his theory of the instinctual drives, and in particular the 'death drive'. Early in the text, Freud discusses a game he witnessed, played by a small boy, who

> very skilfully threw [a wooden] reel [with string tied round it] over the edge of his curtained cot so that it disappeared inside, all the while making his expressive 'o-o-o-o' sound [which Freud understands as the German *fort*, 'gone'], then used the string to pull the reel out of the cot again, but this time greeted its disappearance with a joyful *Da!* ('Here!'). That, then, was the entire game – disappearing and coming back. (Freud 2006: 141)

Freud analyses this scene to suggest that the child uses the game to repeat the pain of his mother's departure from his room, thereby controlling it with the displeasure and wreaking a measure of psychic revenge upon the mother: 'the child may well only have been able to repeat an unpleasant experience in his play because the repetition was associated with a different but direct gain in pleasure' (Freud 2006: 142), one gained by an assumed mastery over the situation and thereby his mother.

The mechanisms that produce psychological pleasure and pain are central to *Beyond the Pleasure Principle*, and to the theory of the instinctual drives. Freud proposes that the cerebral cortex is analogous to the surface membranes of simple living organisms, in that the 'by dint of the constant bombardment of the vesicle's outer surface by external stimuli, the substance of the cell becomes permanently altered down to a certain depth, with the result that the excitation occurs differently in this surface layer from the way it occurs in the deeper layers' (Freud 2006: 153). The surface becomes not an organ of reception, but one of *protection*, filtering out the constant bombardment of stimulation and information; however, excitation still occurs in a sense *within*, in the deepest layers of the organism. This relation between external stimuli and internal processes is one that we discussed in relation to trauma in Chapter 2; and Freud goes on, in *Beyond the Pleasure Principle*, to suggest that 'an event such as external trauma will doubtless provoke a massive disturbance in the organism's energy system' (Freud 2006: 157). From this analogy, Freud draws a conclusion with regard to trauma and the human psychic apparatus: 'I believe we can reasonably venture to regard ordinary traumatic neurosis as resulting from an extensive breach of the protective barrier' (Freud 2006: 158). Roger Luckhurst, in *The Trauma Question* (2008), summarizes by suggesting: 'Trauma is a piercing or breach of a border that puts inside and outside into a strange communication. Trauma violently opens passageways between systems that were once discrete, making unforeseen connections that distress or confound' (Luckhurst 2008: 3).

This leads Freud to diagnose the reason behind the repetition of painful scenarios in his patients, which 'flouts the pleasure principle in *every* way' (Freud 2006: 164). This is the connection between the 'realm of the drives and the compulsion to repeat':

> A drive might accordingly be seen as *a powerful tendency inherent in every living organism to restore a prior state*, which prior state the organism was compelled to relinquish due to the disruptive inelasticity of external forces. (Freud 2006: 164, 165 [italics in original])

This tendency is to find a state of quiescence, of absence of pain and stimulation: 'every living thing dies', Freud argues, 'for *intrinsic* reasons . . . we can only say that *the goal of all life is death*, or to express it retrospectively: *the inanimate existed before the animate*' (Freud 2006: 166, italics in original). Freud then develops a theory of the drives in a state of tension: the 'ego drives arise when inanimate matter becomes animate, and set out to restore the inanimate state'; 'the sexual drives [are bent upon] the continuation of life' (Freud 2006: 172). Here, then are *Eros* and *Thanatos*, the 'death drives [which have been] accompanied from the very beginning by life drives' (Freud 2006: 186).

To speculate further, and to provide an analogy from poetry and myth, Freud refers to the idea of the 'wheel-men' found in Plato's *Symposium* where, in a speech given by Aristophanes, a theory of foundational splitting of the human subject is proposed. As Jonathan Dollimore explains in *Death, Desire and Loss in Western Culture* (1998):

> Originally, he says, there were three sexes: male, female and hermaphrodite. The last of these has characteristics of both male and female. . . . Each type of human was a whole, with four legs, four arms, two faces on one head, two organs of generation, and everything else to correspond. They were formidable and hubristic creatures who even dared to attack the gods. To weaken them, Zeus cut each of them in two. . . . For Aristophanes, each person remains incomplete. Those deriving from the original hermaphrodite sex seek halves of the opposite

sex, those deriving from the female search for other women, while those who are halves of males pursue males. (Dollimore 1998: 12–13)

In this myth, as Dollimore suggests, 'originating in a division which is a kind of death, desire becomes an experience of lack rooted in loss' (Dollimore 1998: 13). Eros, desire, then itself implies a lack, a desire for completion through an ecstatic annihilation of the incomplete self and conjoining with the other in a transcendent whole. This myth of origins presents human beings as always-already traumatized, the 'life drives' (*eros*) bent not towards reproduction, but restitution of the original, whole subject. To find one's 'soul mate' is, then, to heal the self. This is precisely the dynamic of Ward's *What Dreams May Come*, which we shall analyse shortly.

Before doing so, I would like to turn to Herbert Marcuse's *Eros and Civilization* (1956), who proposes a full, unrepressed Eros that combines *both* life and death drives. The book is a meditation upon Freud's late theory of the instinctual drives which attempts to forge a liberationist manifesto by fusing *Beyond the Pleasure Principle* with Marx. While anxious to defend Freud, Marcuse's project in the book is to extend Freud's analysis of the instinctual repression that is the root (and price) of civilization and also to historicize it, wherein the 'reality principle' that determines the repression of libidinal energies, that are then transformed into the work of 'civilization', becomes the 'performance principle'. '[U]nder its rule,' writes Marcuse, 'society is stratified according to the competitive economic performances of its members': an 'acquisitive and antagonistic society in the process of constant expansion' extends its control and rationalization into all areas of life, particularly in relation to libido and desire. 'In the "normal" development, the individual lives his repression "freely" as his own life: he desires what he is supposed to desire; his gratification is profitable to him and to others; he is reasonably and even exultantly happy', Marcuse argues (Marcuse 1987: 44, 46). Marcuse's conception of the performance principle is total domination where even desire is fabricated and internalized by the subject as 'natural'. *Eros and Civilization* is a proposal to resist that domination.

Towards the end of *Eros and Civilization*, Marcuse treads a familiar Freudian path in identifying figures from classical myth as archetypes of human subjectivity. As we saw in Chapter 9, he takes Prometheus, Orpheus and Narcissus as 'culture heroes' who symbolize 'the attitude and the deeds that have determined the fate of mankind'. The first is Prometheus, 'the trickster and (suffering) rebel against the gods, who creates culture at the price of perpetual pain. He symbolizes productiveness, the unceasing effort to master life; but, in his productivity, blessing and curse, progress and toil are inextricably intertwined. Prometheus is the archetype-hero of the performance principle' (Marcuse 1987: 161). For Prometheus, work and utility are all; beauty and Eros are of little account.

By way of contrast, Marcuse offers a countervailing figure, combined of elements from Orpheus and Narcissus (as well as Dionysus, 'the antagonist of the god who sanctions the logic of domination, the realm of reason'). Theirs are the voice 'which does not command but sings; the gesture which offers and receives; the deed which is peace and ends the labor of conquest; the liberation of time which unites man with god, man with nature' (Marcuse 1987: 163). Marcuse argues that Orpheus and Narcissus – who he reads not in terms of self-regard, but one who 'lives by an Eros of his own', not only himself, but also the other that he does not recognize *as* himself – offer images of experience of and in nature that is not about mastery but about liberation. 'The Orphic and Narcissistic experience of the world negates that which sustains the world of the performance principle,' Marcuse writes; 'The opposition between man and nature, subject and object, is overcome. Being is experienced as gratification, which unites man and nature' (Marcuse 1987: 166). When Orpheus moves the trees to listen to his song, or causes the stones to fall in flight, this is an *erotic* relation to 'inanimate' nature, liberating the potentialities of being. Orpheus's song undoes the animate/inanimate binary, and brings forth a fullness or plenitude of being that represents a *different* Eros, not one confined to the repressive regime of genitality.

In rejecting Prometheus's 'rebellion' as one that validates toil and suffering, Marcuse casts Orpheus and Narcissus as figures who 'protest against the repressive order of procreative sexuality' (Marcuse 1987: 171). The Orphic and Narcissistic Eros is one of song, play, beauty and contemplation. It is associated with the death drive (Thanatos) because it engages what Marcuse calls the 'Nirvana principle' (again taken from *Beyond the Pleasure Principle*), the flight from pain and lack towards a state of quiescence. Orpheus and Narcissus offer a full Eros encompassing both life *and* death, love *and* quiescence. Their deaths are indices of their own 'Great Refusal', their unwillingness to accept the normal Eros of repression and toil. Marcuse writes:

> The Orphic-Narcissistic images are those of the Great Refusal: refusal to accept separation from the libidinous object (or subject). The refusal aims at liberation – at the reunion of what has become separated. Orpheus is the archetype of the poet as *liberator* and *creator*: he establishes a higher order in the world – an order without repression. In his person, art, freedom, and

culture are eternally combined. He is a poet of redemption, the god who brings peace and salvation by pacifying man and nature, not through force but through song. (Marcuse 1987: 170)

In the hands of Marcuse, then, Orpheus becomes not the emblem of traumatic loss, but of poetic inspiration, of a pursuit of Eros unto and even beyond death. Orpheus's journey to the underworld is itself a 'refusal' to accept limitations to his love, a refusal which is accounted more powerful than his second loss of Eurydice.

Tom McCarthy, particularly in the non-fictional works written under the aegis of his part-parodic avant-garde group the International Necronautical Society, himself returns (almost compulsively) to the myth of Orpheus, and in particular Jean Cocteau's *Orphée* (1950), as a means by which to bring together several strands of Modernist artistic practice, to interrogate the matrices of transmissions, signifying systems and intertexts that constitute contemporary culture. McCarthy's reading of Orpheus emphasizes an 'aesthetic of repetition' (McCarthy 2012a: 165) that is, of course, true to the orality of Orpheus the poet: he is not an originator, but a weaver and transmitter of images, phrases and stories that are recognizable to the listener. Orpheus thereby compromises the idea of poetic genius and originality that suffuses post-Romantic thinking; in his investigation of the practices of the remix in *Transmission and the Individual Remix*, the very title of which appropriates and repurposes T. S. Eliot's 'Tradition and the Individual Talent', the Orphean mode of transmission becomes the sign under which many forms of artistic making, from electronic music like Kraftwerk, to sampling, to the appropriative strategies that passed into Modernist poetics through Dada, from Tzara to Duchamp. It is Jean Cocteau's *Orphée* that is the cinematic emblem of these practices.

In Cocteau's *Orphée*, Jean Marais plays Orpheus, a poet who fears losing his gifts, and who suffers the loss of his wife when Orpheus's Death (personified by Maria Casares) falls in love with him, and deceives him by sending messages via car radio which he then copies down and presents to the public, to great success, as his own work. Some of these are numbers (referring to the coded broadcasts of the BBC to French Resistance fighters in Occupied France in World War II), but some have a dislocated, surreal quality: 'A single glass of water lights up the world'; 'Jupiter enlightens those he would destroy.' The exogenous nature of Orpheus's poetry – it is actually composed by his great (and deceased) young rival, Cégeste – connects Cocteau's *Orphée* to Rilke, and also to EVP, the disembodied voices we saw in the work of Konstantin

Raudive in the previous chapter, calling via sound broadcast technologies, with mysterious intention. Orpheus asks the angel Heurtebise, 'Where can they be coming from?' It is, of course, from the 'electronic elsewhere'. Tom McCarthy calls these 'found' phrases 'exquisite finds . . . miracle fragments, miniature celebrations of silence and playback, illumination, mourning, and avian transmission, of cards, wisdom and loss' (McCarthy 2012a: 165). This 'aesthetic of repetition' – 'je repète' – is also a poetics of *transmission*, where 'the author of the fragments is not the originator but rather the repeater whose composing consists first and foremost of listening' (McCarthy 2012a: 165). Not only does McCarthy displace an originary integrated subjectivity in his work, then, but he also theorizes his literary or artistic creation through *mediumship*. Orpheus is re-imagined as a listener or *receiver* of broadcasts, the lyre a kind of electronic Aeolian harp which 'sings' to the aetheric broadcasts that surround us. Cocteau's Orpheus does indeed retrieve his Eurydice from the underworld, and although the prohibition about looking back at his wife remains intact, this version of the narrative does not end in disaster (and dismemberment), but in a kind of triumph over Death, albeit mysterious and problematic. It is this element of Death, and the possibility of a journey *into* death, that informs the International Necronautical Society project; Orpheus's own journey to retrieve Eurydice, to explore the space of death, becomes that of the INS itself, philosophically and poetically.

In both *What Dreams May Come* and *Inception*, the journey into the Underworld, into the space of death, is a narrative of restitution for the male protagonist who has suffered the loss of his wife (both by suicide), a means by which to undo trauma and suture together Eros and Thanatos. In *What Dreams May Come*, Robin Williams plays Dr Christy Neilsen, a caring and sympathetic paediatrician who inhabits a rather buttoned-up masculinity, which becomes particularly apparent in the scenes where he interacts with his son Ian (Josh Paddock). As a father, Christy allows the high standards by which he sets his own achievements to determine those he sets for his son; but as a husband, Christy is loving and supportive. Williams plays Nielsen as a variant on his Peter Banning in Spielberg's *Hook* (1991), a yuppified middle-aged businessman whose economic success causes him to neglect his family and, in particular, his relationship with his son, who at one point in the film seems to adopt Captain Hook as a surrogate father as a means by which to punish his neglectful father. Like *Hook*, *What Dreams May Come* is a narrative of learning and healing for the middle-aged, middle-class white male protagonist, who must adjust the model of masculinity he inhabits in order to heal the familial bonds which have been placed under great strain. For Banning, who must discover the 'inner child' (in fact, his 'true' identity as Peter Pan), this is at once a liberation and a means by which to re-establish the loving parental bonds he had neglected; for Christy Nielsen, he must recognize that the 'strong' masculinity he has performed was in fact a place in which to escape the emotional vulnerability and contact that was necessary, in particular, to sustain his wife after the deaths of their children in an automobile accident. The film begins before the children's deaths, with a breakfast scene in which Nielsen is rather withdrawn, but after they and their mother drive away to school and work, a fade-to-white and a title indicating the time has shifted to 'four years later' leaves a narrative gap that will only be filled later in the film. In this gap, Nielsen's wife Annie (Annabella Sciorra) attempts to commit suicide and is confined to a convalescent home, and only at the point at which Nielsen offers to withdraw from their marriage entirely and leave her alone that a reconciliation is effected. This narrative is shown in flashback at points in the main diegesis, often through memories told from Nielsen's point of view. The main narrative follows Nielsen's own death, as he attends an automobile accident in a tunnel, after which he is translated to an afterlife where he must come to terms with the emotional tensions in relation to his children, and then after Annie has succeeded in another suicide attempt, to rescue her from a kind of limbo.

As we saw in Chapter 3 in the Bourne films, *What Dreams May Come* articulates a double narrative, in which a quest or journey is mapped upon a recovery of traumatic memories and a coming to terms with particular constructions of masculinity. For Nielsen, these way points are figured in encounters with other inhabitants of the afterlife, who are, at first, in disguise, though he does not know it. His Virgilian mentor in the afterlife presents himself in the guide of Albert Lewis (Cuba Gooding Jr), 'the only man he would ever listen to', who guides him through his early experiences in 'heaven'. Part-way through their journey into Hell, to find Annie, Nielsen comes to the understanding that 'Albert Lewis' is in fact his son, who has presented himself in the form of another to circumvent pre-existing emotional frameworks. Similarly, his daughter Marie (Jessica Brooks Grant) disguises herself in the form of Leona (Rosalind Chao) before Nielsen is able to realize who she is. This fluidity in terms of subjectivity and disguise is not, however, accorded to Nielsen or his wife. Robin Williams, as Nielsen, in particular, is always *himself*; he must change his appreciation of his life and his family, but there is no flux associated with him. He remains solid.

This is not true of the afterlife that he enters and nor of the other characters in the film. 'Albert Lewis' is first shown, when Nielsen is a ghost haunting his own funeral, as a blurred or smeared body, flickering through the spaces of the film. Annie, an artist, herself has painted a self-portrait which approximates this smearing in a rendition that inevitably recalls the work of Francis Bacon; immediately prior to her suicide, she is shown looking into a mirror, fogged with condensation which visually enacts the same blurring. Annie's personality, her femininity, flagged as fragile and with undefended boundaries, is contrasted with Nielsen's 'strong' masculinity, which, in part, supports her. The failure of this 'strength' is revealed upon Nielsen's own death, whereupon Annie no longer wishes to live; he has simply propped her up, and has not enabled her (and himself) to heal. This marked difference between the two plays against the idea that Nielsen and Annie are 'soul mates', whose fates are unusually closely connected; in a flashback to when they first meet, boating separately on the Swiss border, they are both dressed in white, and she is able to find him on a mountainside seemingly by intuition. This boating scene foreshadows Nielsen's later journey to Hell where, trapped by the naked bodies of the lost, his skiff capsizes and he sinks below the water.

Immersion in water is a recurrent motif in the film. Nielsen is seen in a water fight with his children early in the narrative; an important dialogue with Ian takes place in a deluge; and several times in the afterlife he sinks below the surface of water, to comedic effect (when first met by 'Albert Lewis') and later to more unsettling purpose, when the film's repeated imprecation 'don't give up' is foregrounded. *What Dreams May Come* uses a densely symbolic visual register and an extraordinarily painterly mode of rendition, literally so when Nielsen first enters the afterlife and discovers himself lying in a meadow of painted grasses and wildflowers. (He has entered the visual field of a painting made by his wife.) Drawing upon paintings of sublime and Romantic landscape, the representation of the continuation of life after life is both spectacular and unreal, corresponding to the idea that those who are translated there 'make their own universes'. The 'city' shown to him by Leona is shared, however, and his ability to connect with others is an important sign of the shift in Nielsen's masculinity.

In his journey to Hell, Nielsen is aided by another mentor, the Tracker (Max von Sydow), who eventually reveals himself to be the 'real' Albert Lewis, again in disguise. The Tracker eventually delivers him to his wife (via another fall into deep water), whom Nielsen finds in a ruined version of their shared house built among the arches of what appears to be a vast upturned cathedral built of grey stone. While explicitly repudiating a theological reading that suicides are outside of the state of Grace, the film suggests that the taking of one's own life is a transgression that forms its own punishment in a continuation of self-absorption and pain for 'eternity'. In essence, Annie's female subjectivity is unable to 'carry on', to manage or repress trauma and continue life; in death, she is trapped in a form of repetition-compulsion, eternally reliving her guilt and despair that led to the act of suicide. Annie is no Prometheus, punished for transgression in Tartarus, forced to return again to the same wounding and agony; rather, she is a Eurydice who is unable to recognize her husband and who blames herself for her own death (and those of her children and Nielsen himself). Though cautioned by the Tracker that he will be unable to break through her cycle of self-accusation and punishment, Nielsen ultimately decides to sacrifice himself and stay with his wife in a shared Hell, a gesture that brings Annie to herself again. Nielsen is 'saved' by Annie when he too falls into despair, a reversal that is meant to ameliorate the narrative patterning of feminine passivity and masculine agency encoded by the Orpheus story; but although they are 'soul mates', and although he renounces his 'strong' masculinity as a form of cowardice, it is a masculine sacrifice or self-abnegation that eventually brings narrative closure.

In Christopher Nolan's *Inception*, the inversion of the Orphean narrative, so that the journey of the masculine protagonist is really a quest to save himself rather than his wife, becomes explicit to the extent that this film's Eurydice, Mal (Marion Cotillard) has committed suicide some time before the start of the film, and exists only as a projection in the mind of the Orphean protagonist, Dominic Cobb (Leonardo di Caprio). In fact, *Inception* seems to use an overtly Freudian conception of both dream work and of 'levels' of the subconscious, in which Cobb's guilt about the death of his wife leads to Mal being 'repressed' to the basement of his psychic architecture, but escaping these constraints to haunt other 'levels' of Cobb's mind. The narrative of *Inception* seems to work as a standard thriller narrative with science-fictional trappings: Cobb and his team are hired by a Japanese corporation to implant an idea in the mind of a rival business man, which will result in the willed break-up of the rival corporation. To enable this 'inception', a dream designer known as the 'Architect' (Ariadne, played by Ellen Page) creates 'levels' which are traversed by the team in order for the team's target, Robert Fischer (Cillian Murphy), to confront his own problematic relationship with his father and break away from his legacy, dissolving the corporation in the process. This narrative, at which the action of each level works at different speeds but which all must interlock, is handled masterfully by Nolan and editor Lee Smith; but the narrative is doubled by the sense that Cobb, who is using this 'last job' to 'go home' to his children in the United States, puts his team at risk through the disruptions to his own psychological integrity, the extent of which he does not reveal to them. Cobb is traumatized, and the presence of a residual trace of his wife Mal in his subconscious (she appears unbidden several times in the film, 'haunting' dream space and transgressing borders) is an index of his trauma.

Cobb is an archetypal contemporary wounded masculine subject who longs for a kind of quiescence but, until the end of the film, is unable to confront the source of his own psychological fragmentation, which is his guilt over his wife's death. Cobb knows that inception will work, in the face of scepticism from others, because he has performed it on Mal, to allow them to escape a 50-year-long sojourn in 'limbo' (an 'unreconstructed dream space' many 'levels' from consciousness) that she does not, in fact, want to return from. To enable this, Cobb implants the idea that the real is only apparently so; once Mal returns to the 'real' of consciousness, she is unable to escape the 'viral' nature of this idea, which supposes that the 'real' is a dream. To escape this illusory world, Mal commits suicide; not because she no longer wants to live, but because she has lost contact with life and desires to reconnect with it. Where Cobb desires an absence of pain, Mal desired a return to a kind of plenitude, a fullness of pleasure and pain that constitutes the 'real'. It is as if Freud's 'membrane', the affective shell that prevents the subject from annihilation by the bombardment of stimuli, has become an armour for Mal; she wishes to 'explode' out of it and, indeed, to 'fuse' with Cobb. As Annie and Christy in *What Dreams May Come*, Mal and Cobb are two separate, split parts of the hermaphroditic 'wheel men' in the *Symposium*, who long to return to wholeness. This longing is ultimately rejected by Cobb, towards the end of the film, when he tells his internal construction of 'Mal' that she is only a 'shade' of the perfection and imperfection of his actual wife. 'We had our time together,' he tells her, meaning the 50 'years' spent in limbo, 'I have to let you go.'

In its desire to 'go home' – which Cobb achieves at the end of the film – *Inception* presents itself as an intensely nostalgic narrative for the masculine protagonist. Like *What Dreams May Come*, *Inception* proposes that healing from trauma is possible, that wounds may be addressed and healed. If the unconscious is a labyrinth, it remains one that can be penetrated by the masculine agent and the quest, the 'mission', completed. As in the final stages of the film, the narrative offers a 'short cut' through the maze of memory, trauma and guilt back to a kind of primal scene, whether this is Fischer's bedside visit at the point of his father's death, or Cobb's replaying of his 'betrayal' of Mal to return them both to the 'real'. It is this, rather than the fact of Mal's suicide, which is the crucial traumatic act in *Inception*; notably, it is one perpetrated by the protagonist, both against his loved one and against himself. That the source of trauma in this revision of the Orpheus story is relentlessly internalized completes the logic of the film itself, in which the cinematic 'real' is at the service of a spectacular presentation of internal landscapes. The journey into the space of death is, in *What Dreams May Come* and in *Inception* the journey within, to the 'depths' of despair and pain; but, ultimately, the journey into death, into the Underworld, unlike in *Orphée*, is a return to life.

12

Lecter

For some 30 years now, the figure of the serial killer has been a recurrent and highly visible presence in genre literature, in film and on television. A transgressive figure, the serial killer has gravitated from the masked, monstrous predators of *Halloween* (the character of Michael Myers, wearing a William Shatner mask, 1978) and *Friday the 13th* (the hockey-masked Jason Vorhees, 1978), through the *guignol* burlesque of Freddie Kruger in *A Nightmare on Elm Street* (1984), to the protagonist killers such as *Dexter* (2006–13). Richard Dyer, in his BFI Modern Classic text on David Fincher's *Seven* (1997), notes that the 'serial killer has become a widespread figure in films, novels, television series, true crime coverage and even painting, poetry, opera and rock music', and that 'they have increasingly been seen to be expressive specifically of masculinity in contemporary society' (37). More particularly, Dyer suggests that serial killer masculinity is coded as white masculinity. Where, he suggests, in contemporary culture '[w]hite masculinity occupies the space of ordinariness', films such as *Seven* render this 'notional invisibility' visible (45). They also stage ethnic or racial difference. Dyer continues: 'If [Morgan] Freeman/Somerset's blackness alerts us to the whiteness of serial killing, [Brad] Pitt/Mills's whiteness perhaps suggests the serial killingness of whiteness' (40). Serial killer texts have, therefore, become significant cultural indices of problematic constructions of masculinity and anxieties about masculine desire, subjectivity and violence.

Perhaps the most important argument in Carol J. Clover's *Men, Women and Chainsaws: Gender in the Modern Horror Film* (1992) surrounds the figure of the 'Final Girl' in horror films, the female survivor of the attacks of the killer. Clover suggests that the mode of spectatorship in these films is fluid, moving across genders and between victim and victimizer. Those who revel in the murders and repartee of Freddy Kruger in Wes Craven's *A Nightmare on Elm Street* also identify with the female protagonist Nancy (Heather Langencamp), and enjoy the destruction of her tormentor. More significantly, the 'Final Girl' is implicitly masculinized in the course of the narratives, just as the killer often suffers 'gender distress': both share masculinity, in the phallic symbols (knife, chainsaw) they wield; and both share the potentiality for 'femininity', in that the Final Girl symbolically or physically castrates the killer. 'Male' spectators then identify with both a feminized male killer, and a masculinized female survivor, finding pleasure in the actions and the suffering of both. Clover's seductive explanatory model has been influential, but criticism of horror films often paradoxically de-emphasizes the figure of the killer itself. Clover suggests that sexual repression lies at the heart of the 'killer' male subjectivity:

> The notion of a killer propelled by psychosexual fury, more particularly a male in gender distress, has proved a durable one, and the progeny of Norman Bates stalk the genre up to the present day. (27)

This 'psychosexual fury' is determined by sexual repression. Clover suggests that 'violence and sex are not concomitants but alternatives' (29) in the slasher film. In both, desire for the body is repressed and is represented through aggression, violence and wounds.

The serial killer himself (for, as Clover notes, there are few female killers) is a particularly significant figure, one who exhibits these signs of 'gender distress'. Clover argues that the Final Girl and the killer are, in a sense, doubled: the Final Girl is masculinized by appropriating the excessive phallic symbols of the killer (knife or chainsaw); and the killer is feminized by the threat and execution of a symbolic castration, at the hands of the Final Girl and his own phallic symbols. Richard Dyer also notes, in relation to the serial killer Jonathan Doe in *Seven*, that '[t]here is a slight implication that Doe as a man is sexually inadequate or possibly homosexual' (38). What I shall argue here is that the emphasis on the *mask* in slasher films stages a parodic normativeness, beneath which this gender distress is repressed/expressed. The masked killers include Michael Myers in *Halloween*, Jason Vorhees in the *Friday the 13th* series, Hannibal Lecter in *The Silence of the Lambs*, the killer in the *Scream* series, the prosthetic mask of Freddy Kruger in *A Nightmare on Elm Street* and the blank, affectless face of Jonathan Doe in *Seven*. The mask implies *masquerade*, and this theoretical paradigm (offered by Joan Riviere in relation to female subjectivity) has recently been taken up in relation to masculinity. In the collection *The Masculine Masquerade*, Harry Brod investigates the use of masquerade as a rethinking of male subjectivity, particularly the centrality of *performance* in relation to subjectivity. Drawing on Paul Hoch's *White Hero, Black Beast*, Brod argues:

[w]hat is being masked and repressed to present the face of masculinity is an earlier more 'feminine' anal eroticism, a repression also linked to the suppression of homosexuality. The masculine mask is worn in order to achieve a normative performance-oriented phallic heterosexual male sexuality. . . . There is, however, a crucial difference between the conceptualizations of gender as performance and gender as masquerade, for masquerade invokes a distinction between the artificial and the real. Behind the facade of the mask lies the *real* face, to be revealed when the masquerade is over. (17)

The mask is one of normativeness, but the mask that the serial killer wears is a parodic normativeness, either blank (Michael Myers) or grotesque (Lecter). This excessive or parodic normativeness is paradoxically a revelation of the non-normativeness and violence of the killer's desires. The mask of the serial killer signifies the constructedness of masculinity and cultural anxieties about what desires may boil 'behind' that mask.

Hannibal Lecter

Despite the volumes of films produced in the *Halloween*, *Friday the 13th* and *Nightmare on Elm Street* franchises, the serial killer figure with the greatest pop-cultural longevity is Thomas Harris's Hannibal Lecter, the subject of four novels, five films and a television series. Lecter remains a figure of some interest with regard to masculinity, subjectivity, trauma and agency. One of the ways in which Harris's texts indicate the blurring of the self/other binary, thereby destabilizing unitary subjectivity, is by emphasizing a continuum between the investigating agent (Will Graham in *Red Dragon* or Clarice Starling in *Silence of the Lambs* and *Hannibal*) and their source of knowledge, Dr Lecter. In fact, Graham and Starling's recourse to Lecter's mode of insight – he can understand the serial killers not because of his medical training, but because *he is one himself* – signifies the limits of rational discourse when faced with the seemingly inexplicable actions of the serial killer. In *Red Dragon*, Lecter emphasizes the doubleness of himself and Will Graham when he tells the fleeing investigator: 'Do you know how you caught me, Will? . . . The reason you caught me is that WE'RE JUST ALIKE' (Harris 2000: 75). In *Manhunter*, Michael Mann's 1986 adaptation of *Red Dragon*, Graham (William Petersen) flees Lecter's cell at the run after this dialogue scene (filmed almost in its entirety by Mann), running not only from his nemesis but also from the fatal recognition of his own similarity to, rather than difference from, Dr Lecter. In Demme's *Silence of the Lambs*, shots in which Lecter's face is reflected in near-superimposition on Clarice Starling's, in the Perspex of Lecter's cell, signify the same doubling.

Lecter, the 'monster' (as he is called in all three novels) is, perversely, increasingly placed in the role of the hero, particularly in *Hannibal*, where the narrative of the novel finds perverse resolution in the 'romance' between Lecter and Starling. Lecter's isolation is undone at the end of *Hannibal* through the transgressive 'romance' with Starling, and he seems to achieve his own space of peace and tranquillity. The 'Satanic' traces of the Gothicized Romantic (or Byronic) hero, the destructive individual, are turned into the hero of romance: rescue, seduction and the creation of the *Reich der Zwei*. In the first of the novels, *Red Dragon*, in an analogous way to the positioning of the abject Dracula against the legitimated masculine subjects of the Crew of Light in Stoker's *Dracula* (1897), Lecter is the displaced Other to the 'rational' investigators. This works in *Hannibal* by Harris's use of point of view and our access to Lecter's interiority. Although this is used in a much more pervasive way in *Hannibal*, even in *Red Dragon* we are offered Lecter's point of view: 'Lecter felt much better. He thought he might surprise Graham with a call sometime or, if the man couldn't be civil, he might have a supply-house mail Graham a colostomy bag for old time's sake' (Harris 2000: 78). The role played by the reader's, and viewer's, increasing identification with Lecter's point of view is a vital means by which Harris is able to realign Lecter from the position of monstrous Other to Romantic Self.

The final guarantor of the fixity of Lecter's subjectivity is a reversal of the field of the self/other binary, not its dissolution. Lecter is placed in contradistinction to Dollarhyde and Gumb, rather than Starling and the FBI: the fluid or ruptured subjectivities of the serial killers (Gumb is a 'failed' transsexual, Dollarhyde in *Red Dragon* obsessed with his own 'Becoming') throwing into relief the unitary self of Enlightenment rationality and Romantic feeling. The novels had worked, even from *Red Dragon*, to recruit Lecter into the role of investigator rather than that of the investigated. In parallel scenes in the first two novels, Lecter deduces important information about Will Graham and Starling through his sense of smell. He is able to detect, and name the scent that they wear, in something of an echo of Sherlock Holmes, who is another figure of Enlightenment reason destabilized by excessive behaviour, and a taste for disguise. Lecter *is*: his 'evil' is unchanging. Note the echoes of Milton's Satan in Lecter's self-declared identity (we will return to Lecter's Satanism later in the chapter) in the following passage:

> Nothing happened to me, Officer Starling. *I* happened. You can't reduce me to a set of influences. You've given up on good and evil for behaviorism, Officer Starling. You've got everyone in moral dignity pants – nothing is ever anyone's fault. Look at me, Officer Starling. Can you stand to say I'm evil? Am I evil, Officer Starling? (Harris 2000: 409)

This dialogue is absent from the film, where Lecter brushes off the Behavioural Science questionnaire Starling proffers with the words 'You think you can dissect me with this blunt little tool?' In the novel, Lecter repudiates psychiatric or medical discourse in relation to himself ('Can you stand to say I'm evil?') while using the very same tools of analysis on Starling. Instead, he insists upon the 'I': his is the Cartesian, self-identical subject of the Enlightenment, albeit continually ruptured by a transgressive excess of 'passion'. In Lecter's case, the implication of rationality and non-rationality, reason and 'passion', is all too violently manifest.

It is very curious, then, to note what happens towards the end of Harris's *Hannibal*. It is revealed that Lecter once had a sibling: a sister called Mischa. The Lecter children, growing up on the Baltic, suffer the depredations of fleeing German soldiers on the collapse of the Eastern Front in 1944. Just as Clarice had been haunted by the screaming of the lambs, Lecter is haunted by the memory of his lost sister. In an interior scene of recall (denoted by italics), Lecter remembers his own primal scene of trauma:

> *He prayed so hard that he would see Mischa again, the prayer consumed his six-year old mind, but it did not drown out the sound of the axe. His prayer to see her again did not go entirely unanswered – he did see a few milk teeth in the reeking stool pit his captors used between the lodge where they slept and the barn where they held the captive children who were their sustenance in 1944 after the Eastern Front collapsed.* (Harris 2000: 994; Harris's italics)

The seemingly offhand revelation of Mischa's death through cannibalism is made still more obscene by its association with the 'stool pit': here we find Julia Kristeva's concept of the abject, the tabooed and expelled, in extreme form. It is also close to blasphemous: although it affirms God's presence through the 'answer' the young Hannibal receives, this only confirms a cruel, malignant, even diabolical Godhead. Lecter's later activities, and his Satanic stylings, are decodable first as a rebellion against, yet mirror image of, the God that rules the revolting world of humankind; and second, as the manifestation of the very trauma that deforms him, that makes him monstrous. The discourse of religion as a recourse to the explanation of 'evil' is placed in opposition to a psychological model of trauma and 'acting out'. Throughout the novels, Harris seemingly has an investment in debunking the explanatory power of Behavioural Science and other rational, scientific discourses, when faced with the excessively transgressive acts of the serial killers (Lecter, in *The Silence of the Lambs*, pithily dismisses psychoanalysis, somewhat ironically, as a 'dead religion' (Harris 2000: 546)). In the figure of Mischa, the lost sibling, childhood trauma restores psychiatric discourse (the discourse of reason), evacuating the discourse of the monstrous/'evil', making Lecter finally explicable.

All this returns the narrative, rather surprisingly, to rationality: 'evil' is contained within medical discourse. Discourses for understanding the 'mad' return 'madness' (rationality's other) to reason: history, explanation, psychology.

Harris at first insists that 'Madness' (or the 'evil' subjectivity of the serial killer) exceeds the bounds of rational discourse: 'Senator Martin and Hannibal Lecter considered each other, one extremely bright and the other not measurable by any means known to man' (Harris 2000: 581), but then contains this by reasserting a psychological framework for understanding Lecter not as an incomprehensible 'evil' entity, but a pathological one. The failure to understand madness/the serial killer through reason was outlined in *Red Dragon*:

> Dr Lecter is not crazy, in any common way we think of as being crazy. He did some hideous things because he enjoyed them. But he can function perfectly when he wanted to. . . . They say he's a sociopath because they don't know what else to call him. . . . He's a monster. (Harris 2000: 61)

Throughout the novels, Harris refers to Lecter as 'the fiend', 'the monster', yet ultimately cannot resist psychologizing his protagonist, just as he had Starling, Graham, Dollarhyde and Gumb. While serial killer fictions indicate the limits of rational discourse, and gesture towards the discourse of religion ('monster', 'evil', 'sin') to signify that which lies outside the explicatory powers of science, medicine or reasoned understanding, Harris's Lecter novels cannot embrace this radical destabilization, and in fact work hard to reinstate the unitary subject by repressing the polyvalent subjectivities of Dollarhyde and Gumb, returning us finally to the comforts of reason, and the unitary subject.

Lecter and Romantic Satanism

Lecter first considers Starling to be Mischa's replacement, or a vessel ('a place in the world') for the lost Mischa to inhabit if, through his monstrously transgressive acts, Lecter were able to complete his 'real' project: to reverse time. (This is perhaps his most grandly Satanic aspect, and conforms to another incarnation of Mario Praz's Byronic Fatal Man: he 'dreams of perfecting the world by committing crimes' (Praz 1954: 78). In another echo, the Mischa/ Clarice identification seems to suggest a quasi-incestuous relationship, suggesting Byron's 'incestuous' adultery.) Lecter, at the end of *Hannibal*, stands in his most transgressive guise: the typical Romantic masculine poet/hero. His insertion into a curious (perhaps grotesque) romantic couple with Clarice Starling comes at some cost, however. Lecter's 'silencing' of Starling's lambs is not merely a healing, but also a destruction of the Other. The 'overcoming' of the boundary between self and other here results in the ultimate colonization: the displacement of Starling's identity. The final recourse of the novel is to fix Lecter in the role of the Self, a self that has seemingly absorbed the Other. The serial killer fiction finally makes manifest the violence of the construction of the Enlightenment/Romantic self, a construction of a masculine subject completed by Lecter's symbolic cannibalization of Clarice Starling, the destruction of his own (feminine) Other.

In Harris's *Hannibal* (1999), the eponymous serial killer relocates to Florence. Having disposed of the librarian of the 'fabled Capponi library', Lecter, posing as one 'Dr Fell', proceeds to give a lecture on Dante and Judas Iscariot to the Studiolo, 'the most renowned medieval and Renaissance scholars in the world' (Harris 2000: 934), in order to secure his nomination for the now-vacated position. Lecter proceeds to give a slide show involving death by hanging of avaricious betrayers, of which Judas is the archetype and the policeman who pursues Lecter/Fell, *Commendatore* Pazzi, is the modern analogue. Pazzi is also a member of the audience for the lecture. Lecter/Fell proceeds to read (literally, in a flawless Tuscan 'without accent') Canto XIII of Dante's *Inferno*, which narrates Dante and Virgil's encounter with the seventh circle of Hell, the violent. Dante comes across a wood in the Second Round, filled with trees full of 'poisonous thorns' (Dante 1961: 167). Dante hears voices but presumes they come from people hidden behind the trees; but when he reaches out his hand to unthinkingly pluck 'a twig from a great thorn' (Dante 1961: 169), the tree trunk itself cries out: 'Why dost thou tear me?': 'from the broken splinter came forth words and blood together' (Dante 1961: 169). These are men turned into trees, men who had committed violence against themselves. This is the circle of Hell for the suicides.

The tree explains that he was once the Chancellor of Emperor Frederick II, and who was himself accused of treason, blinded and cast into prison, where he committed suicide. His name is Piero delle Vigne, whose courteous language and reverence towards his former 'master' (he also calls Frederick 'Caesar' and 'Augustus') indicates his undimmed faithfulness, and whose suffering arouses pity in both Virgil (who calls delle Vigne 'wounded soul' (Dante 1961: 169)) and Dante (who cannot question the tree further, 'such pity fills my heart' (Dante 1961: 171)). The tree, impelled to speak truth in Hell, reveals that 'never did [he] break faith with [his] lord' (Dante 1961: 171); but the true horror of his suffering is still to be revealed. When the suicide dies, Minos, the keeper of Hell, throws the soul down to the seventh circle, where it sprouts and grows into a 'savage tree'. Once it bears leaves, 'the Harpies, feeding on its leaves, cause pain and for the pain an outlet' (Dante 1961: 171). To return for a moment to *Hannibal*, this is the point in the lecture that Lecter/Fell begins to quote directly from Dante:

> *Surge in vermena e in pianta silvestre:*
> *L'Arpie, pascendo poi de la sui foglie,*
> *Fanno dolore, e al dolor fenestra.* (Harris 2000: 936)

Lecter/Fell describes the scene in the *Inferno* thus: 'he tells of dragging, with the other damned, his own dead body to hang upon a thorn tree' (Harris 2000: 936). In fact, delle Vigne is describing what will happen on the day of judgement: he, like the other shades in Hell, will drag his own body to be hung on the very thorn tree that sprouts from where their soul fell, a kind of torture that echoes the crucifixion of Christ (the body hung up, the thorns). The lines of Dante that Lecter/Fell quotes are crucial, for they describe the leaves that grow and are eaten by Harpies, causing pain; the leaves grow again and are eaten again. Neither Lecter/Fell nor John D. Sinclair notice what seems to be a clear reference here to the suffering of Prometheus, the Titan of Greek mythology who attempted to amend the fault of his brother Epimetheus (who made Man but was so prodigal in assigning talents to other beings that nothing was left for Man; Prometheus was impelled to steal fire from the Gods and give it to humans to recompense them for the lack of other abilities), and was punished by being chained to a rock while vultures pecked at his liver, which grew back as fast as it was consumed. Prometheus, in the hands of Romantic poets such as P. B. Shelley, becomes the figure of titanic suffering for rebellion against the (unjust) rule of the Gods; I will return to this shortly.

In the *Inferno*, delle Vigne is a pitiable figure, whose suffering stirs great sympathy in Dante and his guide. In *Hannibal*, Lecter/Fell paints a quite different picture. Lecter/Fell avers that 'Dante recalls . . . the death of Judas in the death of Pier della Vigna for the same crimes of avarice and treachery' (Harris 2000: 937). Not so. Delle Vigne in fact offers precisely the reverse of the figure of Judas in his faithfulness. If he were as treacherous and avaricious as Lecter/Fell suggests, delle Vigne would be in a lower circle of Hell, much closer to Satan. Why, then, is Lecter/Fell so wrong? Is it that Harris himself misunderstands the import of Canto XIII, stressing the confluence of hanging, betrayal and avarice to the detriment of Dante's actual text? If it is Lecter/Fell's mistake, wouldn't the 'most renowned' scholars of the Studiolo notice? This is probably unresolvable, but I would like to suggest a possible solution: that Harris introduces the Promethean figure of delle Vigne purposefully to suggest a figure of titanic suffering, but through a quasi-academic sleight of hand, wishes to stress not the Promethean or Satanic rebellion against God – a type that I will argue in this chapter is increasingly identified with Lecter himself – but the Judas-like properties of Lecter's antagonist in this section of the novel, *Commendatore Pazzi*. This typing of the hanged betrayer immediately foreshadows Pazzi's own death by hanging, engineered by Lecter. The greed and betrayal of Pazzi, when seen as analogous to that of Judas (and of Lecter/Fell's creative mis-reading of delle Vigne), almost serves to legitimize his murder. One can, however, trace the lineaments of an alternate reading of this scene, indicated by Lecter/Fell's significant reading of the *Inferno* section in which delle Vigne tells of the Harpies eating the leaves of the thorn trees. In this alternative reading, Pazzi is not Judas, but God's instrument, albeit an avaricious one; and Lecter not the betrayed, but God's Adversary: Satan.

Before attending Lecter/Fell's lecture, Pazzi prays in the Pazzi chapel in Florence, 'one of the glories of Renaissance architecture' (Harris 2000: 931). While Pazzi does not deceive himself about the rather venal nature of what he is about to do (or try to do), he says, 'aloud to God',

> 'Thank you, Father, for allowing me to remove this monster, monster of monsters, from your Earth. Thank you on behalf of the souls We will spare of pain.' Whether this was the magisterial 'We' or a reference to the partnership of Pazzi and God is not clear, and there may not be a single answer. (Harris 2000: 931)

The text here seems to point to Pazzi's presumption in accounting himself God's appointed 'partner', and its rationalization of self-seeking, avarice and corruption, but his gesture to look up at the point of death, hoping 'so much, that God could see' (Harris 2000: 942), does suggest a deeply felt faith. The rhetoric of 'monster', though, repeats that which is used to characterize Lecter from *Red Dragon* through to *Hannibal*, not only by characters within the narrative world of the texts, but also by the putative narrator of the novels, whose presence is particularly intrusive in *Hannibal*. Pazzi's use of it puts him on the side of the sane, if not the side of the angels. Lecter *is* a monster; in a sense, Pazzi is right to plan to dispose of him. However, as I have argued elsewhere, in the development of Harris's fictions involving Lecter, Hannibal 'the cannibal' is increasingly situated at the centre of the narrative, to the extent that we are given access to Lecter's interiority. From a position of monstrous Other, Lecter increasingly becomes stabilized at the centre of the narratives as the Self, offered for identification (and perhaps sympathy). Lecter is re-placed at the centre of the narratives as a redefinition of his subjectivity, achieving a stability guaranteed by his contrast with the fractured, fluid masculinities of the serial killers Francis Dollarhyde (in *Red Dragon*) and Jame Gumb (in *The Silence of the Lambs*). As Sabrina Barton suggests, 'In the economy of selves that the movie sets up, if one marginalized group is allowed to find a subjectivity that feels stable and authentic, another must take its place at the negative pole of performativity' (Barton 2002: 315). As I shall argue in this chapter, however, this re-alignment of Lecter with Self rather than Other does not conflict with his Satanic characterization, but rather follows the Romantic readings of Milton's Satan but as the *hero* of *Paradise Lost* rather than as God's 'evil' adversary.

I would like to stress here both the signs of the diabolic and the heroic in the characterization of Lecter. Part of the stabilization of Lecter's subjectivity is his alignment with the hero of what Peter A. Schock identifies as 'Romantic Satanism', the Romantics' use of Milton's Satan as a symbol for heroic, transgressive rebellion, what Schock further calls 'an idealized antagonist of an Omnipotence embodying the dominant political and religious values of an era' (Schock 2003: 5). Schock writes:

> The presence of various forms of 'Satanism' in Romantic writing has been widely acknowledged. . . . Peter Thorslev identifies the following speech as the *locus classicus* of the Satanic stance in Romantic writing:
>
> > The mind is its own place, and in itself
> > Can make a heaven of hell, a hell of heaven.

> What matter where, if I be still the same,
> And what I should be, all but less than he
> Whom thunder hath made greater? *PL* I, ll.254–8

> Satan's defiant assertion of autonomy, delivered on the burning plain of hell, was so broadly influential [that different types of adaptation of] Satanism have been extended to cover a range of Romantic attitudes or stances – typically individualism, rebellious or defiant self-assertion, and daemonic sublimity. (Schock 2003: 3–4)

For Romantic poets such as Shelley, the figures of Satan (derived from a reading of Milton's *Paradise Lost*) and Prometheus are in close proximity as heroically rebellious figures, as is noted by Mario Praz in *The Romantic Agony*, who writes: 'Milton conferred upon the figure of Satan all the charm of an untamed rebel which already belonged to the Prometheus of Aeschylus' (Praz 1954: 55). In his Preface to 'Prometheus Unbound', Shelley writes:

> The only imaginary being resembling in any degree Prometheus, is Satan, and Prometheus is, in my judgement, a more poetical character than Satan because, in addition to courage and majesty and firm and patient opposition to omnipotent force, he is susceptible of being described as exempt from the taints of ambition, envy, revenge, and a desire for personal aggrandisement, which in the Hero of *Paradise Lost*, interfere with the interest. . . . Prometheus is, as it were, the type of the highest perfection of moral and intellectual nature, impelled by the purest and truest motives to the best and noblest ends. (Shelley 2000a: 734)

Milton's Satan is re-read by the Romantics not as a figure of evil, but as a heroic figure ('courage and majesty') who resists the totalizing power of the monotheistic God ('firm and patient opposition'). Satan becomes not only a figure for Romantic self-assertion, but also (punningly as Lucifer, the 'Son of Light') a curious precursor of Enlightenment emphases on freedom – freedom from arbitrary power, freedom from tradition, freedom of speech and particularly 'freedom of moral man to make his own way in the world' (Gay 1973: l.xii, 3; quoted in Day 1996: 66). This idea of independence, freedom from tutelage, is vital to Immanuel Kant's characterization of the Enlightenment project (such as in his short essay 'An Answer to the Question: What is Enlightenment?') and Aidan Day characterizes it as 'humankind's "resolution and courage" to use the understanding "without the guidance of another"' (Day 1996: 65).

The autonomous Enlightenment and Romantic subject is self-presented in contradistinction to social, political/ideological, hegemonic forces. This, then, is somewhat ironic, as the very nature of this stable unitary subjectivity (inherited from the Enlightenment) recapitulates the hegemon One God (Blake's Urizen) that is rebelled against. The 'tragic rebel' of Milton's Satan simply reflects the One God that is his antagonist. The Romantic Satan finds its analogue in what Mario Praz calls the 'Byronic 'Fatal Man':

> Rebels in the grand manner, grandsons of Milton's Satan and the brothers of Schiller's Robber, begin to inhabit the picturesque, Gothicized backgrounds of the English 'tales of terror' towards the end of the eighteenth century. . . . Certain qualities can be noticed here which were destined to recur insistently in the Fatal Men of the Romantics: mysterious (but conjectured to be exalted) origin, traces of burnt-out passions, suspicion of ghastly guilt, melancholy habits, pale face, unforgettable eyes. (Praz 1954: 59)

At the end of his chapter on 'The Metamorphoses of Satan', Praz connects the Enlightenment libertine 'the Divine Marquis' with the Romantic 'Satanic Lord' Byron (Praz 1954: 81). In these figures, love is implicated in cruelty and violence; desire with destruction; life with death. Here we shade into the Gothic, and Praz himself cites the figure of the vampire (sex/predation, love for/absorption of the Other) as a typical generic form of the *caractère maudit* of both Romantic love and its object of beauty. (Although Harris is careful to assert the cannibal as different from the vampire, the motif of predation and consumption is present in both.) In Ridley Scott's film of *Hannibal*, it is the 'Satanic' figure of the 'mad, bad and dangerous to know' Lord Byron that mediates the characterization of Lecter. In flowing coat and broad-brimmed hat, he is every inch the Gothicized Romantic hero.

Hannibal Lecter is a late avatar of Romantic Satanism, a figure of grand rebellion against a God who boundlessly outmatches Lecter's own appetite for consumption: '*Hannibal Lecter had not been bothered by any considerations of deity, other than to recognize how his own modest predations paled beside those of God, who is in irony matchless, and in wanton malice beyond measure*' [Harris's italics] (Harris 2000: 994). In fact, the ravenous God seemingly present here is much like a deficient demiurge that creates Earth and Man that can be found in the religious teachings of Zoroaster and Gnosticism and is echoed in the rule of Urizen in the works of the Romantic mythographer-poet William Blake. Blake is, of course, himself indebted to Milton, and is an early example of 'Romantic Satanism' to the extent that in *The Marriage of Heaven and Hell*, Blake famously writes that 'the reason Milton wrote in fetters when he wrote of Angels & God, and at liberty when of Devils & Hell, is because he was a true poet and of the Devil's party without knowing it' (Blake 1975: plates 5–6, p. xvii). Lecter's Satanic rebellion takes the form of a denial of God: in *Hannibal Rising*, having found and buried the corpse of his sister, Lecter declares:

> Mischa, we take comfort knowing there is no God. That you are not enslaved in a Heaven, made to kiss God's ass forever. What you have is better than Paradise. You have blessed oblivion. I miss you every day. (Harris 2006: 222)

Traces of Milton can be found even in this denial of God's existence, which at the same time calls up images of servitude (and the key word 'Paradise') that signify a Satanic antagonism.

Lecter, faced with a world in which his sister is a victim of cannibalism, a malign world, also adopts a Satanic position of rebellion against the rule of conventional morality, albeit a transgression relocated as a revenge in the most recent Lecter book, *Hannibal Rising*. Curiously, though, Lecter does come to adopt a kind of code of ethics in the course of the novels. This is proposed most pithily by Barney, the former nurse in the Baltimore State Hospital for the Criminally Insane that houses Lecter in *The Silence of the Lambs*, who says to Clarice Starling in *Hannibal*: 'He told me once that, whenever it was "feasible", he preferred to eat the rude. "Free-range rude," he called them' (Harris 2000: 831). This chimes with Lecter's line to Clarice Starling on their first meeting (when she is sprayed with 'Multiple' Miggs's semen): 'Discourtesy is unspeakably ugly to me' (Harris 2000: 413). Also, at the end of the film of *The Silence of the Lambs*, after Lecter puts down the phone in his last conversation with Clarice, during which he guarantees her ongoing safety from him, he is seen slowly pursuing the oleaginous and undeniably 'rude' Dr Frederick Chilton, once director of the Baltimore State Hospital, somewhere on a street in South America, in order to 'have him to dinner'. In the course of the novels, Lecter is increasingly seen to murder mainly those who threaten him directly or anger him; there is a method in his murderous or monstrous 'madness'.

Lecter is, of course, a serial killer, one of the types of 'evil' in contemporary popular culture, as I noted at the beginning of the chapter. I would like to reiterate here that not only that serial killer fictions signify the boundaries of rational discourse: the incommensurability of the Other to reason is the point at which these texts point towards 'evil', the monstrous and the discourse of religion; but also that serial killer fictions signify the limit case of representations of normative subjectivity and gender roles in contemporary Anglo-American popular culture. Serial killers are archetypal fragmented subjects, emblematic figures indicating the rupture of the unitary subject under the pressures of modernity, particularly in an American context. The serial killers are then non-human or even post-human figures, their fluid or ruptured subjectivities (Gumb is a 'failed' transsexual, Dollarhyde obsessed with his own 'Becoming') throwing into relief the unitary self of monotheism, Enlightenment rationality and Romantic feeling.

Lecter increasingly comes to stand in the place of that unitary self, but it is bound up with evil and particularly with the Satanic: he asks Clarice Starling, 'Can you stand to say I'm evil? Am I evil, Officer Starling?' (Harris 2000: 409). Richard Dyer, in his BFI Modern Classic book on David Fincher's *Seven*, argues as follows:

> The notion of evil, rather than sin, is a common way of dealing with serial killers, often in a context where all other explanations fall short. This is equally true of the coverage of famous cases and in fictions, as at the end of *Halloween* (1978) where the psychiatrist admits that there is no explanation for the remorseless killer Michael other than that he is evil incarnate. Somerset [in *Seven*] himself invokes the notion, when he says that, if, when they finally get the killer, he turns out to be 'Satan himself', that would be satisfying. However, he goes on to say that the sad fact is 'he's not the devil, he's just a man', not an embodiment of the otherness and exteriority of evil, but the common fact of sin. (Dyer 1999: 13–14)

It is interesting that Dyer makes a distinction between 'sin' and 'evil', suggesting the former is quotidian, while the other is transcendent or mythical. In *The Silence of the Lambs*, it is noteworthy that Lecter characterizes Buffalo Bill as sinful rather than evil, particularly considering his own implied self-definition (as evil):

> 'What is the first and principal thing he does, what need does he serve by
> killing?'
> 'Anger, resentment, sexual frus-'
> 'No.'
> 'What, then?'
> 'He covets.' (Harris 2000: 607)

Lecter's assumption of a Biblical discourse in characterizing the serial killer is significant, as is his shutting down of Starling's psychology-based (and perhaps rather pat) answer. It is also, in Dyer's terms, somewhat hierarchical: sin is everyday, while evil is uncommon. Lecter's Satanic grandeur is contrasted with

Jame Gumb/Buffalo Bill's rather ludicrous name, anonymity and occupation as a seamstress. In Demme's film, Ted Levine's performance emphasizes the banality of Gumb, the absence of the quality that ultimately heroizes Lecter: taste.

Lecter is a particular type of serial killer, then, distinct from the fractured, unstable, transformative or masked subjectivities of other fictions (and other serial killers within Harris's fictions). Others do not assume his grandeur, and neither are they surrounded by the signs of the Satanic. For Lecter, these signs abound. In *Hannibal*, the policeman Praz engages a female thief, Romula, to 'botch' a pickpocketing in order to get Lecter's fingerprints (Lecter would seize Romula's wrist, around which was a wide silver bracelet). Romula, clutching her baby as part of her 'act' (an ironic inversion of Madonna and child), awaits Lecter's coming:

> At the moment of touching Dr Fell she looked into his face, felt sucked to the red centers of his eyes, felt the huge cold vacuum pull her heart against her ribs and her hand flew away from his face to cover the baby's face and she heard her voice say '*Perdonami, perdonami, signore,*' turning and fleeing as the doctor looked after her for a long moment. (Harris 2000: 896)

Back with Pazzi, Romula exclaims: 'That is the Devil. . . . Shaitan, Son of the Morning. I've seen him now' (Harris 2000: 897). Later in *Hannibal*, after Lecter has effected his and Clarice Starling's escape from Mason Verger's demonic man-eating pigs, Tommasso, the Sardinian keeper of the pigs, characterizes Lecter as a kind of Lord of the Flies, having supernatural control over other demonic entities:

> [t]he pigs, you must know, the pigs help the *dottore*. They stand back from him, circle him. They kill my brother, kill Carlo, but they stand back from Dr. Lecter. I think they worship him. (Harris 2000: 1165)

Perhaps the most important of the Satanic signs is the name Lecter assumes in Florence, 'Dr. Fell'. Clearly, there is a kind of atrocious punning at work: 'fell' can be connected to hanging and the *Grand Guignol* fate of Pazzi, who, disembowelled, falls to his death (attached to a rope and noose, of course). 'Fell', as used in the phrase 'fell fiend', is also peculiarly apt for the Lecter 'monster'. However, the most insistent allusion seems to be with Lucifer, 'Son of Morning', the 'fallen' archangel of *Paradise Lost*. There, several times in book I, Milton notes Satan's eyes:

> his baleful eyes
> That witness'd huge affliction and dismay

Mixt with obdurate pride and steadfast hate. (Milton 1966: I, ll.56–8);
and

> yet shone
> Above them all th' Archangel; but his face
> Deep scars of Thunder had intrencht, and care
> Sat on his faded cheek, but under brows
> Of dauntless courage, and considerate pride
> Waiting revenge. Cruel his eye, but cast
> Signs of remorse and passion to behold
> The fellows of his crime. (Milton 1966: I, ll.599–606)

Lecter's red or maroon eyes, so powerful that they suck in Romula's consciousness like a vacuum, or command the host of demonic pigs, express his Satanism. The pathos that attends Milton's Satan in his fallen state is not entirely absent from Lecter: he too, as *Hannibal* and *Hannibal Rising* reveal, has witnessed 'huge affliction and dismay', and seems to feel 'remorse and passion' for the memory of his lost sibling, Mischa. In fact, *Hannibal Rising*, which begins with the young Hannibal and his sister playing in the grounds of their home, Lecter Castle in Lithuania, before the arrival of invading German troops during 1941, perhaps suggests some kind of time 'before the fall', a pre-diabolic consciousness lost when his sister is taken from him. *Hannibal Rising* narrates this 'paradise lost', and ultimately the revenge Lecter wreaks upon those who killed and ate Mischa. Its title suggests perhaps a new, self-made Hannibal Lecter, ascending from his 'fallen' state to become the aesthete monster we find in the other books.

In *Paradise Lost*, Satan famously asserts what Peter Schock calls his 'autogeny':

> Who saw
> When this Creation was? Remember'st thou
> They making, when thy Maker gave thee being?
> We know no time when we were not as now,
> Know none before us, self-begot, self-raised
> By our own quick'ning power. (Milton 1966: VI, ll.856–61)

Schock suggests that 'Romantic readers of Milton found the Manichean postulate of Satanic self-assertion compelling' (Schock 2003: 37); 'Romantic Satanism contains a reconception of Milton's fallen angel that is patently an image of apotheosis, an emblem of an aspiring, rebelling, rising human god who insists he is self-created' (Schock 2003: 38). Self-begetting is, then, a form of freedom, not only from the forms and conventions of 'civilized' behaviour, but also from the dominion of God's (deficient) Creation. When Lecter asserts 'Nothing happened to me, Officer Starling. *I* happened' (Harris 2000: 409), it is a declaration of an identity self-begotten, free from the taint of 'influence'. It is noteworthy, of course, that Lecter is also wrong about this, as Harris goes on to demonstrate with *Hannibal* and *Hannibal Rising*, which gives ample evidence of an originary trauma that did 'influence' Lecter and make him into Hannibal 'the cannibal'. Something did indeed happen. Perhaps this is another sleight of hand on Lecter's part, a disavowal of his own history of trauma, and a marker of his difference from, yet similarity to, the other serial killers, Francis Dollarhyde and Jame Gumb, whose subjectivities are not as seemingly fixed as Lecter's ('*I* happened'), but who also wish to transform themselves (to recreate the self or self-beget). The question that Clarice Starling puts to Lecter in *The Silence of the Lambs*, 'Are you strong enough to point that high-powered perception at yourself?' (Harris 2000: 411) remains unanswered in public; but Harris suggests at the very beginning of *Hannibal Rising* that 'pleas and screaming fill some places on the grounds [of Lecter's internal "memory palace"] where Hannibal himself cannot go' (Harris 2006: 1), suggesting Lecter's capacity for self-analysis is limited by the very trauma he disavows.

When Milton's Satan declares his self-begotten status, it is an assertion of radical freedom from the power of God (in the face of the facts of his terrible defeat) to shape subjectivity. Satan's declaration insists that he is *not* a subject at all, but a free individual who exists outside of the dominion of God; Hell becomes a perverse zone of 'liberty'. Satan's famous lines, 'The mind is its own place, and in itself/Can make a heaven of hell, a hell of heaven' (Milton 1966: I, ll.254–5), are echoed by Blake's 'London', wherein humanity suffers under the 'mind forg'd manacles' that are constitutive of human subjectivity and human society. To escape the 'mind forg'd manacles' is to assume freedom, to issue a declaration of independence, but even if 'the mind is its own place', Satan and the other rebel angels are still cast into Hell. For Hannibal Lecter, the mind truly *is* its own place, his 'memory palace' a place of escape when he is incarcerated. Lecter is aware of the deficiency of his internal freedom – '"Memory [he tells Starling] is what I have instead of a view"' (Harris 2000: 406) – and longs for physical liberty, to have a 'view' of the real Florence rather than a memory and a drawing on the wall. Satan's rhetoric of self-begetting as a radical form of liberty, and the insistence on the resources of the self's own mind, is undermined.

In one sense, the sequence of Harris's 'Lecter novels' indicates a trajectory from outside to inside, from Other to Self. Throughout the novels, Lecter is labelled 'the fiend' or 'the monster', not only by the rational characters within it, but also by the narratorial voice. This characterization (as Other) is compromised by the reader's increasing access to Lecter's interiority, and indeed the increasing concreteness of the 'memory palace' within Lecter (which is not even mentioned until *Hannibal*). Just as Lecter moves from monstrous Other to Romantic Satanic hero, the reader is offered the opportunity to move inside Lecter's mind. Perhaps as a consequence or a corollary, the discourse of evil or radical unknowableness/otherness gives way to psychology, just as Starling, Will Graham, Dollarhyde and Gumb are explained by the very psychology Lecter explicitly derides. Harris's novels continually point to the limits of rational discourse, and gesture towards the discourse of religion ('monster', 'evil', 'sin') to signify that which lies outside the explicatory powers of science, medicine or reasoned understanding, but are ultimately conservative in their ultimate recourse to psychology to *explain* Lecter, to make his otherness more explicable (and thereby less troubling).

Lecter's career is not only from outside to inside, but is also inside to outside: from confinement to freedom. In *Red Dragon* and the beginning of *The Silence of the Lambs*, Lecter is imprisoned in his small cell, visited by Will Graham and Clarice Starling. He then effects his escape, and by the end of Harris's *The Silence of the Lambs*, he is recovering from facial plastic surgery, drinking an 'excellent Batard-Montrachet' (Harris 2000: 741) and writing a note to Starling assuring her, 'I have no plans to call on you . . . the world being more interesting with you in it. Be sure you extend me the same courtesy' (Harris 2000: 641). In the film, as I have stated above, he speaks rather more immediately to Starling on the telephone, after which he leisurely pursues Dr Chilton down a South American street. By the end of both texts, then, Lecter is 'at large', physically free, and *Hannibal* narrates his efforts to maintain that freedom. The perverse ending of that novel, with Hannibal and Clarice, the oddest of odd couples, established in romantic happiness somewhere in Buenos Aires, the last image of the pair 'dancing on the terrace' (Harris 2000: 1220), signifies a freedom not only from the cell but also from the past: 'for many months now, he has not seen Mischa in his dreams' (Harris 2000: 1220). Trauma is undone; paradise is regained. Perhaps the word one should use here to characterize Lecter's ultimate state of being is 'unbound'. For the Satanic/Promethean Romantic hero, as I have argued in this paper that Lecter ultimately becomes, destruction is often the end, but at the end of *Hannibal* (which is, in terms of narrative chronology, the end of the sequence:

Hannibal Rising returns to Lecter's youth) Harris follows P. B. Shelley rather than Blake, Milton or Byron. The end of Shelley's 'Prometheus Unbound' offers a kind of cosmic redemption for the suffering Titan, his release an affirmation:

> Neither to change, nor falter nor repent:
> This like thy glory, Titan! is to be
> Good, great and joyous, beautiful and free;
> This alone is Life, Joy, Empire and Victory. (Shelley 2000b: 4, ll.575–9)

The ending of *Hannibal* is not revolutionary, but its implications – that Lecter is 'released' into a quasi-normative heterosexual romantic relationship with an equally happy Clarice – do set the self-delusory 'freedom' of Milton's Satan on its head. For Hannibal and Clarice, their interpenetrating and mutually enveloping minds truly can 'make a heaven of hell, a hell of heaven'.

Revising Lecter: *Hannibal Rising* and the televisual Hannibal

Since the film *Hannibal*, there have been three major cultural works that feature Hannibal Lecter: Harris's novel *Hannibal Rising* (2006) and its screen adaptation (2007), and the television series *Hannibal* (2013–ongoing, 2014). Both *Hannibal Rising* and the *Hannibal* series are, in a sense, origin stories. *Hannibal Rising* narrates Lecter's youth and adolescence, and fills in the gap between the scenes of childhood trauma in *Hannibal* and his arrival in New York; the *Hannibal* series narrates Lecter's first meeting with Will Graham, and his subsequent involvement with Graham up until the point of their violent confrontation that is referred to in *Red Dragon*. *Hannibal Rising*, therefore, is the story of how Hannibal comes to be Hannibal, in part through the ministrations of Lady Murasaki, who enjoys an autonomy not even afforded to Clarice Starling. She explicitly offers Hannibal a pathway out of his traumatic past and into something else, a revision of the imagery to do with transformation that is central to *The Silence of the Lambs*: 'Hannibal, you can leave the land of nightmare,' she tells him. 'You can be anything that you can imagine. Come onto the bridge of dreams. Will you come with me?' (Harris 2006: 81). Hannibal is still haunted, psychologically deformed, by the traumatic loss of his sister (and late in the novel a particularly violent episode is provoked when one of the men he is pursuing suggests that Hannibal had himself ingested Mischa, part of the broth that he was fed during the war). When suspected of a murder, Hannibal takes a polygraph test, and the reaction of the polygrapher – 'He's a blunted war orphan or he has a monstrous amount of self-control' (Harris 2006: 120) – returns the novel to the discourse of monstrosity identified above, but also suggests something else: that Hannibal may be suffering from some kind of 'war neurosis', a psychological disruption caused by his experience of highly traumatic events during World War II. As the novel progresses, the anger and pain Hannibal feels gives way to his 'monstrous control', an armouring of the masculine self that turns him, like Theweleit's *Freikorps* soldiers, into a machine. On the last pages of the novel, Hannibal has left any kind of emotional affect behind: 'He was not torn at all by anger any more, or tortured by dreams. This was a holiday and killing . . . was preferable to skiing' (Harris 2006: 322).

In the *Hannibal* series, Lecter is played by Mads Mikkelsen as an extremely controlled, intellectual, acutely perceptive psychologist. He is first seen cutting and eating some medallions of meat with great precision and finesse, as he would wield a scalpel; later in the first episode, he butchers, cooks and eats human lungs with the approach of a gourmand. In his first meeting with Will Graham (Hugh Dancy), who is played as someone capable of 'pure empathy' but who finds simple human contact almost unbearable, Lecter asks Graham: 'Do you have a problem with taste?', and later visits Graham with a pre-prepared breakfast to establish some form of working relationship. Taste is, of course, in the Lecter texts an extremely loaded word, but Mikkelsen's portrayal of Lecter stresses the aspects of cultivation and consumption still further than that of Antony Hopkins. This Lecter is other, and of course speaks with a European accent, much unlike Hopkins (Brian Cox, in *Manhunter*, does not disguise a Scottish inflection); but his severe, angular tailoring, expressionless, even mask-like face and his demeanour of total control marks him as a disturbing figure from the beginning.

Lecter's ongoing presence in contemporary popular culture and his transformations between textual iterations makes him a curiously labile figure. There is not one Lecter, but many, even within Harris's own texts. Lecter is not emblematic of contemporary masculinity in his 'serial killingness', as Richard Dyer has it, but in his very mutability.

13

The Angels and the Damned

David Peace's Red Riding Quartet, *Nineteen Seventy-Four* (1999), *Nineteen Seventy-Seven* (2000), *Nineteen Eighty* (2001) and *Nineteen Eighty-Three* (2002) can be described as British hyper-noir fiction, drawing upon the generic acceleration produced in James Ellroy's *LA Quartet* of novels (1987–92), in which South Yorkshire in the 1970s and 1980s is presented as a crucible for developments in post-war British society and culture, from the fraying of the fabric of the 'post-war consensus', to the nascent entrepreneurial capitalism that characterized the Thatcher years (which itself exacerbated social and economic tensions and conflict), to renegotiations of masculinity through the figures of corrupt policemen, obsessional investigative journalists and, in particular, the Yorkshire Ripper, whose presence haunts three of the books and who serves to manifest the latent misogyny and violence that Peace diagnoses as being part of post-war British masculinity. As we saw in Chapter 4, in relation to *The Damned United* (2007), Peace's male protagonists are embedded in homosocial environments, but in the Red Riding Quartet, these social environments are toxic and particularly corrosive to the investigative protagonists who try to penetrate this masculine culture.

Just as with the Ellroy crime novels that he emulates, Peace's narratives encompass murder, conspiracies, betrayal, power, violence, and have an overt moral coding: these narratives of bad white men, involved in corrupt struggles for power, advancement or revenge are portrayed in terms of good and evil, redemption and damnation, angels and the diabolic. South Yorkshire, and in particular the city of Leeds, is haunted not only by its bloody history but also by visions, of hell and of salvation, that accompany the narrative. In this, Peace draws his moral world directly from Ellroy. In *White Jazz* (1992), which, as Katy Shaw has pointed out in her book on Peace, is an acknowledged major influence on the entirety of the Red Riding Quartet and in particular *Nineteen Seventy-Four* (Shaw 2011: 66), Dave 'The Enforcer' Klein, who harbours incestuous desires for his sister, is a lieutenant in the LAPD, but is also a trained attorney, a hit man for hire and a bag man for organized crime. The language of the novel is accelerated, compacted, staccato: the compressed rhythms, demotic register and liberal use of obscenity present an urban masculinity deformed by the pressures and speed of the contemporary American city, and a protagonist who slides from amorality into perpetrating acts that he knows to be wrong. Many of Ellroy's protagonists are obsessed, pursuing their own psychological journeys and imperatives while attempting to maintain their grip on a more legitimated place in the city's economy, as cop or as part of the media or entertainment industries, but often sliding towards organized crime, outright criminal activity or the margins of Hollywood's economy (scandal sheets, exploitation movies, pornography). These damaged men are also often in search of redemption, represented by an idealized heterosexual relationship with a *femme fatale* who also wishes to escape 'the Life'. There is, therefore, a strong dose of the romantic in the narrative resolutions, and the Romantic/Gothic in the narratives in which titanic male figures struggle with themselves and each other for power, but also for the condition of their own souls. Los Angeles is itself a city of angels and a city of the damned; Leeds, a northern British city that was surrounded by coalfields and heavy industry and is now a financial centre, is far from the material fabric and cultural representations of Los Angeles and Hollywood, but Peace uses the history of the industrial north of England as the site of 'dark satanic mills' to present the city of Leeds as emblematic of certain elements in British post-war society and culture in a way parallel to Ellroy's Los Angeles.

In fact, Peace uses Ellroy's model to fabricate a 'secret history' of the 1970s in Britain, one in which police conspiracies and corruption, financially irregular real estate speculation, political and social repression and violence (particularly against women) form a kind of fabric against which the connected stories of the four books are narrated. Characters recur, as do key images and symbols, particularly those inflected by the Gothic: the West Yorkshire police HQ at Millgarth, for instance, becomes a kind of dungeon, its cells the site of torture and horror, where confessions are extracted by force, and where the writ of law does not run. Millgarth, the place of 'law and order', is in fact the emblem of the reverse. Once inside, suspects (and even outsider policemen) are subject to power in its most physical form, unrestrained by either legal frameworks or codes of civility. Leeds is explicitly Concrete Gothic, a place of darkness and secret histories of sexual transgression, physical abuse and psychological malformation.

One of the problems that are encountered in reading Peace's texts is the same as that one encounters with Ellroy: that there is an emphasis on *conspiracy* over *history*. Peace's narratives of corruption, violence, murder, revenge and so on largely exclude history or replace it with an occult one (literally in the first novel, *Nineteen Seventy-Four*, where the child killer sews a swan's wings on to the backs of his victims in ritual and symbolic acts performed underground). There is no sign of Prime Ministers Heath or Callaghan or Thatcher, no 3-day week, no oil shocks and power cuts, and certainly no elections (although they have a brief role in *Nineteen Eighty-Three*, the final novel of the Quartet). In fact, much of the civic as well as political fabric of post-war Britain simply is not present; this absence of history allows conspiracy to fill this space. Fredric Jameson, in 'Totality as Conspiracy', suggested that paranoia and a belief in conspiracies is a function of the subject's dislocation in the contemporary 'world system': that conspiracy itself signifies 'some deeper incapacity of the postmodern subject to process history itself' (Jameson 1992: 16). In the same terms he uses in the famous essay on 'Postmodernism', Jameson also suggests that 'conspiracy . . . is the poor person's cognitive mapping in the postmodern age; it is a degraded figure of the total logic of late capital, a desperate attempt to represent that latter's system' (Jameson 1992: 16). Because contemporary globalized capital's matrices of power and its socioeconomic systems are so complex, they may no longer be grasped as a totality. Conspiracy allows us to do so, but this is a false totalization which, in fact, promotes a very different analysis of the relations between subject and ideology, individual and society, than a more rigorous analysis would provide. The answers that conspiracy theories provide – in Ellroy's and Peace's hands, that history is made in secret by very bad men – not only disempowers the subject but also diverts attention from a truer understanding of the social and cultural forces that produce the kinds of subjectivity, and the kinds of masculinity, that both writers diagnose.

From conspiracy to theology

The first novel in the Quartet, *Nineteen Seventy-Four*, is narrated by Eddie Dunford, a callow journalist on the *Yorkshire Post* newspaper, who has returned from London, having failed there as a 'crime correspondent' for a national newspaper. The newsrooms of the *Post* and the relationships between the cynical men who work in them mirror the corruption that Dunford attempts to investigate in the Yorkshire 'establishment', including policemen, politicians and local businessmen. Dunford is an outsider and treated with something close to contempt by his colleague (and antagonist) Jack Whitehead, who himself narrates *Nineteen Seventy-Seven*. The locus for Dunford's investigations is a series of abductions and murders of young girls, which the Leeds police fail to solve. The central figure in the matrix of corruption and conspiracy that Dunford uncovers is the architect John Dawson, who was based by Peace on the real-life Yorkshire architect John Poulson. Poulson, according to Dominic Sandbrook, was the centre of a culture of 'cash[ing] in on the redevelopment boom in the North of England' in the early 1970s (Sandbrook 2006: 509), which was attended by a massive network of 'bribes, retainers and kickbacks' (Sandbrook 2006: 510). Where Poulson was implicated in bribery and corruption scandals that implicated important political figures all the way up to Conservative Party grandee Reginald Maudling, Dawson's desire to build a shopping mall in Hunslet Carr (close to Leeds) is implicated in child murder: Dawson's construction foreman, George Marsh, is the killer and is protected by Dawson to enable his project to be completed. This is a diagnostic Peace technique, where economic factors are occulted and Gothicized, the horror of the murders inflecting the sociopolitical developments of which they are emblematic. The economic victims of the development of Hunslet Carr – Dunford witnesses the violent breaking up and incineration by police squads of a traveller's camp on the land Dawson wants to develop – are symbolized by the Gothic/*noir* victims of crime. This is a recurrent trope in the Quartet: the victims of the Yorkshire Ripper, in particular, stand in for society's marginalized and victimized, those who suffer at the hands of (white male) power while others look away and prosper. The swan's wings, prefiguring the wings of angels and those blackened and rotten appendages felt by 'damned' men in later books, are an index of innocence, compounding the moral (even theological) codings of the Quartet.

George Marsh's 'workshop', where the children die and where he fits swans's wings onto their backs, is underground, a Bluebeard's cave of horror and terror. Katy Shaw notes that 'the concept of the subterranean connects the many hidden histories of Yorkshire to highlight covert truths operating under the surface of the public gaze' (Shaw 2011: 16), and that the 'Belly' (the maze of cells beneath the station at Millgarth) 'echo the underground world of George Marsh' (Shaw 2011: 16). Both spaces reflect (in a dark glass) the source for much of Yorkshire's prosperity in the age of Industrial Modernity: coal mining, itself taking place in darkness underground, and a formative site for a class-oriented construction of masculinity. Marsh, as a skilled working-class male, reveals the misogyny and violence latent in the normative masculinity of his place, time and class; his particular deformation is partly expressed in the spatialized environment of the book, where the underground 'workshop' signifies occluded or repressed histories and desires. This underground space is also hellish, infernal. When he locates the 'cave', Dunford finds Marsh already dead; in an act which presents his own moral deformation, he forces Marsh's wife, who knew of her husband's crimes but covered them up, into the cave in anticipation that she will die there. There is little sense of the redemptive at work in *Nineteen Seventy-Four*; at the end of the novel, Dunford shoots other corrupt businessmen at a bar called 'The Strafford', an act that reverberates in the remaining three novels, and he waits for the police to arrive outside in the car park. Even the 'shoot-out', the violent means by which narrative resolution can be effected (and redemption gained) in genres such as the Western and crime/*noir* narratives, becomes ambiguous. The deaths at The Strafford are in no sense an ending, even for Dunford.

That references to Orwell's *Nineteen Eighty-Four* recur throughout the novel indicates that there is more than an intertextual or allusive purpose to Peace's choice of titles for the Quartet. In Chapter 2, Dunford is told 'Big Brother Is Watching You', and a section title is 'We Are the Dead', a song from David Bowie's 1974 album *Diamond Dogs* (itself deeply influenced by *Nineteen Eighty-Four* and, in fact, a phrase taken from Orwell's novel). *Nineteen Seventy-Four* is, in a sense, an Orwellian dystopia, as well as a hyper-*noir* novel, and Dunford is its alienated protagonist. The hellish and hopeless quality of Peace's narrative reflects Orwell's vision of a 'boot stamping on a human face forever', a symbol of violent power and subjugation that is physically enacted in Millgarth and elsewhere in Yorkshire.

The next novel in the quartet has some claim to be the strangest. *Nineteen Seventy-Seven* has two first-person narrators: Sgt Bob Fraser, an Ellroy-style anti-hero whose sense of his own corrosion accompanies the ethically problematic acts he embarks upon; and Jack Whitehead, the journalist-antagonist of the previous novel who has undergone a kind of transformation. Fraser is, in a sense, a 'good man' gone to the bad, undone by his sexual obsession with the prostitute Janice Ryan and the subsequent neglect of his wife and son. Fraser's fragmentation is itself accompanied by visions of a murder done in a Preston lock-up, a doubling of policeman and rapist/murderer that recurs in the rest of the books, dominated as they are by the 'real' crimes of the Yorkshire Ripper,

Peter Sutcliffe. Whether the Preston murder is a Ripper murder remains ambiguous, but it becomes another of the nodal points of the Quartet's occulted history, like the multiple shooting that Dunford perpetrates at The Strafford. Peaces's 'history' of West Yorkshire in the 1970s and 1980s is less a chronology than a series of nodal events, the consequences of which form ripples in the social and cultural fabric which intersect and interfere with the other violent psychosexual events narrated in the book. This model of waves or transmissions is repeated in the actual 'transmissions' that are found in *Nineteen Eighty*, wherein the voices of Ripper victims are given in blocks that punctuate the main diegesis. It also echoes the model of 'concentric circles' that Nicole Ward Jouve uses in her critical book on the Yorkshire Ripper, *The Street-cleaner* (1988), where she proposes a series of concentric circles emanating from Bingley, Bradford and Heaton (where Sutcliffe lived, sequentially) that the *Sunday Times* 'Insight' investigation team marked out as a 'Geography of Terror', 'Sutcliffe's homes . . . like the eye of a hurricane wreaking havoc in its eddies' (Jouve 1988: 156). We will return to Jouve later in the chapter.

Whitehead is also subject to visions. His visions take the form of the ghost of his murdered ex-wife Carol (killed by a follower of the Revered Martin Laws, another of the shadowy bad men who proliferate in the Quartet) and five other angels, who visit him serially throughout the narrative. Jack Whitehead, who feels himself damned, is then psychologically (and perhaps really) haunted by figures whose winged forms echo the horrifying mutilations to the child victim Claire Kemplay in *Nineteen Seventy-Four*. In Chapter 8 of *Nineteen Seventy-Seven*, Jack Whitehead finds himself in a Leeds cathedral, where he is consumed by his knowledge of murder and evil. The scene that Whitehead witnesses indicates a turn in *Nineteen Seventy-Seven* from conspiracy to theology in his conception of the consequences of crime. What the murder of Clare Kemplay or the victims of the Yorkshire Ripper indicates is not simply a function of a certain time or place, a *social* manifestation of domination and violent (perverse) male desire; rather, it is the blackening of men's, and by extension Yorkshire's, 'soul'. Whitehead watches as

> the child led the old woman by the hand down the aisle and when they reached my pew they paused under the statues and the paintings, the shadows against the altar, and the child held out his open prayer book and I took it from him and watched them walk away.
>
> And I looked down and I read aloud the words I found. (Peace 2000: ch. 8, 132)

The words that follow are from Psalm 88, which runs as follows:

> For my soul is full of troubles,
> And my life draws near to Sheol,
> I am counted among those who go down into the pit;
> I am like those who have no help,
> Like those forsaken among the dead,
> Like the slain that lie in the grave,
> Like those whom you remember no more,
> For they are cut off from your hand.
>
> . . .
>
> But I, O Lord, cry out to you;
> In the morning my prayer comes before you.
> O Lord, why do you cast me off?
> Why do you hide your face from me?
> Wretched and close to death from my youth up,
> I suffer your terrors; I am desperate.
> Your wrath has swept over me;
> Your dread assaults destroy me.
> They surround me like a flood all day long;
> From all sides they close in on me.
> You have caused friend and neighbour to shun me;
> my companions are darkness.

Psalm 88 elucidates a moment of extremity, of despair and fear of abandonment by God. It does not fit neatly into a narrative of redemption; the Psalm ends with darkness, terror and isolation. The Psalm comes to emblematize Whitehead's own disturbed state of mind, but also that of all the other men who narrate Peace's narratives. As we shall see shortly, this is a correlative of an absolute failure of male homosociality and collectivity in the novels; all the men act, and in fact are, alone.

Little wonder then that Whitehead, at the end of *Nineteen Seventy-Seven*, goes to the Reverend Laws for his own, elective, trepanning (the means by which his former wife died), which will either kill him or symbolically 'let out' the demons and angels that pursue him. He survives, and is seen in *Nineteen Eighty-Three* by the policeman Maurice Jobson (who had murdered, in turn, the killer George Marsh, and narrates part of the novel) as a figure transformed into Christ, 'bleeding from his hands and feet' (Peace: ch 61), surrounded by children. Whitehead is a kind of obscene saint, who speaks in parables: 'During an eclipse there is no sun . . . only darkness. . . . The sun is still there . . . you just can't see it' (Chapter 61). This speech reveals a persistence in hope, in faith, in the things *unseen*, which will defeat material evil. 'How can you fucking believe, after the things you've seen?' shouts Jobson. 'It's the things I've not seen,' replies Whitehead (Chapter 61). At this point, Jobson himself receives a *vision*, but an intensely material one, in fact, tactile:

> A ten-year-old girl with blue eyes and long straight fair hair, wearing an orange waterproof kagool, a dark blue turtleneck sweater, pale blue denim trousers with a distinctive eagle motif on the back left pocket and red Wellington boots, holding a plastic Co-op bag in her other hand. (Chapter 61)

This is Clare Kemplay, who haunts the narratives of the Quartet but here becomes more than a ghost, a trace of a secret and criminal history, but a material and redemptive presence, a symbol of innocence sacrificed to the desires of evil men. As well as a turn to theology, this moment also signifies a turn to sentimentality, albeit one that leavens the almost hermetically sealed environments of moral darkness and corruption found elsewhere in the novels. It also restores the idea of paternity, which is terribly damaged throughout the Quartet, to the extent that only Bob Fraser of all the narrators in the novels is a father (Peter Hunter and his wife, in *Nineteen Eighty*, have 'tried' to conceive by natural and artificial means prior to the beginning of the novel, a 'failure' that estranges husband and wife), and by the end of *Nineteen Seventy-Seven* Fraser's wife has left him for his colleague John Rudkin, and the very paternity of Fraser's son is in doubt.

The mobility and geography of murder

The narrative of *Nineteen Eighty* is dominated by considerations of space and mobility to an extent even greater than the other texts in the Quartet. The novel is narrated by Peter Hunter, a policeman from Manchester who is appointed to head an investigation or reappraisal of the Ripper case files and the failed hunt to find the murderer, and (more covertly) to conduct an inquiry into the murders themselves. He and his team, who all come from the Greater Manchester police force, meet with hostility and obstruction from their West Yorkshire colleagues. They are 'outsiders', a team who can form no further solidarity with the policemen and women with whom they must work. Hunter can make no friends in Yorkshire; although it is revealed towards the end of the novel that he and a female member of his team, Helen Marshall, have been having an affair, he becomes increasingly isolated, prey to the obsessional and alienated masculinity that is dominant in Peace's narratives. This corrosion of collectivity is a legacy of Ellroy's re-negotiation of *noir* tropes, but where 'bad men' like Dave Klein in *White Jazz* can operate in a social vacuum, the trajectory of Peace's protagonist involves atomization, demoralization and ultimately destruction by the forces of institutionalized corruption.

Nineteen Eighty begins with the Yorkshire Ripper investigation in limbo. The investigation has been confused by false leads (such as the notorious 'Wearside Jack' audio tape received by police and mistakenly assumed to be genuine, or the ambiguous connection to the murder of Clare Morrison in the Preston lock-up of which Bob Fraser has visions in *Nineteen Seventy-Seven*); and the doubling of cop and killer, implicit throughout the Quartet, has become a highly problematic locus of sympathy among the policemen themselves. In a statement to the *Yorkshire Post*, George Oldman implicitly reveals that the Ripper's 'feelings' towards the fallen state of Leeds are mirrored in those of the police:

> *I feel after all this time, I feel that I really know him. . . . I don't regard him as evil. The voice is almost sad, a man fed up with what he's done, fed up with himself. To me he's like a bad angel on a mistaken journey and, while I could never condone his methods, I can sympathise with his feelings* (Peace 2001: ch. 1)

Shaw notes that Hunter also 'identifies the shared humanity of the Ripper' with himself and others (Shaw 2011: 74), but does not analyse the insistently theological note that is struck in Oldman's words. The Ripper is a 'bad angel', perhaps a fallen one; if Leeds is infernal, then the Ripper is Satanic, an emblem of its hellish social fabric. If the Ripper is 'from Hell' (a phrase from a letter purporting to be from 'Jack The Ripper' at the time of the 1888 Whitechapel murders), then Hunter and his team are on its outskirts, in limbo, and heading towards its centre. The road to Hell is the M62. This motorway, which crosses the Pennine hills and connects Leeds with Manchester, is recurrently traversed by Hunter, is a primary symbol in *Nineteen Eighty*: it is a space *between*. While in *Nineteen Seventy-Seven* Bob Fraser and others travel across to Preston, indicating a wider geography of murder and corruption (and by implication, wider networks of corruption and 'evil'), Hunter commutes backwards and forwards, no longer at 'home' in Manchester but alienated from, and corroded by, the city of Leeds. The M62 becomes another kind of limbo, a spatial index of Hunter's (and all Peace's protagonist's) isolation).

Just as we saw in Chapter 1, mobility is a crucial motif in articulating masculine subjectivity. In contrast to female characters who are rooted in domestic space, such as Paula Garland in *Nineteen Seventy-Four*, masculinity is bound up with automobility: Eddie Dunford drives his father's Vauxhall Viva; Peter Hunter shuttles between Manchester and Leeds; and Peter Williams (Peace's half disguise for Peter Sutcliffe) is a truck driver, though the Yorkshire Ripper is presumed by the police to be a taxi driver, as this allows a degree of licensed mobility across the space of West Yorkshire. In Chapter 1, I suggested that Bond's licensed mobility as an agent is itself 'haunted' by that of the terrorist, whose problematic mobility is also enabled by the mobile circuits of globalized late capital. Peace's novels, where such a world is just coming into being, is more limited in its terrain, but the same structure of gendered mobilities is in place.

The crucial loci of the problematic of mobility are the murder sites: Chapel-town in Leeds, Manningham Road in Bradford, the lock-up in Preston. These form an archipelago across the north of England, nodal points in a network of violence that are established by the unlicensed double of the police force (the Yorkshire Ripper) and then visited and revisited by the policemen who hunt him, but reflect his misogyny. In the note 'Clueless', sent by Peter Sutcliffe to the *Sheffield Star* newspaper, this obscene itinerary is at once concrete and ambivalent: 'Bradford was not me/But just wait and see/Sheffield will not be missed/Next on the list.' The physical relation between Bradford and Sheffield is re-imagined as a transit of sexual murder, the city and the female victim explicitly connected. The forms of masculinity inhabited by Williams/Sutcliffe, as well as Oldman, Jobson and Hunter, are placed in problematic relation to the female sex-workers who are, to begin with, the victims of the Ripper's crimes. This is most revealingly anticipated in Bob Fraser's sexual obsession with Janice Ryan, which engages an erotic relation at the same time that it engages a hegemonic masculine need to *protect* the vulnerable (whether that is Clare Kemplay or the sex-workers). Fraser's confused and corrosive inability to separate out his emotional or sexual relation to Janice Ryan from the ethical and tactical necessities of his role as a policeman is diagnostic of the compromised positions nearly all of Peace's men find themselves in. That the policemen sympathize with the Ripper's 'feelings' suggest a similar failure to separate out 'protector' and 'violator' masculinities that I analysed in terms of post-war British hegemonic masculinity in *Masculinities in Fiction and Film, 1945–2000*, or that Peace's texts acknowledge the mutual implication of one in the other.

The streets of Leeds or Bradford are less a psychogeography which, in the imagination of writers such as Iain Sinclair, has been used as a means to uncover lost or occluded urban histories (not least, in Sinclair's first novel *White Chappell, Scarlet Tracings* (1987) in relation to Jack the Ripper and the mythologies surrounding the Whitechapel murders), than a liminal terrain, not only in which marginalized or displaced subjects live and work but also in which they are vulnerable to violence and oppression. The 'streetwalker', the female prostitute or sex-worker, is particularly vulnerable in these liminal spaces, for they offer no protection against the violent desires of damaged men. Unlike the domestic females of Peace's novels, from Paula Garland to the wives of senior policemen, who are rooted in a particular – if socially and emotionally imprisoning – space (the house), even this problematic security is unavailable to the streetwalkers. In fact, the unlicensed and dangerous masculine mobility represented by the Ripper reflects that of the sex-workers themselves who have long been culturally encoded as themselves inhabiting a dangerous and unlicensed female mobility: sexually; in terms of sexually transmitted disease (as 'contagion' or 'plague' or 'blight'); in terms of a wider 'moral contagion' that threatens the social fabric; and in terms of being workers whose clients may come from a range of social classes. It is significant that Sutcliffe, the 'real' Yorkshire Ripper, presented himself as 'the Street-cleaner', self-defining as a masculine subject whose responsibility it is to secure the streets and make them hygienic.

Nicole Ward Jouve's book on the Yorkshire Ripper case, *The Streetcleaner* (1988), reads Sutcliffe psychoanalytically, suggesting the murders were, in part, to overcome 'feminization' through a deficient performance of masculinity in a deeply retrograde patriarchal culture, where violence against women was accepted as a fact of everyday life. In a sense, although George Oldman suggests that '*if we do get him, we'll probably find he's had too long on the left breast and not enough on the right*' ([italics in original], Peace 2001: ch. 1), almost burlesquing a psychoanalytical interpretation, Jouve suggests that a basic continuity between the masculine culture of Yorkshire, of those of the police force and of the Ripper himself indicates a deep-rooted problem in the production of masculinity in post-war Britain. It is not that the Ripper is a pathologically aberrant masculine subject, but that his desires and attitudes mirror those of 'mainstream' masculine culture. His acts are an extension, not a perversion of it. Jouve asserts the socioeconomic and political dimension of the Yorkshire Ripper's crimes in a way that Peace does not; she notes that

> it [the Yorkshire Ripper case] occurred during the period in which recession began to make itself felt, to scar and depress the industrial North in particular.

1974 happens to be both the date of the first petrol crisis in the wake of the Yom Kippur war, and that of Sutcliffe's marriage. He begins to kill in 1975. (Jouve 1988: 170)

While only 'offer[ing] this for what it is worth' (Jouve 1988: 170), not over-pressing the sense that Sutcliffe manifests a violence that is present within the social and cultural order of that period in British post-war history, Jouve skewers (in anticipation) Peace's own imaginative practice when she describes the Yorkshire Ripper's murders as a 'mythical contagion . . . made to spread from [run-down alleys and waste ground to children's parks and campus grounds], a sense of the overwhelmingly seedy, violent, dark, industrial North. . . . Male violence is displaced into one extreme Northern example. It can be ignored elsewhere' (Jouve 1988: 171). To be fair to Peace, his insistence that all his male protagonists are in some sense complicit and 'damned', that there is no division between the 'sane' and the pathological, helps to defray the potential cost of placing the Ripper events at the centre of the narrative of the books, of occluding other parts of political, social and cultural history.

Jouve suggests that a psychiatric testimony at the trial, proposing that Sutcliffe was marked by 'four of the eight first-rank signs that indicated paranoid schizophrenia: bodily hallucinations; influence of thought; delusional percep-tion; passivity (thinking he was controlled by someone else' (Jouve 1988: 115), tends to reinstate a sense of pathological exception to the masculinity inhabited by Sutcliffe. While I agree with this argument, the idea that Sutcliffe 'thought he could read the thoughts of his victims' (Jouve 1988: 115) offers an intriguing line into *Nineteen Eighty* and its deployment of sections which can be counted as 'transmissions' of the voices of the victims:

echo test transmission one a citizens band broadcast of pictures at an atrocity exhibition from the shadows of the sun out of the arc of the searchlight joyce jobson in halifax on friday the twelfth of july nineteen seventy-four more life in a graveyard the rain keeping them in time for a look in the royal oak one more lager and then a fish supper with donald the lift home the chat the banter the chip shop shut out of the shadows the darkness he steps five foot four inches and quite good looking slightly wavy hair dark long sideboards he would not frighten anybody and says in a yorkshire way he says the weather is letting us down again and e know e am going to be in trouble severe cuts above both eyes and lacerations on the head her skull had suffered double fractures from an iron bar or hammer and for a moment the living soul is here among the dead who are suspended and soon will die get away from here (Peace 2001: 'Saint Cunt')

This 'giving voice' to the victims attempts to avoid the gender problematic that attends all texts which deal with such material, in that masculine violence is written upon the bodies of female victims, who are denied subjectivity and voice in their own right. It is clear that Peace's texts are deeply masculine ones, not only in the narrative foci but, as I have attempted to investigate in this chapter, also in their presentation (and interrogation) of damaged masculine subjects and the cultures that produce and sustain them. Jouve's approach connects language with gender and power; Sutcliffe developed a stammer in childhood because of his own 'feminization'. Violence silences women; and silences internal feminization which, Jouve suggests, is compounded in Sutcliffe's relation with his wife Sonia: 'She would tell him to shut up. Dress the way she liked.' (Jouve 1988: 192). Towards the end of Jouve's text, the very language of the critical text itself becomes staccato, compacted, a foreshadowing of that used by Ellroy and Peace:

> She's been branded. She is a victim. She is a martyr. She's got stigmata. Being female is being a victim. She wants success. She wants power. Election. That's Peter. He offered her a Durex. Secret contempt in her heart perhaps. She clings to him. There is only him. At least she can vent her frustration on him, punish him for the misery she feels. She lashes out at him.
>
> He cannot give her what she wants. But he's like her. Divided like her. Alone like her. He too wants to get out of the pit. She deeply resents him. She also loves him.
>
> Together they may make a go of it. (Jouve 1988: 193)

Jouve's rhetorical strategy here both replicates the masculine language of *noir* and subverts it, in ascribing division, isolation and agency to the female subject, Sutcliffe's wife. We should also note the seemingly insistent theological register that writing on this subject slips into: she is a 'martyr', 'has stigmata' and he wants to get 'out of the pit' (Jouve 1988: 193). Despite Jouve's insistence on a psychological and social reading of the Yorkshire Ripper case, a sense of 'evil' haunts these texts.

Towards apocalypse

A strong apocalypticism lurks within the Red Riding Quartet, a sense that the hellish city of Leeds (the damned united) has been forsaken by God and awaits judgement: this is the implication of Psalm 88, read by Jack Whitehead in

Nineteen Seventy-Seven. As noted above, however, Whitehead's own (suicidal) visit to the Reverend Laws for elective trepanning results not in death, but a form of revelation; he is transformed into a kind of holy man, speaking in parables. This is the counterpart to the sense that the Red Riding Quartet is an eschatological text, one that narrates the End of Days: both Whitehead and Maurice Jobson, one of the narrators of *Nineteen Eighty-Three*, achieve a vision of faith and hope that countermands the materialism and corruption of *this*, fallen world. This almost seems arbitrary, nothing to do with their deeds nor any sense of their moral worth: Peter Hunter in *Nineteen Eighty* or the journalist Piggott in *Nineteen Eighty-Three* go to their deaths with the feeling of rotten, leaden wings attached to their backs, and these can be accounted 'good' men in some ways. Even though the Reverend Laws is himself killed by the male sex-worker B. J., a victim of child abuse at Laws' and others' hands, the novels of the Quartet resist a resolution based upon a conventional sense of ethics, on 'just desserts' or even divine retribution. B. J.'s murder of Laws is retributive, but is really cast in the *noir* trope of revenge.

A structural and narrative principle of repetition (murders, investigations, interrogations) is then placed in tension with a theological and eschatological principle of apocalyptic endings, a revelation of the 'secret history' of the period at the moment at which that very history (of the 1970s) itself comes to an end. With Margaret Thatcher's Conservative Party winning a large majority in the 1983 election in the lee of reclaiming the Falklands/Malvinas in the war with Argentina, the social and political landscape of Britain (not to say the beginning of the remaking of Britain's urban centres, especially London, with the rapid acceleration of de-industrialization and the dominance of financialized global capital) alters significantly from the fragmenting 'post-war settlement'. While Peace anticipates the rise of the entrepreneur, property speculation and the domination of the economics of consumption in the Hunslet Carr development, John Dawson proposes in *Nineteen Seventy-Four*, the last book of the Quartet ends at the point at which these nascent developments will begin to alter the social and cultural fabric of Britain entirely, to come into full flower. This, of course, is not to say that Thatcherism 'sweeps away' corruption, masculine violence or the physical and psychological horrors of abuse and oppression that Peace foregrounds in his 'secret history' of the years between 1974 and 1983; these things begin to manifest in other forms.

Part of the ethical problem of the Quartet is interwoven into the narrative inheritance of the *noir* or crime genre. The masculine hero, the 'righteous man' who will clean the streets of the fallen metropolis, is at once the *noir* hero *and* the figure of the Yorkshire Ripper, the former haunted by the potential deeds of the latter. It is probably undecidable whether Peace's narratives are an indictment of masculine 'heroism' and agency, or whether they rather encode, in their flawed and compromised protagonists, a wish for a 'purer' and more moral heroism; but it is certainly true that the Quartet offers the reader the hyper-*noir* pleasures of a rather retrograde individualist and violent masculine subject, while at the same time suggesting that such agency is a fantasy. Enmeshed in conspiracies and morally compromised, black symbolic wings hanging from their shoulder blades, Peace's men both fail and succeed in their tasks to pursue the 'truth'. They uncover horrible crimes, but are signally unable to bring the perpetrators to justice, and nor are they able to change the cultural circumstances which produce such acts. The 'truth', for Fraser and for Hunter, leads to despair, to trauma, to suicide; even, as Katy Shaw suggests, to a 'sense of time shifting, of temporal flow . . . traumas are so profound that they cause characters to re-imagine time and space' (Shaw 2011: 60), where history itself no longer adheres to chronology but is as fragmented as the masculine subjects who experience it.

As we saw in Chapter 4, particularly in relation to the film *Four Lions*, the agency of the masculine 'hero', as presented in narratives that focus upon men whose alienation from the social mores and cultural fabric of contemporary Britain leads them to validate violence as a means of 'cleaning the streets', is deeply ambiguous in many of the films and novels produced since 2000. In 2009, three screen adaptations were made of Peace's novels, *1974* (directed by Julian Jarrold), *1980* (James Marsh) and *1983* (Anand Tucker) and shown on television to great critical acclaim, eventually finding a theatrical release in the United States. The absence of *Nineteen Seventy-Seven* has the effect of somewhat displacing the Yorkshire Ripper murders from the centre of the narrative, and the three films instead focus upon the abduction, murder and sexual abuse of children. Clare Kemplay, the symbolic innocent sacrificed in *Nineteen Seventy-Four*, haunts the text to the extent that the abduction of Hazel Atkins, whose walk home from school is re-enacted for the cameras at the beginning of the *1983* film, is seen as a repetition of past events: 'it's happened before, it's happening again', the medium Mandy Wymer (Saskia Reeves) tells policeman Maurice Jobson (David Morrissey). *1983* is itself a recapitulation of the events of nine years before as well as a closing of the circuit; flashbacks to 1974 are inserted regularly into the diegesis, from the point of view of Jobson in particular, but also seen by the solicitor John Piggott (Mark Addy), whose father had been a part of the abuse and conspiracy in the 1970s, and who seeks to investigate both the Kemplay murder and the Atkins abduction. The other character, who is given a voice-over but relatively little screen time, is B. J. (Robert Sheehan), who is released from prison and seeks out the Reverend Laws to enact revenge for his abuse. The two time periods are interwoven, but there is a strong sense of the end of a particular era; Jobson's senior officer, Harold Angus (Jim Carter) tells Jobson that in 5 years everyone will be gone, and in fact forces Jobson's resignation from the force. Curiously, the main musical markers used are from the 1970s soul records that Piggott plays, alone, in his rather squalid bachelor flat. This version of 1983 is very definitely the last year of the 1970s.

Jobson acts as a kind of witness to many scenes in the film, present at the violent 'interrogations' and at the dispersal of the traveller camp at Hunslet Carr, but an unwilling participant and more often a bystander. (During the interrogation of a suspect in *1983*, which involves the beating of the suspect's hands and burning with cigarettes, he leaves the room, to his colleague's remark: 'Maurice gone soft, has he?') Jobson, an archetypal 'good man' who has allowed himself to be complicit in cover-ups, police brutality and the jailing of an innocent man, bears the traces of his knowledge; he is taciturn, withdrawn, isolated; his wife and children left him, it is revealed; and his colleague Dickie Alderman (Shaun Dooley) almost certainly suspects him of no longer being 'one of us', and it is implied that he is sent along to chaperone the doubting Jobson. Clearly exasperated with Jobson's wish for the truth to be revealed, rather than politically and personally expedient cover-ups, Angus says, 'you and your guilty fucking conscience, Maurice', as though such a thing is an unnecessary and debilitating appendage for 'one of us'. Jobson acts not only as witness but also as the bearer of some kind of ethical residue which, at the end of the film, forces him to act. When B. J., who has come to Laws' house to kill him, is disarmed by the Reverend and is to be killed by trepanning with an electric drill, Jobson appears and shoots Laws with a shotgun. Murder, extra-legal violence, here becomes itself a redemptive act, which is ethically problematic, to say the least. Just as in other vigilante-cop movies (such as *Dirty Harry* (1971)), the violent 'heroics' of the rogue cop are validated by the portrayal of the legal system as itself corrupted and in the service of the wealthy and powerful. The suborning of the law is another effect of the matrix of power and domination at work across the terrain of the novels and films.

If the temporality of the film interweaves the two time frames, 1974 and 1983, then the film is spatially patterned on repetition, and, in particular, in institutional spaces. The film returns, almost obsessionally, to the enclosed spaces of the prison in which Michael Myshkin (Daniel Mays), who was framed for the Kemplay murder, is interviewed by Piggott, Jobson and Alderson; the cells in Millgarth's Belly, where we are witness to the 'interrogations' of Leonard Cole, the suspect in the Atkins abduction, and Martin Laws; the hospital room where Myshkin is restrained after he harms himself; and the various police station offices and foyers that are marked by hostility and exclusion. A crucial scene plays out in the interview room in the prison, one that will eventually connect with Jobson's own experience of the physical torture endured by suspects in Millgarth's cells. Jobson and Alderson sit on one side of the table, Myshkin on the other; when Myshkin claims he did not kill Clare Kemplay, but knows who did, Alderson presses him for the name. (Myshkin had already shouted 'put your hands on the table!' at the beginning of the interview.) Alderson strikes up a cigarette; as the conversation unfolds, the camera lingers on the lit cigarette. Eventually Myshkin cowers and urinates on himself in terror, while reaction shots of Jobson's face show that he is trying to diagnose the exact psychological dynamic at work. When we are witness soon after to Cole's 'interrogation', which involves stubbing out lit cigarettes on his hand, the meaning of Alderson's gesture and Myshkin's fear is made clear. What is not revealed until the end of the film is that the policeman who persuaded Myshkin to confess, by threatening him that he would not see his mother again while in jail, was Jobson himself. The repetition of the space of the cell in the Red Riding films (Peter Hunter is shot dead at the end of *1980* in a cell beneath Millgarth and his death faked as a shoot-out) makes the insistently carceral aspects of Peace's Concrete Gothic Leeds a claustrophobic and material presence. The connection to Orwell and *Nineteen Eighty-Four*, that this world is one where the boot stamps upon a human face forever, is explicitly signified in the scene of Laws' torture in *1974*, when a rat in a cage is brought in and an open end held to Laws' face; both novels and films share a hellish representation of the city.

Where *1983* markedly differs from the novels is in the ending. Where Piggott dies at the end of the novel, with the sensation of black, rotting wings on his back (like Peter Hunter), in the film Piggott is thrown by Laws into the underground chamber that had been George Marsh's in the novel *Nineteen Seventy-Four*, but there he finds Hazel Atkins alive. When Jobson goes to the shed and opens to trapdoor, Piggott emerges into the light surrounded by a cloud of white pigeon feathers, holding the girl in his arms. This becomes a masculine *pieta*, a moment of redemption not only for Jobson and Piggott but also the ending of the cycle of abuse and terror, a closing of the circuit. B. J. is given the last lines, in voice-over; over images taken from his memory (home movies of a boy and his young mother skipping along a British beach), which he ultimately seems to disappear into, B. J. begins: 'here is one that got away, and lived to tell the tale'. This is a reference to himself, of course, but it could also signify any other of the characters at the end of *1983* who escape: Jobson, Piggott and Hazel Atkins. The ending of the film offers more hope than do Peace's novels, with their complicated and partial redemptions; as Piggott carries the girl across the fields, and B. J. wanders on the beach of the imagination, there is a final emergence out of darkness and into the light.

Life on Mars?

The cultural terrain traversed by the Red Riding texts finds its analogue in popular culture in the BBC television series *Life on Mars*, which ran from 2006 to 2007. This time-travelling cop show, which featured Sam Tyler (John Simm) as a police officer from Greater Manchester in the 2000s who is displaced back in time to the 1970s, played versions of masculinity against each other in a playful revision of 'cop show' tropes familiar from such British television staples as *The Sweeney* (1975–78). In a contribution to an edited collection of essays on *Life on Mars*, John Curzon noted the difference between Tyler's 'sophisticated "metrosexual" variant of work and lifestyle which contrasts with the unreconstructed masculinity of his fellow officers' (Curzon 2012: 74), most notably Gene Hunt (Philip Glenister). Curzon proposes a reading of the series in which 'Sam Tyler and Gene Hunt represent two different ideas of the north . . . which are associated with contrasting representations of masculinity and male gender roles' (Curzon 2012: 75). This is cultural work that seems unavailable to either Peace's novels or the Red Riding films, and perhaps indicates their deficiencies: change, even within short historical time scales (1970s/2000s) seems impossible. The same difficulty noted above with regard to the ideological nature of (and problematic audience sympathy for or identification with) the vigilante-cop is present here, for Curzon notes that 'the series seems to invite greater sympathy with, and nostalgia for, the unrefined masculinity of birds and boozers represented by Gene' (Curzon 2012: 75–6). In another essay from the same collection, Ruth McElroy proposes a form of masculinity inhabited by Hunt as 'retrosexuality', characterized by 'a disavowal of technology, a rejection of reflexive analysis of the self, a renewal of traits deemed traditionally masculine and a disavowal, when adopted by men, of those traits and practices deemed feminine' (McElroy 2012: 121). The nostalgic popular response to Gene Hunt suggests that the satiric intent of *Life on Mars* partially works against itself, and restores the very thing that it holds up to burlesque. Nostalgia is certainly not part of any of the Red Riding texts, for what Harold Angus calls the 'good old bad old days'; instead, these texts are unremittingly bleak in their plotting of the social, economic and civic fabric of the 1970s. As I suggested above with regard to conspiracy, theology and politics, this does not tell the whole story of the period, and reflects a rather despairing political moment from which the events are seen in retrospect, as the world of Red Riding is implicitly proposed as the crucible that forms our own. Although the Red Riding texts return compulsively to its 'year zero' or even primal scene, the abduction and murder of Clare Kemplay, the ending of both the novel Quartet and the film Trilogy offers the possibility that the cycle, at least, may be broken.

Conclusion

What we have seen in the preceding chapters suggests that, in terms of masculinity, crisis is the new dominant. Such a conception might suggest, however, that there was a time when constructions of masculinity in capitalist Modernity were ever untroubled, when male subjects were whole and not produced by conflicting ideological, social and cultural structures, or when men existed in an unchallenged patriarchy not striated by class or ethnicity. If I have tried to diagnose different kinds of male subjectivity in this book, this is not only because of the different and deeply various ranges of representations of masculinity available in contemporary culture, but also because I believe that masculinities are not reducible to one 'self' or type. My understanding of the production of gender is performative in the way proposed by Judith Butler in *Gender Trouble* (1990) – that gender roles are enacted, and do not presume an underlying 'real' identity. (In fact, in this book, there is no male 'identity', as this implies a self-consistent, unitary subject, which is contrary to my methods and approach.) Individual men do not simply reproduce patriarchal formations in their behaviours and performances of masculinity, but are in negotiation with it; even hegemonic forms of masculinity, the ones that are most validated by the ideologies of capitalist modernity, are not simple reflections of those imperatives. Representations are a step more estranged; even popular texts are able to offer critical, even dissenting forms of masculinity. That is not to say, of course, that popular fictions may not do ideological work; indeed, as Hamilton Carroll demonstrates in *Affirmative Reaction* (2011), dominant fictions negotiate forms of white male entitlement in the changing political landscape of the United States.

Despite the traumatized narratives of the contemporary James Bond films, there are some fictions that offer the pleasures of a 'traditional', heroic masculinity. Though I have mentioned the BBC TV series *Life on Mars*, whose Detective Gene Hunt (Philip Glenister), an unreconstructed 1970s man, was a popular phenomenon during its run (and its sequel, *Ashes to Ashes* (2009–10)), it is the American TV series *Mad Men* (2007–15) that symbolizes the ambiguous means by which contemporary texts can valourize and criticize formations of masculinity, particularly in relation to a simplified, even sentimentalized past. *Mad Men*, whose male lead Don Draper (Jon Hamm) inhabits a hard-drinking, smoking, womanizing aspirational ultra-competitive masculinity, exposes these masculine performances to critique, while allowing a measure of identification and even nostalgia. The contemporary televisual success of series which are set in a past prior to second-wave feminism, filled with fashionably dressed men and women (particularly men) whose mores are no longer quite acceptable, indicates that the imperatives of display (male dandyism), homosociality and masculine consumption and pleasure, which Steven Cohan in *Masked Men* (1997) analysed as subordinate or resistant masculinities, have become backward projections of contemporary hegemonic formations.

The 'Mad' men are from Madison Avenue, the heart of New York's advertising empire, of course; but the pun reveals the beckoning-yet-threatening potentials of retrograde masculinity. These men may have more old-fashioned 'fun', but the price is corrosion, pain and potential psychological dislocation. As we saw with David Peace's Red Riding novels, in more directly critical hands the recent past can become a lens by which to articulate 'traditional' masculine agency in a way which distils the destructive, malign forms of 'traditional' masculinity. The 'good' men who are drawn in to the matrices of murder and corruption are themselves driven 'mad', destroyed by their own sense of guilt and complicity. Insanity becomes an understandable response to exposure to social and moral 'evil'. Peace's men seem 'fated' to destruction, but it is the world they negotiate (and which they help bring into being, the world of financialized global capitalism) that destroys them.

Can masculinity be healed? In *A Dangerous Method* (2011), David Cronenberg's film investigating the relationship between Sigmund Freud (Viggo Mortensen) and Carl Gustav Jung (Michael Fassbender), the analysts and their friendship are themselves in need of analysis and healing. When Jung conducts an affair with one of his patients, lies to Freud, and then rejects the influence of his 'father' to pursue his own lines of psychological and philosophical inquiry (which Freud dismisses as mysticism), Cronenberg presents this not only as a form of Oedipal conflict, but Jung's rejection of the therapeutic basis of Freud's practices. At the end of the film, he declares that he is not content to leave the patient and world as it is: he wants to change and to heal his subjects, and thereby change the world. Jung's own journey into 'dangerous methods', an acceptance of tabooed desire and pleasure, is one in which his own authority is necessarily compromised. His break with Freud comes after Freud refuses to share his dreams with Jung, in order, he jokes, to preserve his authority; Jung does not see the joke, nor the tension between the two that provokes it, but uses this idea of authority (and his discomfort with it) to establish the ground upon which his break with Freudianism can be established. Neither of these physicians may heal themselves, an emblematic failure that bespeaks a deeper irrecuperability in terms of male subjectivity. If these men's capacity for healing themselves (and others) is so circumscribed, what may be said for others?

Therapeutics largely exists beyond the disciplinary boundaries of this book, though it draws significantly upon Freud's work, particularly in theorizing trauma, and also the death drive. Yet, I do not mean it to be entirely negative. Contemporary (white, hegemonic, Anglo-American) masculinities are undoubtedly troubled, ill at ease with their own aspirations and pleasures, uncomfortable with the systems of privilege and power that differently enable individual men economically, socially and culturally. The relationships between men and women are rarely entirely positive either, and fatherhood is an anxious role, one in which the compromised happiness and aspirations of the father is transmitted to the sons (and daughters). Therapeutics, however, cannot take place only upon the stage of the individual psyche. This is where the diagnoses of the texts I have studied might be put to more progressive purpose: in representing exclusions, or 'bare life', or the alienated or dispossessed, the radical edge of these texts are in their potential to help us to understand the conditions of alienation and disenfranchisement – what is common to male subjects across cultures and locations – and to form a practical cultural politics from it.

Bibliography

Agamben, Giorgio (1998), *Homo Sacer: Sovereign Power and Bare Life* (Stanford, CA: Stanford University Press).

Aldiss, Brian W. (1973), *Billion Year Spree* (London: Weidenfeld and Nicolson).

Anderson, Perry (2013), 'American Foreign Policy and Its Thinkers'. *New Left Review* 83 (September/October): 5–167.

Augé, Marc (1995), *Non-Places: An Introduction to the Anthropology of Supermodernity* (London: Verso).

Banks, Joe (2001), 'Rorschach Audio: Ghost Voices and Perceptual Creativity'. *Leonardo Music Journal* 11: 77–83.

Baker, Brian (2006), *Masculinity in Fiction and Film 1945–2000: Representing Men in Popular Cultures* (London: Continuum).

Barker, Pat (1992), *Regeneration* (London: Penguin).

Barton, Sabrina (2002), 'Your Self Storage: Female Investigation and Male Performativity in the Woman's Psychothriller', in *The Film Cultures Reader*, ed. Graeme Turner (London and New York: Routledge), pp. 311–30.

Benjamin, Walter (1992), 'On some motifs of Baudelaire', in *Illuminations*, Hannah Arendt, ed. and trans. Harry Zohn (London: Fontana), pp. 152–96.

Blair, Tony (2011), *A Journey* (London: Arrow).

Blake, Linnie (2008), *The Wounds of Nations: Horror Cinema, Historical Trauma and National Identity* (Manchester: Manchester University Press).

Blake, William (1975), *The Marriage of Heaven and Hell* (Oxford: Oxford University Press).

—(2000), 'London', in *The Norton Anthology of English Literature*, eds. M. H. Abrams and S. Greenblatt, 7th edn, vol. 2 (New York: W. W. Norton), pp. 56–7.

Botting, Fred (2010), 'A-ffect-less: Zombie-Horror-Shock.' *English Language Notes* 48, 1 (Spring/Summer): 177–90.

Bould, Mark (2012), *Science Fiction Cinema* (London: Routledge).

Bradley, Arthur (2006), 'Originary Technicity: Technology and Anthropology', in *Technicity*, eds. Arthur Bradley and Louis Armand (Prague: Literraria Pragensia), pp. 78–100.

Brooker, Will (2009), *Star Wars* (London: BFI/Palgrave Macmillan).

Brown, Wendy (2010), *Walled States, Waning Sovereignty* (New York: Zone Books).

Brown, William (2008), 'Not Flagwaving but Flagdrowning: Postcards from Post-Britain', in *The British Cinema Book*, ed. Robert Murphy, 3rd edn (London: Palgrave Macmillan/BFI), pp. 408–16.

Bruzzi, Stella (2005), *Bringing Up Daddy: Fatherhood and Masculinity in Post-War Hollywood* (London: BFI).

Bukatman, Scott (1993), *Terminal Identity: The Virtual Subject in Postmodern Science Fiction* (Durham, NC and London: Duke University Press).

—(1999), 'The Artificial Infinite', in *Alien Zone II: The Spaces of Science Fiction Cinema*, ed. Annette Kuhn (London: Verso), pp. 249–75.

—(2003), *Matters of Gravity: Special Effects and Supermen in the 20th Century* (Durham, NC and London: Duke University Press).

Burroughs, William S. (1985), 'It Belongs to the Cucumbers', in *The Adding Machine: Collected Essays* (London: John Calder), pp. 53–60.

Butler, Judith (1990), *Gender Trouble: Feminism and the Subversion of Identity* (London and New York: Routledge).

Carroll, Hamilton (2010), *Affirmative Reaction: New Formations of White Masculinity* (Durham, NC and London: Duke University Press).

Castells, Manuel (2000), 'Toward a Sociology of the Network Society'. *Contemporary Sociology* 29, 5 (September): 693–9.

Castle, Terry (1995), *The Female Thermometer: Eighteenth-Century Culture and the Invention of the Uncanny* (New York and Oxford: Oxford University Press).

Clarke, I. F. (1992), *Voices Prophesying War: Future Wars 1763–3745*, 2nd edn (Oxford and New York: Oxford University Press).

Cohan, Steven (1997), *Masked Men: Masculinity and Movies in the Fifties* (Bloomington and Indianapolis: Indiana University Press).

Conrad, Joseph (1994), *Heart of Darkness* (London: Penguin).

Cornea, Christine (2007), *Science Fiction Cinema: Between Fantasy and Reality* (Edinburgh: Edinburgh University Press).

Crary, Jonathan (2001), *Suspensions of Perception: Attention, Spectacle, and Modern Culture* (Cambridge MA and London: The MIT Press).

Creed, Barbara (1986), 'Horror and the Monstrous-Feminine: An Imaginary Abjection'. *Screen* 27, 1 (January–February): 44–70.

Cresswell, Tim (2006), *On the Move: Mobility in the Modern Western World* (London: Routledge).

Curzon, John (2012), 'Sam Tyler and the "New North"', in *Life on Mars: From Manchester to New York*, eds. Stephen Lacey and Ruth McElroy (Cardiff: University of Wales Press), pp. 69–78.

Dante (1961), *The Divine Comedy*, volume 1: *Inferno*, trans. John D. Sinclair (Oxford and New York: Oxford University Press).

Davis, Mike (1998), *City of Quartz: Excavating the Future in Los Angeles* (London: Pimlico).

Day, Aidan (1996), *Romanticism* (London and New York: Routledge).

Deleuze, Gilles and Felix Guattari (1983), *Anti-Oedipus: Capitalism and Schizophrenia*, trans. Robert Hurley, Mark Seen and Helen R. Lane (London: Athlone).

—(2004), *A Thousand Plateaus*, trans. Brian Massumi (London: Continuum).

Denning, Michael (1987), *Cover Stories: Narrative and ideology in the British Spy Thriller* (London and New York: Routledge and Kegan Paul).

Derrida, Jacques (1976), *Of Grammatology*, trans. Gayatri Chakravorty Spivak (Baltimore: Johns Hopkins University Press).

Derrida, Jacques and Bernard Stiegler (2002), *Echographies of Television*, trans. Jennifer Bajorek (Cambridge: Polity).

Dery, Mark. (2012), *I must not Think Bad Thoughts* (Minneapolis: University of Minnesota Press).

Dick, Philip K. (1994), 'The Minority Report', in *The Days of Perky Pat: The Collected Short Stories of Philip K. Dick*, volume 4 (London: HarperCollins), pp. 99–140.

Dollimore, Jonathan (1991), *Sexual Dissidence: Augustine to Wilde, Freud to Foucault* (Oxford: Clarendon Press).

—(1998), *Death, Desire* and *Loss in Western Culture* (London: Penguin).

Donald, Ralph and Karen MacDonald (2011), *Reel Men at War: Masculinity and the American War Film* (Lanham, Toronto and Plymouth: Scarecrow Press).

Dyer, Richard (1999), *Seven* (London: BFI).

Eklund, Tof (2007), 'A Magic Realism of the Fuck'. *ImageText: Interdisciplinary Comics Studies* 3, 3 (Spring), http://www.english.ufl.edu/imagetext/archives/v3_3/lost_girls/eklund.shtml. Accessed 29 July 2014.

Ellroy, James (1992), *White Jazz* (New York: Alfred A. Knopf).

Fisher, Mark (2009), *Capitalist Realism* (London: Zero Books).

Foucault, Michel (1980), 'The Eye of Power', in *Power/Knowledge: Selected Interviews and Other Writings, 1972–1977*, ed. Colin Gordon, trans. Colin Gordon et al. (Brighton: Harvester), pp. 146–65.

—(1990), *The History of Sexuality. Volume 1: An Introduction*, trans. Robert Hurley (Harmondsworth: Penguin).

—(1991a), *The Foucault Reader*, ed. Paul Rabinow (Harmondsworth: Penguin).

—(1991b), *Discipline and Punish: The Birth of the Prison* (Harmondsworth: Penguin).

Freud, Sigmund (1951), *Moses and Monotheism*, trans. Katherine Jones (London: Hogarth Press).

—(1955a), 'Introduction to *Psycho-Analysis and the War Neuroses*' (1919), *Standard Edition of the Complete Psychological Works of Sigmund Freud*, vol. XVII, trans. and ed. James Strachey (London: Hogarth Press), pp. 207–1.

—(1955b), 'Appendix: Memorandum on the Electrical Treatment of War Veterans' (1920), in *Standard Edition of the Complete Psychological Works of Sigmund Freud*, vol. XVII, trans. and ed. James Strachey (London: Hogarth Press), pp. 211–5.

—(2006), 'Beyond the Pleasure Principle', in *The Penguin Freud reader*, ed. Adam Phillips (London: Penguin), pp. 132–95.

—(2010), *The Wolf-Man*, trans. Louise Adey Huish (London: Penguin).

Freud, Sigmund and Joseph Breuer (1956), *Studies on Hysteria*, trans. James and Alix Strachey (London: Hogarth Press).

Friedberg, Anna (1993), *Window Shopping: Cinema and the Postmodern* (Berkeley, Los Angeles and London: University of California Press).

Friedman, Lester D. (2003), 'Minority Report: A Dystopic Vision'. *Senses of Cinema: an online journal devoted to the serious and eclectic discussion of cinema* 27, July-Aug 2003. http://www.sensesofcinema.com/contents/03/27/minority_report.html. Accessed 13 August 2008.

Frost, David, with Bob, Zelnick (2007), *Frost/Nixon: Behind the Scenes of the Nixon Interviews* (New York and London: Harper Perennial).

Gamer, Michael (2000), *Romanticism and the Gothic: Genre, Reception and Canon Formation* (Cambridge: Cambridge University Press).

Gay, Peter (1973), *The Enlightenment: An Interpretation*, in 2 vols, *The Rise of Modern Paganism* and *The Science of Freedom* (London: Wildwood House).

Halloran, Vivian (2005), 'Tropical Bond', in *Ian Fleming and James Bond: The Cultural Politics of 007*, eds. Edward P. Comentale Stephen Watt and Skip Willman (Bloomington and Indianapolis: Indiana University Press), pp. 158–77.

Hardt, Michael and Antonio Negri (2000), *Empire* (Cambridge, MA: Harvard University Press).

Harris, Robert (2010), *The Ghost* (London: Arrow).

Harris, Thomas (2000), *The Hannibal Lecter Omnibus: Red Dragon, The Silence of the Lambs, Hannibal* (London: BCA).

—(2006), *Hannibal Rising* (London: William Heinemann).

Hayles, N. Katherine (1999), *How We Became Posthuman: Virtual Bodies in Cybernetics, Literature, and Informatics* (Chicago: University of Chicago Press).

Hendershot, Cyndy (2001), *The Animal Within: Masculinity and the Gothic* (Ann Arbor, MI: University of Michigan Press).

Hunter, I. Q. (1999), 'Introduction: The Strange World of the British Science Fiction Film'. *British Science Fiction Cinema*, ed. I. Q. Hunter (London: Routledge), pp. 1–15.

Hurley, Kelly (1996), *The Gothic Body: Sexuality, Materialism, and Degeneration at the* fin de siècle (Cambridge: Cambridge University Press).

Iain Boal, T. J. Clark, Joseph Matthews, Michael Watts [RETORT collective] (2005), *Afflicted Powers: Capital and Spectacle in a New Age of War* (London: Verso).

James, P. D. (1992), *The Children of Men* (London: Faber).

Jameson, Fredric (1992), *The Geopolitical Aesthetic: Cinema and Space in the World System* (London: BFI).

Jarvis, Brian (2007), 'Anamorphic allegory in *The Ring*, or, seven ways of looking at a horror video'. *The Irish Journal of Gothic and Horror Studies* 3, November 2007. http://irishgothichorrorjournal.homestead.com/ring.html. Accessed 1 July 2009.

Jeffords, Susan (1994), *Hard Bodies: Hollywood Masculinity in the Reagan Era* (New Brunswick, NJ: Rutgers University Press).

Joll, James (1979), *The Anarchists* (London: Methuen).

Jouve, Nicole Ward (1988), *'The Streetcleaner': The Yorkshire Ripper Case on Trial* (London: Marion Boyars).

Kaplan, E. Ann (2005), *Trauma Culture: The Politics of Terror and Loss in Media and Literature* (New Brunswick, NJ and London: Rutgers University Press).

Kelley, Mike (2003), 'An Academic Cut-up, in Easily Digestible Paragraph-Size Chunks; Or, the New King of Pop, Dr. Konstantin Raudive'. *Grey Room* 11 (Spring): 22–43.

King, Geoff (2006), 'Spectacle and Narrative in the Contemporary Blockbuster', in *Contemporary American Cinema*, eds. Linda Ruth Williams and Michael Hammond (Maidenhead and New York: Open University Press/McGraw-Hill), pp. 334–55.

Kirby, Lynne (1997), *Parallel Tracks: The Railroad and Silent Cinema* (Exeter: University of Exeter Press).

Kittler, Friedrich (1999), *Gramophone, Film, Typewriter*, trans. Geoffrey Winthrop-Young and Michael Wutz (Stanford, CA: Stanford University Press).

Landon, Brooks (1992), *The Aesthetics of Ambivalence: Rethinking Science Fiction Film in the Age of Electronic (Re)production* (Westport, CT: Greenwood Press).

Latimer, Heather (2011), 'Bio-reproductive Futurism: Bare Life and the Pregnant Refugee in Alfonso Cuaron's *Children of Men*'. *Social Text* 108 29, 3 (Fall): 51–71.

Lauro, Sarah Juliet, and Karen Embry. 'A Zombie manifesto: the Nonhuman Condition in the Era of Advanced Capitalism'. *Boundary 2* 35, 1: 85–108.

Lawrence, T. E. (1997), *Seven Pillars of Wisdom* (London: Wordsworth).

Lifton, Robert Jay (1973), *Home from the War: Vietnam Veterans, neither Victims nor Executioners* (New York: Simon and Schuster).

Luckhurst, Roger (2008), *The Trauma Question* (London: Routledge).

Marcuse, Herbert (1987), *Eros and Civilization: A Philosophical Enquiry into Freud* (London: Ark).

McCarthy, Tom (2010), *C* (London: Jonathan Cape).

—(2012a), 'Calling All Agents', in *The Mattering of Matter: Documents from the Archive of the International Necronautical Society*, ed. Leah Whitman-Salkin (Berlin: Sternberg), pp. 162–205.

—(2012b), 'INS Declaration on the Notion of the "Future"', in *The Mattering of Matter: Documents from the Archive of the International Necronautical Society*, ed. Leah Whitman-Salkin (Berlin: Sternberg), pp. 266–76.

—(2012c), *Transmission and the Individual Remix* (London: Jonathan Cape).

McElroy, Ruth (2012), 'Consuming Metrosexualities: The Past Live on Screen, Online Now', in *Life on Mars: From Manchester to New York*, eds. Stephen Lacey and Ruth McElroy (Cardiff: University of Wales Press), pp. 117–29.

Mellor, Anne (1993), *Romanticism and Gender* (London and New York: Routledge).

Miles, Robert (1993), *Gothic Writing 1750–1820: A Genealogy* (London: Routledge).

—(1999), 'The Eye of Power: Ideal Presence and the Gothic Romance'. *Gothic Studies* 1: 10–30.

Milton, John (1966), *Poetical Works*, ed. Douglas Bush (Oxford: Oxford University Press).

Moore, Alan and David Lloyd (1990), *V for Vendetta* (New York: Warner Books).

Moore, Alan and Melinda Gebbie (2008), *Lost Girls* (New York: Top Shelf).

Mulvey, Laura (1975), 'Visual Pleasure and Narrative Cinema'. *Screen* 16(3): 6–18.

Murphy, Robert (ed.) (2008), *The British Cinema Book*, 3rd edn (London: Palgrave Macmillan/BFI. 2008).

Niffenegger, Audrey (2004), *The Time-Traveler's Wife* (London: Vintage).

O'Brian, Patrick (2002), *Master and Commander* (London: HarperCollins).

—(2003), *The Far Side of the World* (London: HarperCollins).

—(2010), *The Mauritius Command* (London: HarperCollins).

Paterson, Don (2006), 'Afterword' to *Orpheus: A Version of Rilke* (London: Faber), pp. 61–72.

Peace, David (1999), *Nineteen Seventy-Four* (London: Serpent's Tail).

—(2000), *Nineteen Seventy-Seven* (London: Serpent's Tail).

—(2001), *Nineteen Eighty* (London: Serpent's Tail).

—(2002), *Nineteen Eighty-Three* (London: Serpent's Tail).

—(2007), *The Damned United* (London: Faber).

Penley, Constance (1992), 'Feminism, Psychoanalysis, and the Study of Popular Culture', in *Cultural Studies,* eds. L. Grossberg, C. Nelson and P. A. Treichler (New York and London: Routledge), pp. 479–500.

—(1997), *NASA/Trek: Popular Science and Sex in America* (London: Verso).

Phillips, Kathy J. (2006), *Manipulating Masculinity: War and Gender in Modern British and American Literature* (Basingstoke: Palgrave Macmillan).

Praz, Mario (1954), *The Romantic Agony*, trans. Angus Davidson (London and New York: Oxford University Press).

Raudive, Konstantin (1971), *Breakthrough: An Amazing Experiment in Electronic Communication with the Dead*, trans. Nadia Fowler (New York: Taplinger).

Rieder, John (2008), *Colonialism and the Emergence of Science Fiction* (Middletown, CT: Wesleyan University Press).

Robbins, Bruce (1996), 'Murder and Mentorship: Advancement in *The Silence of the Lambs'. Boundary 2*, 23, 1 (Spring): 71–90.

Roberts, Adam (2000), *Science Fiction* (London: Routledge).

Rodger, N. A. M. (1988), *The Wooden World: An Anatomy of the Georgian Navy* (London: Fontana).

Rutherford, Jonathan (1997), *Forever England: Reflections on Masculinity and Empire* (London: Lawrence and Wishart).

Said, Edward W. (1993), *Culture and Imperialism* (London: Chatto and Windus).

Sandbrook, Dominic (2006), *Never had it so Good: A History of Britain from Suez to the Beatles* (London: Abacus).

Savran, David (1998), *Taking it Like a Man: White Masculinity, Masochism, and Contemporary American Culture* (Princeton, NJ and Chichester: Princeton University Press).

Schock, Peter A. (2003), *Romantic Satanism: Myth and the Historical Moment in Blake, Shelley and Byron* (Basingstoke: Palgrave).

Sconce, Jeffrey (2000), *Haunted Media: Electronic Presence from Telegraphy to Television* (Durham, NC: Duke University Press).

Sedgwick, Eve Kosofsky (1985), *Between Men. English Literature and Male Homosocial Desire* (New York: Columbia University Press).

Shaw, Katy (2011), *David Peace: Texts and Contexts* (Eastbourne: Sussex Academic Press).

Shelley, Percy Bysshe (2000a), 'Preface to *Prometheus Unbound*', in *The Norton Anthology of English Literature*, eds. M. H. Abrams and S. Greenblatt, 7th edn, vol. 2 (New York: W. W. Norton), pp. 733–6.

—(2000b), 'Prometheus Unbound', in *The Norton Anthology of English Literature*, eds. M. H. Abrams and S. Greenblatt, 7th edn, vol. 2 (New York: W. W. Norton), pp. 736–62.

Silverman, Kaja (1992), *Male Subjectivity at the Margins* (New York and London: Routledge).

Smith, Andrew (2004), *Victorian Demons: Medicine, Masculinity, and the Gothic at the fin-de-siècle* (Manchester: Manchester University Press).

Sobchack, Vivian (1990), 'The Virginity of Astronauts', in *Alien Zone: Cultural Theory and Science Fiction*, ed. Annette Kuhn (London: Verso), pp. 103–13.

Stacey, Jackie (2010), *The Cinematic Life of the Gene* (Durham and London: Duke University Press).

Sterling, Bruce (2008), 'The Life and Death of Media', in *Sound Unbound: Sampling, Digital Music and Culture*, ed. Paul D. Miller (Cambridge, MA: MIT Press), pp. 73–82.

Sterne, Jonathan (2003), *The Audible Past: Cultural Origins of Sound Reproduction* (Durham, NC: Duke University Press).

Stevenson, Robert Louis (1999), *Strange Case of Doctor Jekyll and Mr Hyde* (1886), ed. Martin A. Danahay (Peterborough, OH: Broadview).

Stewart, Garrett (1999), 'Body Snatching: Science Fiction's Photographic Trace', in *Alien Zone II: The Spaces of Science Fiction Cinema*, ed. Annette Kuhn (London: Verso, 1999), pp. 226–48 (p. 226).

Stiegler, Bernard (1998), *Technic and Time I: The Fault of Epimetheus*, trans. Richard Beardsworth and George Collins (Stanford, CA: Stanford University Press).

Stiegler, Bernard and Jacques Derrida (2002), *Echographies of Television: Filmed Interviews*, trans. Jennifer Bajorek (London: Polity).

Stoker, Bram (1992), *Dracula* (1897) (Kerry, Eire: Brandon).

Tasker, Yvonne (1993), *Spectacular Bodies: Gender, Genre and the Action Cinema* (London and New York: Routledge).

—(2002), *The Silence of the Lambs* (London: BFI).

Theweleit, Klaus (1989a), *Male Fantasies I: Women, Floods, Bodies, History*, trans. Stephen Conway, Erica Carter and Chris Turner (London: Polity).

—(1989b), *Male Fantasies II: Male Bodies: Psychoanalysing the White Terror*, trans. Stephen Conway, Erica Carter and Chris Turner (London: Polity).

Toop, David (1995), *Ocean of Sound: Aether Talk, Ambient Sound and Imaginary Worlds* (London: Serpent's Tail).

Urry, John (2002), *The Tourist Gaze*, 2nd edn (London: Sage).

—(2007), *Mobilities* (Cambridge: Polity).

Verstraete, Gillian (2001), 'Technological Frontiers and the Production of Mobilities'. *New Formations: A Journal of Culture/Theory/Politics* 43 (Spring): 26–43.

Vidal, Gore (2004), 'The Day The American Empire Ran Out Of Gas', in *Imperial America: Reflections on the United States of Amnesia* (New York: Clairview), pp. 41–54.

Virilio, Paul (1989), *War and Cinema: The Logistics of Perception* (London: Verso).

Vonnegut, Kurt (1998), *Timequake* (London: Vintage).

Wade, Robert (2006), 'Choking the South'. *New Left Review* 38 (March/April): 115–27.

Wald, Priscilla (2008), *Contagion: Cultures, Carriers, and the Outbreak Narrative* (Durham and London: Duke University Press).

Walton, Jo (2005), 'Who Survives the Cosy Catastrophe?', *A Celebration of British Science Fiction (Foundation Studies in Science Fiction 4)*, ed. Andy Sawyer, Andrew M. Butler and Farah Mendelsohn. *Foundation 93*, 34, 1 (Spring): 34–9.

Warner, Marina (2006), *Phantasmagoria* (Oxford: Oxford University Press).

Weber, Cynthia (2005), 'Securitising the Unconscious: the Bush doctrine of Pre-emption and *Minority Report*'. *Geopolitics* 10 (2005): 482–99.

Whitehead, Stephen (2008), 'Metrosexuality! Cameron, Brown and the Politics of "new masculinity"'. *Public Policy Research* 14, 4 (December–February): 234–9.

Wood, Gillen D'Arcy (2001), *The Shock of the Real: Romanticism and Visual Culture, 1760–1860* (London: Palgrave).

Wordsworth, William (1970), *The Prelude* (London and New York: Oxford University Press).

Žižek, Slavoj (2002), *Welcome to the Desert of the Real! Five Essays on September 11 and Related Dates* (London: Verso).

Filmography

2001: A Space Odyssey. Dir. Stanley Kubrick. MGM, 1968.

28 Days Later. Dir. Danny Boyle. DNA Films/UK Film Council, 2002.

28 Weeks Later. Dir. Juan Carlos Fresnadillo. 20th Century Fox/DNA Films, 2006.

A Dangerous Method. Dir. David Cronenberg. Recorded Picture Company/Telefilm Canada, 2011.

A View To A Kill. Dir. John Glen. Eon Films/MGM/United Artists.

Alien Nation. Dir. Graham Baker. 20th Century Fox, 1988.

Alien Resurrection. Dir. Jean-Pierre Jeunet. Brandywine/20th Century Fox, 1997.

Alien. Dir. Ridely Scott. Brandywine/20th Century Fox, 1979.

Alien3. Dir. David Fincher. Brandywine/20th Century Fox, 1992.

Aliens. Dir. James Cameron. Brandywine/20th Century Fox, 1986.

Altered States. Dir. Ken Russell. Warner Bros, 1980.

Apocalypse Now Redux. Dir. Francis Coppola. Zoetrope Studios, 2001.

Apocalypse Now. Dir. Francis Coppola. Zoetrope Studios, 1979.

Blade Runner. Dir. Ridley Scott. The Ladd Company, 1982/1991/2007.

Casino Royale. 2006. dir Martin Campbell. Eon Films/MGM/United Artists.

Children of Men. Dir. Alfonso Cuarón. Universal, 2006.

Code 46. Dir. Michael Winterbottom. BBC Films/Revolution Films. 2003.

Contact. Dir. Robert Zemeckis. Warner Bros., 1997.

Contagion. Dir. Steven Soderbergh. Warner Bros, 2011.

District 9. Dir. Neil Blomkamp. Wingnut Films/TriStar, 2009.

District 9. Dir. Neill Blomkamp. Wingnut Films/QED International/Key Creatives/
    Wintergreen Productions, 2009.

Elysium. Dir. Neill Blomkamp. Alphacore/Media Rights Capital/QED International.

Event Horizon. Dir. Paul W. S. Anderson. Paramount/Golar Productions/Impact
    Pictures, 1997.

Four Lions. Dir. Chris Morris. Film 4/Wild Bunch/Warp Films, 2010.

Frequency. Dir. Gregor Hoblit. New Line, 2000.

From Russia, With Love. Dir. Terence Young. Eon Films/United Artists, 1962.

Frost/Nixon. Dir. Ron Howard. Imagine Entertainment/Working Title/Studio Canal/
    Relativity Media.

Frozen. Dir. Juliet Mckoen. Liminal Films, 2005.

Gattaca. Dir. Andrew Niccol. Jersey Films, 1997.

Gladiator. Dir. Ridley Scott. Universal, 2000.

Goldfinger. Dir. Guy Hamilton. Eon Films/United Artists, 1964.

Gravity. Dir. Alfonso Cuarón. Esperanto Filmoj/Heyday Films, 2013.

Hannibal Dir. Ridley Scott. MGM/Universal, 2000.

Hannibal. NBC television, 2013–14.

Inception. Dir. Christopher Nolan. Legendary Films/Syncopy Films, 2010.

La Haine. Dir. Matthieu Kassowitz. Canal Plus, 1995.

Life on Mars. Kudos Film and Television/BBC television, 2006–7.

Mad Men. Lionsgate Television, 2007–14.

Manhunter. Dir. Michael Mann. Red Dragon Production/De Laurentiis
    Entertainment, 1986.

Master and Commander: The Far Side of the World. Dir. Peter Weir. Universal/
    Miramax/Samuel Goldwyn Films, 2003.

Minority Report. Dir. Steven Spielberg. Amblin/Cruise/Wagner Productions, 2002.

Monsters. Dir. Gareth Edwards. Vertigo Films, 2011.

Moon. Dir. Duncan Jones. Stage 6 Films, 2009.

Never Let Me Go. Dir. Mark Romanek. DNA Films/Film 4, 2010.

Orphée. Dir. Jean Cocteau. 1950.

Outland. Dir. Peter Hyams. The Ladd Company, 1981.

Poltergeist. Dir. Tobe Hooper. SLM Productions/MGM, 1982.

Prometheus. Dir. Ridley Scott. Scott Free Productions/Brandywine/Dune Entertainment, 2012.

Red Riding 1974. Dir. Julian Jerrold. Revolution Films, 2009.

Red Riding 1980. Dir. James Marsh. Revolution Films, 2009.

Red Riding 1983. Dir. Anand Tucker. Revolution Films, 2009.

Solaris. Dir. Stephen Soderbergh. Lightstorm Entertainment, 2002.

Star Trek: Into Darkness. Dir. J. J. Abrams. Bad Robot/K/O Paper Products/Skydance, 2013.

Star Wars Episode I: The Phantom Menace. Dir. George Lucas. Lucasfilm/20th Century Fox, 1999.

Star Wars Episode II: Attack of the Clones. Dir. George Lucas. Lucasfilm/20th Century Fox, 2002.

Star Wars Episode III: Revenge of the Sith. Dir. George Lucas. Lucasfilm/20th Century Fox, 2005.

Star Wars: The Clone Wars. Lucasfilm/Lucasfilm Animation, 2008–14.

Stargate. Dir. Roland Emmerich. StudioCanal/Centropolis Film Productions/Carolco, 1994.

Sunshine. Dir. Danny Boyle. Moving Picture Company/DNA Films/UK Film Council/Ingenious Film Partners, 2007.

The Bourne Identity. Dir. Doug Liman. Kennedy/Marshall Company/FilmColony, 2002.

The Bourne Supremacy. Dir. Paul Greengrass. Kennedy/Marshall Company/Ludlum Entertainment, 2004.

The Bourne Ultimatum. Dir. Paul Greengrass. Kennedy/Marshall Company/Ludlum Entertainment, 2007.

The Damned United. Dir. Tom Hooper. BBC Films/Left Bank Pictures/Screen Yorkshire, 2009.

The Deal. Dir. Stephen Frears. Granada Television, 2003.

The Ghost. Dir. Roman Polanski. R. P. Productions/France 2 Cinema/Studio Babelsberg, 2010.

The Hurt Locker. Dir. Karthyn Bigelow. Voltage Pictures/Grosvenor Park Media/Film Capital Europe Funds/First Light Production/Kingsgate Films/Summit Entertainment.

The Man Who Fell to Earth. Dir. Nicholas Roeg. British Lion Films, 1976.

The Queen. Dir. Stephen Frears. Granada Productions/BIM Distibuzione/Pathé Renn
 Production/France 3 Cinema/Canal+.
The Silence of the Lambs. Dir. Jonthanan Demme. Orion, 1991.
The Sixth Sense Dir. Shyamalan, M. Knight. Spyglass/Kennedy/Marshall, 1999.
The Special Relationship. Dir. Richard Loncraine. Rainmark Production, 2010.
The Time Traveler's Wife. Dir. Robert Schwentke. Plan B Entertainment, 2009.
V for Vendetta. Dir. James McTeigue. Virtual Studios/Silver Pictures/Anarcho
 Productions.
War of the Worlds. Dir. Steven Spielberg. Amblin/Cruise/Wagner, 2005.
What Dreams May Come. Dir. Vincent Ward. Interscope Communications, 1999.
White Noise. Dir. Sax, Geoffrey. Gold Circle Film/Brightlight Productions, 2005.
You Only Live Twice. Dir. Lewis Gilbert. Eon Films/United Artists, 1967.

Index

443475

Lightning Source UK Ltd.
Milton Keynes UK
UKOW05f0727081116

287128UK00015B/324/P

9 781501 320095